How Fantasy Becomes Reality

How Fantasy Becomes Reality

Information and Entertainment
Media in Everyday Life

REVISED AND EXPANDED

KAREN E. DILL-SHACKLEFORD

OXFORD
UNIVERSITY PRESS

OXFORD
UNIVERSITY PRESS

Oxford University Press is a department of the University of
Oxford. It furthers the University's objective of excellence in research,
scholarship, and education by publishing worldwide.

Oxford   New York
Auckland   Cape Town   Dar es Salaam   Hong Kong   Karachi
Kuala Lumpur   Madrid   Melbourne   Mexico City   Nairobi
New Delhi   Shanghai   Taipei   Toronto

With offices in
Argentina   Austria   Brazil   Chile   Czech Republic   France   Greece
Guatemala   Hungary   Italy   Japan   Poland   Portugal   Singapore
South Korea   Switzerland   Thailand   Turkey   Ukraine   Vietnam

Oxford is a registered trademark of Oxford University Press
in the UK and certain other countries.

Published in the United States of America by
Oxford University Press
198 Madison Avenue, New York, NY 10016

Library of Congress Cataloging-in-Publication Data
Dill-Shackleford, Karen, 1969–
How fantasy becomes reality : information and entertainment media
in everyday life / Karen E. Dill-Shackleford. — Revised and expanded.
   pages cm
Includes bibliographical references and index.
ISBN 978-0-19-023929-9
1. Mass media—Social aspects.   2. Mass media—Psychological aspects.
3. Social psychology.   I. Title.
HM1206.D55 2015
302.23—dc23
2015013950

9 8 7 6 5 4 3 2 1
Printed in the United States of America
on acid-free paper

For my students

CONTENTS

Welcome to the second edition of *How Fantasy Becomes Reality*. I wrote the original in 2008 and as I sit down to write this, it is now the fall of 2015. A lot has happened in the media landscape and in my life between then and now.

In terms of the media landscape, the changes have continued to come fast and furious. My son Jason, a teenager now, keeps me up to date on what's popular with his friends. We've spent time watching funny Vines and YouTube videos on his iPad, like one of his current favorites called Super Café, which involves scenes of Batman and Superman chatting over coffee. My daughter Regan and I watch cat videos, laugh, and make "angry cat" noises together.

My son Jason has started high school and my daughter Regan is finishing up elementary school. Since 2008, I also got divorced and then remarried, hence the name change. My husband Lee Shackleford, whom I've known now for nearly 25 years, is a playwright, screenwriter, and a college professor. He's brought so much joy and adventure to my life.

When I wrote the first edition of *How Fantasy Becomes Reality*, I was just finishing more than 10 years of undergraduate teaching and a great deal of speaking about media violence. I cannot tell you how tired I was of people telling me that what they watch has zero percent influence on their lives. The disdain and emotional energy with which people said this to me on a regular basis was starting to get under my skin. I couldn't believe that many people did not understand the simple idea that what you consume becomes part of your psyche. Not that it's always a simple maneuver and not that media are just like pills we take with single outcomes, but that the messages we think about become part of us in some way.

Now, leading up to the second edition, as a professor at Fielding Graduate University in Santa Barbara, California, I have taught only adult graduate students for five years. I've done new and exciting research. I also edited the *Oxford*

Handbook of Media Psychology (2013). In the six years that have intervened, my perspective has shifted. While I've always been of the mind that there are positive influences in the media, I wanted to emphasize that fact more in this edition. In the intervening years, I have also had the opportunity to conduct more research showing the difference in outcomes between positive and negative media exposure, which I write about in this edition. My colleagues and I have conducted research on everything from music in film, to social media sobriety support, to using live theater for entertainment-education, to using podcasts to teach meditation for psychological benefit. We've shown how good and bad entertainment magazine writing about social issues makes a real difference in the readers' minds. My colleagues and I have demonstrated that how you portray African American men in the media makes a great deal of difference in how your audience reacts to African American men.

I've also written more about how polarizing this topic of media effects or media influence tends to be. People tend to flock to a false division of media lovers and media haters. Some people seem to say only good things about media, while others only emphasize the bad. It's a shame because surely we can all see that media choices are vast and varied and could not possibly result in either all bad or all good outcomes.

Logically speaking, if you believe that exposure to media can lead to positive outcomes, you must believe it can also lead to negative outcomes. How could something so complex have only positive consequences? Or only negative ones? That just doesn't make any sense. Media are as varied as people are. As I explain in these pages, we get reactionary when we feel threatened. And then we tend to polarize. Let's get over that phase together and move into a new era in the understanding of media, with the knowledge that our media choices mean a lot to us and that they can influence our lives in many ways—some positive, some negative, some mixed. The trick is just to be open and to be mindful and to make our choices. Whoever you are and whatever perspective you are coming from, thanks for reading.

Karen E. Dill-Shackleford

ACKNOWLEDGMENTS

I'd like to thank the staff I have worked with at Oxford over the years. This is our third project together, and I hope we have more adventures in the years to come. Without exception, everyone I have worked with at Oxford has been amazing. I want to thank Lori Handleman, without whom this book would not exist, and Abby Gross and Molly Balikov, who worked with me on this second edition.

As a professor of social psychology and media psychology, I am a teacher, a mentor, and a researcher. All of these roles are social. All are symbiotic. I am grateful to all of my students, mentors, and collaborators. I want to thank Craig Anderson and Russ Geen, who have inspired me since I was a very green apprentice researcher (not to mention a very green apprentice human). They continue to inspire me. I cannot thank Brad Bushman enough for his editorial advice on the first edition. Thanks also to Melinda Burgess, Katherine Larsen, Sam Osherson, Cynthia Vinney, Elizabeth Braun, and Bruce Bartholow for feedback on parts of this new edition.

I am endlessly grateful to my students, to whom I dedicate this volume. I will not thank them here by name because I do not want to slight anyone by leaving out a single name. (Trust me on this decision: you do not want to instigate the competitive nature of highly competitive people. It gets weird fast!) Seriously, each of you has added so much to my life. Words cannot adequately express how much I value you.

To my family and friends, my love and thanks for all you do. Thank you to my parents for buying lots of copies of the first edition. Thanks to my children for inspiring me and making my life much more interesting than it would be without them. And thanks to my husband Lee, for his love, respect, support, and for just being awesome. Thank you for the many conversations inspired by the issues in this book. And thank you, Lee, for reading the first edition—four times.

Fantasy and Reality

A Primer on Media and Social Construction

Right now, at this moment in history, Americans are having a love affair with mass media. While this romance is sometimes sublime, as with many affairs of the heart, many of us are still seeing the object of our affections through rose-colored glasses, unable to acknowledge the flaws that may end up hurting us. On the other hand, the reason we fell in love with mass media in the first place is understandable. It's like one of those relationships where the chemistry is good, so we ignore those niggling problems that are always in the background. We know we should do something about it, but we just keep muddling through, hoping for the best. But if this is going to be the kind of relationship that adds to who we are, rather than one that does more harm than good, the relationship is going to need work.

The benefits of a healthy relationship with media are also too great to miss. It's no accident that we are so drawn to media—drawn to the stories and people we encounter there. Stories and information in the media help us make sense of our own lives.

This book is essentially about media influence—it's about how media matter to us, and how we can avoid the pitfalls and take advantage of the opportunities they offer. Throughout this book, I view the role of media in our culture through a wide-angle lens, telling the story of what social scientists have learned about the psychology of mass media. Exactly how and why do the media change us and mold us? What active role do we play in the process?

A broad premise of the book is that mass media are a persistent and pervasive influence in our lives and that their influence is meaningful. Though far from the only factors that influence our behavior, the effects of media are not trivial. Early in the book, I explore several reasons for a persistent dichotomy: if media are indeed so influential, why are many of us are under the impression of being almost entirely unaffected by media exposure? And before we're through, I'll give concrete suggestions about how we can become much more savvy about how we use media and how it uses us. There are many positive uses and effects of media, and I explore these as well, so that we can best harness the potential of media.

Speaking of risks and benefits, lately the conversation about media use has focused on social media. Are selfies great new forms of self-expression, or signs that we are hopelessly self-centered? Are online social networking sites like Facebook avenues for enhancing social contact, or are they turning us into a society with worsening social skills? Is binge watching harmful, or a great idea whose time has finally come?

The very questions we ask speak to the trend to polarize around media issues, dividing into two groups: the lovers and the haters. I think this represents overly simplistic, reductionist thinking. Media are neither "bad" nor "good" in general—media are channels through which we send messages, which can be judged as positive, negative, neutral, or mixed. One of my suggestions is that we open our minds to accepting that some effects of media exposure are going to show benefits, some are going to show risks and harm, and others will be mixed or neutral. You don't have to pick a "side." You can intelligently consider each issue that arises in the media landscape and see both the dark and the light. A friend once told me that an intellectual is someone who can see both sides of any argument. I invite you to be an intellectual, rather than a "team player," when it comes to thinking about the roles of media in our everyday lives. Don't play just one note over and over: play a symphony!

As an example of what I hope is a balanced approach to media research, Don Grant and I studied the role of social media in sobriety support. We did not enter into the discussion to say that social media would be the ruination of sobriety support or that they would be the panacea. We simply asked this question: How can social media play a role in sobriety support? We surveyed over 200 adults who had used both face-to-face and social media forms of sobriety support (for example, face-to-face alcohol recovery groups and social media recovery groups). We found that this group of people said that the face-to-face support was the most crucial recovery modality. At the same time, the consensus was that social media support was also valuable, and that some facets of the social media support experience seemed superior to their face-to-face counterparts. Interestingly, we discovered a trend that users of both modalities found it easier to be honest about their sobriety in a social media venue than in a face-to-face venue. Surprisingly (to us!), they also reported being more likely to show up at a face-to-face support group while drunk or high than to use a social media support group while drunk or high.

I find it valuable to approach our everyday mediated and unmediated lives, not as mortal enemies of each other and not as valuable and valueless, but as a subject that is full of nuance and complexity. I recommend looking for benefits and avoiding harm in our media diets. I also recommend becoming mindful about what media you use and what they do for you. These questions are so pertinent because this is a new era of media use. In the history of humanity, the speed of change and the pervasiveness of media in our everyday lives play vital roles in our human psychology and our well-being. Now, let's move to a discussion about the pervasiveness of media in our lives.

OUR COLLECTIVE ATTRACTION TO MEDIA

Over the last 50 years, and most especially in the last decade, there has been a revolution in the way Americans spend their free time. How many hours per week do you think the average American child spends staring into an electronic screen? Take a guess. Currently the statistic stands at about 45 hours per week of what is now termed "screen time." All told, American children spend more time watching TV and movies, playing video games, surfing the net, and the like than they spend in school each year. When you factor in going to school, sleeping, and basic maintenance tasks like grooming and chores, it's easy to see that American kids are basically devoting their lives to consuming media. When they have a choice about how to spend their time, they almost always choose media.

What about statistics that include adults? According to data from the last US Census (www.census.gov), the average US citizen spends 3,700 hours per year using mass media. If you are like the average person, you spend about two-thirds of your waking hours using media in one form or another. Americans spend more money annually on entertainment media than they do on healthcare and clothing. What's your impression? Do you think we realize just how much time and energy we devote to media? As media critic Marshall McLuhan famously asked, "Does a fish know it's wet?" In other words, we probably fail to notice just how much we are immersed in media for the very reason that they are so pervasive.

Since we live in a culture where clearly the great majority of our free time is spent staring into electronic screens, don't you think it's about time all of us were taught to think intelligently and critically about our media diets? Like the saying goes, knowledge is power. In a country where we are free to choose, we should marry that freedom with some wisdom to help guide us in making those choices. We've turned a major corner with media use in America—in terms of both the percentage of our lives that media use occupies and the diverse forms of media now available to us—and it's time we followed those major changes with some major changes in how we understand the psychology of how we are affected by media. I have also come to believe that we remain undereducated about what benefits we derive from our experiences with entertainment media and that maximizing the benefits of media is important for our continued evolution. These are just some of the many issues to ponder as we explore what it means to be a social creature in a media-saturated world. Before we continue these explorations, let's look at a road map for the rest of our journey together.

THE MAGICAL MYSTERY TOUR IS WAITING TO TAKE YOU AWAY

When I read a book, I see it as taking a trip with the author. Reading an author's thoughts means looking out at the world through that person's eyes for a short time, while still using your own head to filter the author's perspective. Because you are climbing on board with me, let me tell you more about your traveling companion.

First, I'm a social psychologist. Social psychologists mostly study how people influence each other. My special area of interest is media psychology, which involves understanding how social influence is carried out through mass media (TV, the Internet, video games, music, etc.) rather than in face-to-face interactions between people. Much of my early research centered on understanding how violence and portrayals such as stereotypes in the media affect people. For example, when we see a stereotype in the media (an African American woman playing a maid on TV or a woman who says "no" when she means "yes" in a movie), often the effect is for the stereotypical idea to be reinforced and acted upon. On the other hand, when we see a person of color portrayed with great respect and humanity, this opens the door to increased respect and understanding in the real world. These are examples of how social psychology and media psychology come together. The social aspect involves learning either a stereotype or a progressive example of race by watching others. The social interactions in question were mediated; and since a medium is something in the middle, a mediated interaction involves something coming *between* the people in question. In other words, two real people didn't interact; rather, someone watched a television show or movie and learned through a representation about what other people are like.

To move again toward the positive side, a landmark television show like *All in the Family* can change viewers' thoughts, feelings, and even behaviors toward people from other races. Did you know that by simply being exposed to a show in which people of different races form friendships, viewers develop more positive feelings about members of the other race and can more easily see themselves interacting with members of the other race in their own lives? The viewer, by engaging in the simple act of watching a television show, has learned a valuable life lesson: that African American and White people really can break down racial barriers and become friends. *All in the Family* was therefore not "just a TV show" but was in fact a real force for social change. Some people missed the joke, but many did not. Who knew that Archie Bunker, that stereotype of stereotype holders, could be such a powerful influence for positive change on untold numbers of viewers? But indeed he was.

A show or film that we find meaningful can really rock our worlds. It can change the way we look at life, and inspire our plans for how we want to live in the future. Some music, for example, can bring with it a sense of transcendence and importance. Nicole Phinney, Mary Beth Oliver, and I have studied the role of music in bringing us deeper into the characters and stories portrayed in film. We discovered that a film score can indeed bring us deeper into a story and connect us more closely with characters. Part of the reason for this is that music evokes emotion in a way that can't easily be changed with logical thought. A film score, in a way, tells us how to feel about what we're seeing. We also learned that if the score doesn't fit the film, then we will enter that story world more superficially than we would have if the score's emotional tone fit the scene well. (We also learned that many women are drawn more deeply into a story if Tom Cruise takes his shirt off. But I think the producers probably knew that already.)

Since this book is a social psychological analysis of mass media, I will use many examples like this, including both research findings and real-world illustrations, to show the power the mass media exerts in our individual lives and in our culture, affecting us in both positive and negative ways. For example, movies like *The Shawshank Redemption, The Color Purple*, and *Talk to Me* make us feel the power of oppression, injustice, and discrimination. Just as strong is the feeling of inferiority we get from the illusions often conjured in the media of people who have something we want desperately, whether that be social status, beauty, or popularity. And as sad as it may be to realize that the people who make commercials, for example, really would sell us out (defined as jeopardizing or damaging our well-being and our pocketbooks), we must face the fact that even though it is sad and pathetic, it's still true. The good news is that we do have power, and that power starts with acknowledging plain truths such as these. I hope that what you gain from reading this book is a savvy, progressive perspective on the role of media in modern life, a view that inspires you to think critically about your use of media in everyday life and to maximize the benefits of media for yourself and your family.

MEDIA CRITICISM MAKES FOR STRONG OPINIONS

Every college professor hopes that her dissertation will (a) be published and (b) be well received. When my dissertation was published in the top journal in social psychology, I was thrilled. Having exhausted myself to produce the best research I could manage, I hoped my colleagues would notice. Well, they did. Some days it seems that everybody noticed. My dissertation became the most-cited paper in the field on the effects of violent video games on aggression. When it was published, the American Psychological Association put out a press release. My phone rang nonstop for two weeks. I did interviews with CNN, *Time* magazine, and *USA Today*. The Japanese broadcasting company (NHK) sent a crew to North Carolina to film a documentary on my dissertation, and a company in California also shot documentary footage for a video on research methodology, now packaged with one of the most popular introductory psychology textbooks in the United States. To this day, I still get calls for interviews that begin with, "I was just reading your dissertation ... " (to which I mentally reply, "Oh, I'm sorry!" because I realize that dissertations are generally regarded as pretty dry stuff and that I am among the few living people who actually *like* reading research reports).

Some years and two US congressional testimonies (not to mention two children) later, I have a perspective on the field of media psychology that comes with international exposure to people from all walks of life. I have spoken about my research and about media psychology in South Korea and South America, in front of television cameras and senators, in high school classrooms and churches, on sidewalks and in bathroom stalls, as well as in my own college classrooms. Because of the intense interest in these issues and because of their potential to polarize, I have been vilified and deified by various stakeholders and in the end have been left with the unmistakable feeling that there is something fundamental about mass media that we're not quite getting yet as a society. I hope this book will sharpen the dialogue about the role of mass media in our lives and our understanding of how that relationship works.

> The most effective kind of propaganda is that which is not recognized as propaganda.
>
> —JEAN KILBOURNE, *Can't Buy My Love*

Now let's focus more deeply on the paradox that we live in a culture where entertainment and information media hold a place of great importance in our lives but where many of us misread the potential influence of media—both positive and negative—because we think we are largely unaffected by it. I believe that when we deny the potential power of media we are actually increasing the degree to which we can be manipulated, as well as missing real opportunities to more fully realize the benefits of media. On the negative side, if you do not know you are vulnerable—indeed, if you think you are invulnerable—you will not think and act in ways that protect you. Likewise, on the positive side, if you do not understand the potential benefit, you are less likely to use it to your best advantage. Two basic errors in judgment that we make are (1) believing that fantasy stories in no way shape our realities, and (2) believing that media's reason for being is to passively entertain rather than to move us and make a difference to us.

Jean Kilbourne has written bestselling books and videos and has lectured widely about the many ways in which advertising influences us. In her award-winning film, *Killing Us Softly 3*,[1] she says that wherever she goes, people always tell her that they are not affected by advertising—that they don't listen to or remember ads at all. "This usually comes from a person wearing a Gap T-shirt," she quips in the film. I certainly identify with both her experience and her incredulity at the extent to which people seem unaware of the influence of media. How is it, do you think, that advertisers make such enormous profits if indeed none of us is influenced by advertisements? Where is this silent majority of malleable individuals?

My own experience is very much like Jean Kilbourne's. Everywhere I go, people tell me that exposure to media violence does not cause increases in aggressive thoughts, behaviors, or feelings. And this is not just my experience. Research also shows that, by and large, people believe that entertainment media have no effect on them. Teen video game enthusiasts look at me with thinly veiled disgust and say, "It's only a game." (Subtext: Chill out, lady. You are so uncool.) I testified before the US House of Representatives subcommittee on Commerce, Trade and Consumer Protection in 2007,[2] speaking about the effects of sexist and racist stereotypes in the media. A rap singer who was there giving testimony threw his hands up in the air and said, "It's only a song." Recently, a friend told me that he mentioned my name to a student and the student responded that he was so angry with me for doing media violence research that he wanted to make a version of the violent video game *Grand Theft Auto* where I shoot everyone. (At this point, I'm just glad he didn't want to make me the victim.) To me, the passion behind people's rejection of the premise that media affect them is very telling.

AFFECTED BY MEDIA? NOT ME!

Recent research out of the University of Maryland[3] reported that college students, in general, are apt to think of media as "just harmless entertainment."

Young people were asked whether "it matters" if there are violent scenes or sexist stereotypes in video games. Most did not believe that this violent or sexist content could possibly change people's behavior or attitudes. Even more interesting, those who played violent video games *the most* were also *the most likely* to see media violence exposure as consequence-free. The more we do something that is regarded as controversial or potentially harmful, the more we need to justify doing it. It's also true that the less we really think something is harmful, the more we can feel free to do it. Opinion polls have documented that many Americans believe that media exposure is harmless. For example, one poll showed that 57 percent of American adults and children believe that playing violent video games is "safe" for children.[4] (Hmmmm, do you smell a psychological explanation coming? I do!)

These studies are consistent with a large body of research documenting what scholars call the "third person effect." The third person effect is the phenomenon that people believe others are affected by exposure to media, but that they personally are not affected. If you probe more specifically, you will learn that many people believe the only ones subject to media effects are basically young children.

What do scholars think? I'll completely ruin any suspense by saying that often mainstream scholars believe the opposite of what the public tends to believe about the effects of media on people. "OK, well, how exactly do media affect people?" you might be wondering. Let's take a look at an intriguing study reported by Glasser in *Television and the Social Construction of Reality*.[5] It occurred to Glasser that while people watch a lot of TV shows about cops and lawyers, the average person (perhaps mercifully) does not actually have much direct experience dealing with either the police or the judicial system, especially when it comes to relatively serious criminal activity. So he asked everyday people some specific questions about how the criminal justice system in America works. He found that people believe things work the way they see them on TV, which turns out to be consistently different from the way they work in real life in a number of documentable ways. For example, on TV the detective often knows "who dunnit" right away and spends his time trying to "get his man." As a matter of fact, in the seriously less glamorous world of actual police work, cases have a bothersome tendency not to resolve themselves neatly, to involve "victimless" crimes and tedious duties such as arresting disorderly drunks and filing paperwork. On TV, being a detective is way cooler. For famous TV detective Lieutenant Columbo, all he has to do is have a two-minute conversation with someone and he immediately knows he has found his perpetrator. The same is true for the USA Network's obsessive-compulsive detective, Adrian Monk. Monk will inevitably discover a quirky clue about the way the murderer ate his sandwiches or tied his shoes and he'll throw out his catch phrase, "He's the guy." And Monk is never wrong. Columbo is never wrong. And what do we believe, fantasy or reality? Fantasy. Every time. If someone asked us where we get our facts about police work, would we ever say, "I learned it by watching TV?" You know we wouldn't. We wouldn't know that we learned it from watching TV, and we would think the very notion was absurd.

Craig Haney and John Manzolati also recognized the pervasive role of television in informing us about crime. In their article "Television Criminology: Network Illusions of Criminal Justice Realities,"[6] they relate how crime depictions on TV are often very different from real-life crime. For example, the crime we usually see on TV is street crime, including violent crime like murder. Very little crime on TV is white-collar or corporate crime. The truth, however, is that these (possibly less dramatic) crimes are vastly underrepresented on TV, and street crime and murder are vastly overrepresented. And it follows that Americans are very concerned about street crime as opposed to white-collar crime. This is because TV is constructing a reality in which street crime is rampant but white-collar crime is almost nonexistent. Similarly, TV criminals are often motivated by a pathological level of greed, or they commit the crime because they are insane. In real life, anger and frustration brought about by realistic circumstances—such as stealing caused by chronic unemployment—are far more likely than the "made for TV motives" we've grown accustomed to seeing. We see it on TV, so we think it is real. And still we don't understand or admit that we learned about crime by watching TV, when that is precisely what we have done. This is how it is in our relationship with mass media.

FANTASY AND REALITY

When I discuss the effects of exposure to mass media with various audiences, one of the comments I hear most often is that anyone old enough to "know the difference between fantasy and reality" is not affected by media content. In other words, fictional stories do not influence us because we "know they are not real." This fantasy/reality argument represents a major misunderstanding of the psychology of the media. In fact, it is so pervasive that it merits a thorough discussion.

Now, let's look more closely at the words "fantasy" and "reality." When an adult says she knows the difference between fantasy and reality, how is she defining each word? I think by "fantasy" she means fiction. According to dictionary.com, the word "fiction" has a variety of meanings. Fiction can mean a creation or an invention of the imagination. Fiction can mean a lie. Stories are classified either as truth or fiction, literature as nonfiction or fiction. When someone says media do not affect him because he knows the difference between fantasy and reality, I think he means that he knows the people and situations on TV are contrived or invented. We know, for example, that the TV show *Friends* was a fictional story about the relationships and exploits of a group of twenty-somethings. In what ways is the story based in fiction rather than fact? Well, the adult audience is aware that the people in the stories are actors who are paid to play parts. A young woman whose name is Rachel in the story is played by an actress named Jennifer Aniston, for example. The "apartments" that the characters live in are actually sets. The friends' dialogue is the creation of professional writers.

So the stories on *Friends* were products of the imagination of the writers and producers of the series. When we watch a fictional TV show, we're essentially imagining "what if" these were real people and these situations and events really took place. We are entertained by a story that we imagine in our mind's eye as really happening. I don't think people would be much entertained by fiction if they thought of it purely as a lie that could never happen. I think the truth is quite the opposite: to the extent that we believe these characters and their circumstances and relationships are plausible and valuable, we take an interest in them. To the extent that we buy into the fantasy, we are drawn into the show.

So where does the reality come in, and what is a more meaningful definition of "reality" in this context? The reality of a fictional story is not whether it is a fantasy or a creation; it is whether it is believable and attractive. One definition of fiction (again from dictionary.com) is something artificial or counterfeit—specifically, a likeness made to pass for the real thing. So fiction can actually mean a story created to pass for the real thing. Paradoxically then, the best kinds of fantasies are the ones that strike us as in some way real or genuine. I think one of the joys of experiencing really good fantasy and fiction is the very fact that they allow us to imagine "what if"—to feel as though a very interesting or gratifying story could be true.

THE VALUE OF ENTERTAINMENT MEDIA

One consequence of misunderstanding media's place in our everyday lives is that we can misconstrue or undervalue the benefits we can gain through cultivating a rich relationship with media. As a scientist, for years I longed to know more about our obsession with media. Why can't we seem to live without it? Why do we enjoy it to the exclusion of so many other things in life? One answer to this question lies in understanding the deep meaning and value we carry away from our healthy experiences with media.

Have you ever watched a movie that changed your life? Has a song, a video, a story, or other work of art taken you to new places, leaving you with a feeling of transcendence and value? I have experienced all of these positive effects of media, and I bet most of you have as well. Media psychologists are just beginning to understand the complexities behind what we instinctively know about the value of really good media. A great film, play, game, or song is a work of art and can have profound influence on our lives. True, some entertainment media experiences may be shallow and without lasting value. But some entertainment experiences are so profound that they change us and stay with us.

Psychologists have begun to unravel the difference between a shallow and a deeper media experience. Going back to the work of the great American psychologist William James, psychologist Gerald Cupchik's work illuminates the division between the shallow and the deep media experience. On the shallow level is what Cupchik calls "low art"—which flashes images before us that are perhaps merely pleasant or mildly interesting, but that do not inspire deeper consideration. In a film, for example, low art would mean a shallow plot line with no surprises, perhaps one catering to provide pleasant experiences, but no real challenge. Cupchik refers to these as "sentimental" works of art. When I think of this kind of sentimental low art, I think of the "Hallmark Channel." (Sorry, Hallmark Channel: I'm sure some of your stuff is more artistic.) Another example of low art might be a poster of a cute kitten. The kitten is surely sentimental, evoking simple pleasurable emotions and no real challenge. Sometimes, in fact, we manage our media diet simply by saying that we are exhausted after a complex emotional day and we just want to watch cat videos. And that's fine. (I've spent many a happy time watching Internet cat videos with my daughter or humorous videos with my son.)

On the other hand, some entertainment media can be rightly classed as "high art." Whatever the medium (film, music, gaming), these works of art offer us enough familiarity to connect with the story, and enough novelty to engage us. We also desire a maximal amount of stimulation, not wishing to be either too bored or too stimulated.

The real difference starts when these works are complex enough to inspire divided emotions, or what Cupchik refers to as "polyvalent" reactions—"poly" meaning many, and "valence" meaning value. It turns out that we are more likely to be moved by a work if it inspires these polyvalent or mixed emotions and is accompanied by a sense of psychological challenge, inspiring us to think and feel more deeply then we do in experiences with low art. When we have a story that we can connect to, but one that is novel enough and nuanced enough to inspire challenge, we can make meaning from the experience. When we enter this kind of relationship with media, the work of art "rings true." We imagine "what if" the messages inherent in the art were really happening.

Finally—and this is key—we come away from the experience seeing the world through fresh eyes.

I recently attended an exhibit of surrealist art that left me with this feeling of mixed emotions and of deep meaning. Surrealism juxtaposes the ordinary with the extraordinary, challenging the meanings of both. The result was an experience of energy and transcendence. We can get the same feeling of meaning and transcendence from a favorite gaming world, fiction novel, television series, or from music. Exploring these transcendent and meaningful experiences more fully, we can more fully realize a life well lived. This is perhaps our greatest aspiration in our relationship with media—that it would help us more fully realize optimal human experiences.

NARRATIVE PERSUASION

Aside from finding meaning through our experiences with media, we can emerge changed from the experience in other ways. One way in which we are changed is when the experience of a story world changes our thinking. Research has documented the persuasive power of fictional narratives to change what we believe. For example, studies have shown that if you build false information into a fictional narrative, people actually come to believe the false information. For example, in one study,[7] German college students read a fictional story called "The Kidnapping" into which either true or false information had been inserted. A control or comparison group read a comparable story without the information inserted. One true assertion was that exercise strengthens one's heart and lungs. The false assertion was this statement's opposite—that exercise weakens one's heart and lungs. Results showed that the college students were persuaded by the factual information in the story regardless of whether the information was true or false. So, if you read in a fictional story that exercise weakens your heart and lungs, you are persuaded that this is true. These researchers also studied a phenomenon called the sleeper effect—that persuasion through fictional narratives increases over time as the source of the information becomes remote. While at first the students' confidence in their newly formed attitudes was relatively low, two weeks later their confidence had returned to baseline levels. What this research shows is that we can be persuaded to believe false information that is inserted into a fictional story. Also, over time, we forget where we learned this information, and our confidence in its truth increases. As another example, reading romance novels has been shown to increase negative attitudes about using condoms. So, misleading information can be stated as a fact or woven into the story line. Also, to the degree that one forms an emotional connection with a character, the persuasive power becomes stronger. So, if a reader is attached to a character in a novel who dislikes using condoms, that can change the reader's own attitudes and behaviors.

My husband Lee Shackleford and I collaborated with Melanie Green, Ericka Scharrer, and Craig Wetterer on a research study about the value of entertainment education in the domain of live theater.[8] In this study, we presented theater audiences with either a play that communicated the realities of intimate partner violence, or a comparison play—one that presented people in difficult dramatic relationships, but did not relate to intimate partner violence. Lee is a theater professor and playwright, and he wrote the play about intimate partner violence in consultation with the research team. Because there are common myths about intimate partner violence, the play was written in such a way as to debunk these myths. We found that audiences were highly engaged with both plays, but that watching the play about intimate partner violence resulted in more elaborate knowledge of the subject, as well as less endorsement of common myths about intimate partner violence, as compared to controls. We titled this paper, "Setting the Stage for Social Change." This research is one example of the potential power of fictional narrative to change our knowledge and beliefs about important social issues. Although very little research of this sort has focused on theater, entertainment education has been studied more thoroughly in other genres that present fictional narrative, such as literature, radio, and television.

One important theory explaining why people are persuaded by information in fictional stories is called transportation theory. People reading a book, watching a movie or TV show, or playing a video game become transported, swept up, or lost in the story, even feeling like they themselves are part of the story. This is one of the appealing properties of media: being transported is a state of flow in which the person loses track of time because of deep engagement. When a fictional story transports us, we are persuaded rather uncritically because transportation decreases counterarguing (questioning assertions) and increases connections with the characters and the sense that the story has a reality to it.[9] Engaging with a story means that we have suspended our disbelief, and this facilitates our persuasion to the points of view embedded in the story. In fact, some theorists believe that we accept beliefs not only uncritically but involuntarily.[10]

This discussion of fantasy and reality reminds me of a funny story line from the movie *Galaxy Quest*. *Galaxy Quest* is a good-natured spoof of popular science fiction and its fans. Basically, *Galaxy Quest* asks, what if *Star Trek* were real? In the film, the actors who play science fiction characters become embroiled in a real-life encounter with aliens and spaceships. When the situation becomes life threatening, the "commander" enlists the help of some extremely devoted fans he's met at a scifi convention. Earlier in the story the fans had indicated that they knew the spaceship and its crew's adventures weren't really real. However, when the commander needs their help, he tells them the news that those things that were supposed to be fantasy really are real. The fans reply with great excitement that they knew it all along! I think fans of Star Trek and similar shows and films found this scene amusing because they've personally experienced what it's like not only to wish that the fictional universe really existed, but actually found it so compelling that somewhere deep in their psyches it really is real to them. We want Spock to be real. We want beaming from one place to another to be real. And there is another gray area in the fantasy/reality distinction. In the 1960s, the communicators and computer disks used as props in the show did not have real-life counterparts, but later in history these things really did come to fruition in the form of real mini-disks and cell phones.

Speaking of Star Trek, Nichelle Nichols, the actress who played the role of Lieutenant Uhuru on the original series, often speaks of another kind of reality that her appearance on the show created. In the fictional universe of Star Trek, people believed in the notions of interracial harmony and equality. The ship's officers, who were from a variety of racial backgrounds, exemplified these values. Nichols the actress has told of a conversation she had with the late Dr. Martin Luther King Jr. in which she told him she was thinking of quitting the show. Dr. King reportedly responded that she could not because her being in a respected position in this fictional story was affirming and uplifting for African Americans in America. Whether they watched the show or not, it was part of our culture, and having an African American officer on Star Trek was a real victory for civil rights.

How Fantasy Becomes Reality

What Martin Luther King Jr. understood about the positive influence of an African American actress on real American race relations is a great example of how fantasy becomes reality. When writers produce a fictional story that asks, "What if an African American woman were an officer on a futuristic space ship? What if people in the future really acted as if they were color-blind?" this excites the imaginations of those who watch the show and even those who know of its existence. Seeing a story about racial equality demonstrates that it could happen, and maybe that it should happen, in real life. So you see, on one level we know that Star Trek isn't real, but on another level it is very real. Real people have been changed by watching Star Trek, or even by hearing about it. Dr. King understood that.

And what about *Friends*? As one of the most popular television shows in recent history, *Friends* has not only influenced fashion and hairstyles, but it has even influenced the way we speak. Researchers at the University of Toronto[11] argue that *Friends* both reflects changes in American language usage and has *caused* changes in that usage. For example, *Friends* is credited with influencing the American usage of the word "so" in the sense of totally and completely, as in "you are *so* dead." This is a great example of a fairly subtle, but direct, media effect. Everyday people watching *Friends* were exposed to a novel way to use the word "so" and started to imitate it. (Wow, we are *so* influenced by media!) Part of the power of social influence behind that change was undoubtedly that the people on *Friends* are seen as hip, and therefore imitating their speech, mannerisms, dress, and so forth would presumably make the imitator seem more hip to her actual—well, *friends.*

This social influence extends, of course, to other attitudes and behaviors. For example, the actresses in *Friends* were examples of Hollywood's thin beauty ideal for women. An educational video I sometimes play in my college class-room refers to a billboard that featured the female stars of *Friends* with the caption "Cute anorexic chicks." You may know that many studies document how exposure to very thin women in the media has a host of negative effects on both female and male viewers, including increasing eating disorders, body dissatisfaction, mate dissatisfaction, feelings of guilt and shame, and desire for oneself or one's mate to undergo plastic surgery. This is another example of watching stylish people in the media and wanting to imitate them. Do you think the latest actresses are just as thin as the stars of *Friends*, or do you imagine it is getting worse? How would you compare Evangeline Lilly from *Lost*, Keira Knightly from the *Pirates of the Caribbean* movies, or Katherine Heigl from *Grey's Anatomy* to the female stars of *Friends*? How about to the top actresses of decades past?

The idea that viewing a steady diet of underfed actresses and models can make us feel fat and unattractive is an example both of the pervasiveness of certain media messages and of the power of those messages to affect us. There are myriad other ways that media exposure affects us. How about our view of the standard of living and habits of people we see on TV? Did you ever notice that people's houses and apartments on TV and in the movies never look much like the places real people live? If you've never noticed, take a close look at the digs of your favorite characters next time you are watching TV. Apartments have more in the way of architectural and design elements than real dwell-ings almost ever have. Think about your first apartment and how it looked before you moved in—probably it featured box-like rooms with standard ceil-ing heights, plain windows, white walls, and beige carpet. Even the humblest characters on TV and movies have interesting, chic apartments. My husband

and I were watching the detective show *Monk* recently and noticed that the apartment of a supposedly shifty character featured a very spacious living room with wood floors and an artfully designed color scheme and his kitchen boasted a beautiful vintage oven. This apartment was supposed to be in San Francisco, no less, where such an apartment would be beyond most people's means. As for Rachel from *Friends*, ask a real Manhattan resident what the apartment of a waitress looks like, or how many roommates she would need to be able to make rent in Manhattan.

What does all this mean from a social psychological perspective? When we watch TV, we don't think we are actively learning anything, but in fact we are. One thing, for example, we learn from watching *Friends* is that you can be a waitress and live in a nice apartment in Manhattan. As for lifestyle, notice that on TV people regularly hang out in interesting places during the day having long, funny conversations with their friends. For the *Friends*, these conversations often took place at their favorite coffeehouse, the Central Perk. On *Frasier*, it was Café Nervosa. In the end, what this amounts to is the projected image that other people's lives are more interesting and rich than our own. We naturally compare ourselves to others; this is a basic premise of social psychology known simply as social comparison theory. When watching these stylized, idealized lives play out before us, we wonder why we can't get as many dates with glamorous, educated women as *Frasier* does, why our conversations are not as witty, our jobs as interesting, our standard of living as high. In short, watching idealized lives makes real lives seem substandard and can result in a personal sense of dissatisfaction or ennui. This dissatisfaction is a blow to our personal well-being, but a boon to advertisers who want to sell us more products than we can afford by marketing the promise that their products will make us happy and fulfilled.

Unintended Consequences

Now we come to an important and recurring theme in media psychology—namely, that very real media effects can absolutely be unintended consequences of media producers' desire to get our attention for their advertisers. Producers want us to enjoy watching *Frasier*, so they give him a splendidly decorated apartment, witty repartee, and gorgeous dates. Many times, I don't imagine the producers do this with the goal of making us feel inferior (although the advertisers do have that as an explicit goal); those feelings are an unintended consequence of the natural process of social comparison meeting the plastic world of Hollywood, where appearance is everything and where depth and substance don't translate as well.

MEDIA PSYCHOLOGY MEETS EVOLUTIONARY PSYCHOLOGY; OR, DARWIN DIDN'T ANTICIPATE HOLLYWOOD

According to evolutionary psychology, we are motivated most deeply, albeit unconsciously, to procreate. Therefore, we are naturally attracted to anything that will help us do that. For example, men are attracted to youthful women because younger women are more likely to be able to conceive and give birth to healthy offspring. Women are attracted to men with the resources to sustain children more than they are attracted to youth. This is, in part, because older men are perfectly capable of impregnating women, and more experienced men may actually be better at protecting and providing for offspring. Furthermore, women are attracted to socially dominant men for the same reasons. Psychologists have actually analyzed what men and women say in personal ads[12] and have found that women emphasize their good looks, while men emphasize their material resources and social status. From an evolutionary perspective, this makes total sense.

Now, enter Hollywood, and Darwin gets thrown on his ear. If you think about it, we human beings were designed under the premise that we'd be interacting with other real live humans (insert booming voice from above saying, "Well, duh!"). For example, we were designed to function in a system where we choose mates from the group of people around us. And, true enough, before modern media we were pretty much only exposed to other real-live people in our communities. Now many of us spend more time with media images than we do with real people (so sad!). The—again, I think largely unintended—result is that we've unconsciously changed our standards to encompass media ideals.

What are the consequences of exposing oneself to a steady diet of images of people created artificially and for other purposes altogether? What are the consequences of this to an entire society? If you want to know, then read on; we will discuss more of those consequences—what psychologists call "media effects." In fact, we've already talked about a number of them. Let's take a closer look at one consequence relevant to our last example of mate selection. Scientists from Arizona State University[13] showed undergrads photos and profiles of young people of the same sex, supposedly for the purposes of evaluating the formats used by a dating service. Actually, the researchers were interested in seeing how the viewers' perceptions of their own "market value" as a mate changed in comparison to the competition. What they discovered was that women felt their market value decreased after seeing photos of physically attractive women. Not so for men. Young men felt their market value took a punch after reading about socially dominant young men (for example, a leader who was the editor of the university newspaper). In a nutshell, people see themselves as less desirable mates if the competition is steeper. The authors point out that in the past, nature provided the competition, whereas now the media provide us with "massed exposure to desirable others."[14] In fact, we may see in the course of one hour of screen time competition at a level our ancestors weren't likely to see even in the course of one lifetime. If we operated purely on logic, when a woman saw Angelina Jolie or a man saw Bill Gates on TV, they would mentally stamp these individuals as crazy-unfair competition and make no adjustments whatsoever to their image of themselves as desirable mates. But that's simply not the kind of animal we are. We were created under a system in which it made sense to compare ourselves to the competition that we *saw*. No adjustments have been made to that system to accommodate modern media exposure and the corporate desire to get our attention by any means possible in order to make large profits. In sum, we simply weren't designed to navigate this media-saturated environment in which we find ourselves.

Let's think about this more deeply for a second. Let's assume that Darwin and contemporary sociobiologists are right and that our primary goal in life is to produce healthy offspring. We aren't so much consciously aware of this, but it is the deepest unconscious motive of our lives. Part of the drive to produce healthy offspring includes assessing the competition and positioning ourselves favorably within it. So, if other eligible mates are physically fit, we are motivated to keep ourselves fit as well. Our competition comes from within our own gene pool and shares our environment, so comparing our physical desirability to that of other suitable mates from within this group seems fair. Within this system, keeping ourselves fit is adaptive because it tends to increase our likelihood of winning a suitable mate. Now imagine moving from this set of rules, where our desirability as a mate was compared to that of our neighbors, to one in which we compare ourselves to the top actors and actresses, models, and business tycoons. How can we compete with the best in the world? What does this do to our sense of self-worth and desirability? The situation sounds pretty grim for us. But let's move a little deeper into the picture. If we assume that it is adaptive to make ourselves as desirable as we can as mates and that this is not really a choice but a biological imperative—and then suddenly we feel woefully inadequate—that makes us vulnerable. We are now vulnerable to sales pitches that promise to make us slimmer and more attractive or to make us more successful and socially dominant. You see where I am going with this. Mass media provide us with images of extreme people—extremely beautiful or extremely successful people. That gets our attention, which means we are watching the commercials, which means we are more likely to buy the advertised products. Now we are feeling vulnerable and inadequate. What do the media do next? Why, they provide us with a host of products and services that promise to make us beautiful and successful. To complicate matters, they also sell us images of delicious looking foods that will make us feel fat and unattractive, and this just adds to the vicious cycle. So the mass media play on our deepest needs, creating needs and selling products to meet those needs, but this is a vicious cycle and most of us end up simply caught up in the cycle—unhappy with our progress but unable to escape. Do we react, as a society, by condemning this unhealthy struggle? Do we ask for reform in the media, or at least demand that our schools educate our children about the vicious cycle? A few do, but for the most part we pretty much do the opposite. Since we, by and large, do not accept the idea that the media manipulate us, we do not find fault with this painful cycle of creating need and providing empty promises of fixing those problems that media created for us. In the next section, let's explore why that might be.

APOLOGISTS

When people passionately deny that media affect them, another interesting state of affairs takes place, namely, that these same people start to defend media executives. We call this condition being a media *apologist*. Now "apologist," I know, is a funny kind of word because it sounds like it means exactly the opposite of what it does mean. If you remember (and this might come under the category of what Michael Feldman, host of NPR's *What Do You Know?* calls "[t]hings you should have learned in school, had you been paying attention"), a Christian apology is a defense of the Christian perspective. Likewise, a "media apologist" defends media producers' rights to basically do whatever they want to do to make money. So, people can be manipulated by big business, and not only not realize it, but also defend businesses' right to use us. Ironically, in part this springs from a desire to feel that we are not being manipulated. The further irony, though, is that when we let ourselves be manipulated, do not realize it is happening, and then go so far as to defend big business's right to manipulate us, we become the perfect pawns of the profiteers. We let them stick it to us, and we jump to their defense when anyone questions it. This is a sad state of affairs. I think those of us who can see through this smokescreen ought to do something about it. We ought to educate others about the power of the media and the absurdity of becoming a media apologist.

This reminds me of something that happened when I was giving expert testimony before a congressional committee about the power of sexist rap lyrics. During the conversation, we heard truly dark and vulgar hardcore rap lyrics such as "if your daughter is 14, I'm gonna rape her." One congressman defended the media corporations' rights to produce any musical content they saw fit. He said simply, "If you don't like the song, turn it off." I replied in my testimony that "you can turn off the song, but you can't turn off your culture." I will talk more about both media apologists and media producers later on, but first I want to address the reasons that I think we have become pawns caught in the vicious cycle of vulnerability to the greed of big business, even to the point of becoming media apologists.

THE PSYCHOLOGY OF WHY

As mentioned earlier, there are many positive sorts of media influence, such as some of my own studies I mentioned above. It is more common for the public to accept that there are benefits of media use, such as the value of children watching Sesame Street. When it comes to potential risks, let's talk about the social psychological reasons that we might deny that these risks exist. These explanations are, for the most part, not mutually exclusive, but they often do coexist and interact with each other. I also want to stress that there are undoubtedly more reasons for this phenomenon than the ones I list below. In fact, I sincerely hope this book will start a conversation about why the current state of affairs exists and what we can do to move on to a new era in our relationship with media.

Cognitive Dissonance

In the 1950s, social psychologists Festinger and Carlsmith[15] brought naïve college students into their lab and asked them to do boring, repetitive tasks. Then some of those students were offered a trifling $1 to lie to other students by telling them the experiment they were about to do was enjoyable. Others were offered a better reason for lying, namely $20. Funny thing, the students who told these lies for no good reason ended up reporting that they actually liked these boring tasks, at least more than students who were given a good reason for lying. Why would students suddenly think boring tasks were not so very boring after all? Because of "cognitive dissonance"—the idea that mental inconsistencies cause discomfort that we are motivated to change, often through rationalization. The idea that we would lie to our peers and that we had no good reason for doing so makes us feel uncomfortable, and maybe even immoral or stupid. We make ourselves feel better by rationalizing; in this case, we soften the extent of the lie—"oh, the tasks weren't really that bad," we tell ourselves.

If Sigmund Freud (or more properly, his daughter Anna, but that's another story) had been alive to read social psychologists' work on cognitive dissonance, he probably would have explained that this is a psychological defense mechanism. Our egos can be quite fragile, and we human beings are motivated to defend ourselves from, well, ourselves. We don't want to think we are bad people, so often we rationalize. There are many ways to do this. We can tell ourselves we didn't have a choice. We can trivialize our behavior, for example, by saying that, in perspective, the behavior wasn't that bad. We can remind ourselves that we are generally good people and/or that other people are much worse than we are. We can deny responsibility for our actions (in this case, we could say that the experimenter made me do it).

Freedom of Choice Does Not Mean Freedom from Consequences

As cognitive dissonance researchers from the University of Paris[16] point out, responsibility is the consequence of making a choice. These dissonance researchers had Parisian university students write arguments in favor of a new application process for French universities. The students were given either a choice or no choice about writing these arguments. Parisian students are generally Universalists who oppose an application procedure for universities, and this attitude is tied to their general moral beliefs in justice and equality; therefore, the arguments they wrote were against their beliefs. Results showed that those not given a choice about writing these immoral arguments reduced their dissonance about having done so by denying personal responsibility (again, the experimenter made me do it). Furthermore, the authors noted that this denial of personal responsibility was a stronger rationalization than trivializing their behavior ("it's no big deal"). For all the students, once they rationalized sufficiently, they no longer felt bad (guilty, ashamed, etc.) about their behavior.

So how does dissonance reduction apply to our media habits and our views about those habits? If we spend most of our free time using media and if media exposure exerts powerful consequences on us, changing our attitudes, feelings, and behaviors, and if some of those changes are negative (such as negative body image, increased eating disorders, and increased aggression), then knowledge of these phenomena undoubtedly produces dissonance. If we are to protect our egos, it is quite likely that we will resort to rationalization. One rationalization for concerns about our media diet is to deny that media exposure affects us. Ah, but what consequences this brings! If we can't face the truth of our own manipulation, then we open ourselves to becoming pawns of big business, vulnerable to its many attempts to manipulate us. Paradoxically, the stronger our unconscious fear that we might be the victims of harmful manipulation, the more powerful becomes our drive to reduce dissonance and therefore defend media. Thus some media apologists are probably those who experience the most cognitive dissonance and therefore are among those with the most powerful needs to rationalize their behavior. (Others are probably those who are truly ignorant that they are manipulated and thus have no dissonance to reduce.) When some media apologists passionately defend big business, what they're really doing psychologically is defending their own egos by rationalizing behavior that they themselves are not comfortable with.

An alternative to rationalization, of course, is to change our attitudes or behaviors. Instead of defending the right of big business to manipulate us and denying that media affect us, we could face the truth and take steps to do something positive about it. But that would require real strength—strength of character, strength of intellect, and the strength to make real social change. I think many of us are strong enough and savvy enough to do this. I bet, in fact, that if you are reading this book and following my arguments, you are just the person I want to talk to about this. Maybe you, like me, have come to the realization that we are raising our children in a media-saturated environment that makes them vulnerable to manipulation and that it is time we all got smart about it. It's time for us to become more powerful and less vulnerable to manipulation. Rationalization will, after all, get us only so far. It's at best a short-term fix that will keep the symptoms at bay, but it won't cure the underlying problem. Like staying in a bad relationship, we can ignore it for only so long before it blows up in our face.

In the end, whatever our viewpoint on media effects, we must come to understand that when addressing our media diets, freedom of choice does not translate into freedom from consequences. All things considered, negative choices most likely lead to negative consequences, whether we want to believe it or not. Likewise, wise media use will tend to lead to healthy consequences. A subtly different point is that regarding the choices we make concerning media consumption, freedom of choice also does not mean true liberation. Simply put, poor choices do not free us; they ensnare us with their consequences. As great parents have been explaining forever, "just because you *can* doesn't mean you *should*." For example, research shows that small children who watch more television enter schools with lower vocabularies than their peers who watch less television. Choosing poor media habits did not liberate these children. Just the opposite: it put them at risk for failure. On the other hand, an experience with good media can also have lasting effects. For instance, I use a health and fitness tracking app called myfitnesspal. I hope that in the years to come I will look back on how this app helped me, and I will be grateful. In terms of fictional media, there are films, plays, shows, and other mediated stories that I use to inspire healthy choices—things that make life better. I'm glad I have these experiences in my life.

Truth and Consequences

Turning back to negative media effects, another reason people don't clearly see how media may affect them negatively involves another kind of perception of choice. We have the feeling that we freely choose what media to expose ourselves to. We decide when to turn the TV, game, or movie on and off, for example. *We* decide. No one forces us to buy a particular video game or to go to a certain movie. Sometimes we believe that when we choose freely, those choices cannot harm us.

How true is it that we choose our media diet freely? When US adults were surveyed about their TV viewing habits, the majority said they watch more TV than they want to watch.[17] Wait a minute—they watch more TV than they *want* to watch? How is that possible? Who's forcing them to watch? Well, I don't think anyone is forcing them, in the traditional sense of the word. No one is strapping them into their Lazy Boys and forcibly directing their eyes toward *America's Funniest Home Videos*. But mass media's job is to suck us in—to get our attention at a deep, emotional level. At this level, our viewing is not actually a 100 percent rational choice. To use an extreme example, this argument strikes me as being like the alcoholic who says he chooses to drink and that he can stop drinking at any time. How likely is the average American to stop "choosing" to plug into media so much that it takes up almost all his spare time? How likely is he even to significantly reduce the amount of time he spends with media? Kubey and Csikszentmihayli noticed a phenomenon that happens daily in living rooms across America. The television is on and people are talking. During the conversation, something happens on the TV, and all eyes go to the screen in a reaction called the orienting response (like when we turn our head toward a sudden noise). This is because TV is produced to get our attention. The methods for doing this will be discussed later. For now, let me just say that mass media artfully, skillfully, and adeptly use knowledge of human psychology to get our attention, and yes, even when we don't necessarily "want" to give it. In their article, "Television Addiction Is No Mere Metaphor," Kubey and Csikszentmihayli[18] put it well—and with a nod toward evolutionary psychology—when they said, "Perhaps the most ironic aspect of the struggle for survival is how easily organisms can be harmed by that which they desire. The trout is caught by the fisherman's lure, the mouse by cheese. . . . Realizing when a diversion has gotten out of control is one of the great challenges of life."

And what of the notion that anything that is freely chosen cannot harm us? To push the alcohol comparison further, it would be like the alcoholic deciding that drinking will not damage his liver or shorten his life span—that he somehow had control over the effects of the substance on his body and mind. This would be a dangerous fantasy, but one that is quite compelling. It's so tempting to believe a lie that covers up our messy problems, like sweeping dirt under a rug. It's probably why we believed cigarette executives for so many years when they told us that cigarette smoking does not lead to lung cancer. It's easier to believe it than to face the truth. In fact, some of the top media violence researchers[19] have suggested that the link between media violence exposure and aggression is comparable to that of smoking and lung cancer. Again, put this in the context that a large percentage of Americans do not believe there is any connection between media violence exposure and aggression, recognizing that this belief is in direct contradiction to our best scientific evidence, and that it is also what media executives and advertisers want us to believe.

There is another reason for this belief that our freely chosen habits do not harm us. This reason relates to our political perspective, placed in the context of recent world history.[20] When we think of manipulation, we are likely to think of strong-arm techniques: fascist dictators and terrorists manipulate, and they do it with an iron fist. Think of George Orwell's *Big Brother*. Think of the motto of the Borg on TV's *Star Trek: The Next Generation*: "Resistance Is Futile." Think Hitler, Stalin, Saddam Hussein, Osama Bin Laden, or the general view that Americans had of Russia in the mid-twentieth century. The idea is that we'll know when people want to manipulate us because they'll publicly declare their intention or brag about how we're powerless against their strength.

This is actually similar to how villains operate in the movies, on television, and in video games (and in "professional" wrestling, for that matter). In the *Die Hard* movies (Figures 1.1A and 1.1B), we know when someone wants to control the nice people by the way he hijacks their building, terrorizes them, shoots some of them, and brags about his domination over them and his evil scheme for great personal profit. And, in true American cowboy form, we fight back with one rugged, wise-cracking individual who can overpower an entire militant organization with a wry smile and a little "Yippee-ki-yay Motherfucker."

This vision of conquering the brutal, heartless thieves and avenging the innocent victims is a compelling fantasy. I understand, believe me. *I* want to be Bruce Willis. *I* want to run unflinching in bare feet over broken glass while firing my weapon *and* my witty retorts. *I* want to see clearly who is good and who is evil and to always have the power to take down the bad guys—and look cool while doing it. I think we all do. What I'm saying is that when people want to take our money and manipulate us, they generally don't show up in our building with a German brute squad and a pithy, high-tech-savvy sidekick. The truth is much more boring: they generally manipulate us through our hands-down favorite pastime: the media. They make TV commercials and

Figures 1.1A and 1.1B Americans have an Orwellian view of manipulation—that if I want to control you, I'll strong-arm you like the iconic villains in the *Die Hard* films. This leaves us vulnerable to the more subtle forms of mass media manipulation that are more likely to take our money and change our minds. (Pictured here: Alan Rickman as Die Hard baddie Hans Gruber, and Bruce Willis as John McClane, the "ordinary cop" out to stop him.)

print ads designed to make us feel bad about ourselves and give us the illusion that if we buy their stuff, we will be happy. And rather than responding by opening fire at them, we're more likely to defend their right to manipulate us for all we're worth.

MASS MEDIA, AUTOMATICITY, AND MIRROR NEURONS

In 1890, the great American psychologist William James wrote about the principle of "ideomotor action"—the idea that just thinking about a behavior makes you more likely to do it. Research shows that we unconsciously imitate the behaviors of those around us. A baby imitates her mother's smile. If your date rubs her nose, you will probably unconsciously rub your nose, too. But if someone were to ask you about it, you'd probably say that you didn't notice you were doing it. The reason is that the behavior is outside conscious control—we do it automatically and we're not aware of it. Scholars think we're hard-wired to imitate because it helps us learn adaptive behaviors and survive. Socially, it is also the glue that can bind us to other people, in part because people like others who act the way they do. Social imitation, then, is often unconscious and it is often adaptive.

Exciting new research has identified what may well be the physical structures in the brain responsible for our ability to imitate and our inclination to do so. Called "mirror neurons," these complexes of feeling, thinking, and doing help us imitate actions. Simply put, when we see another person doing something, it is reflected directly in our mirror neurons. In fact, seeing someone else perform a behavior provokes a response in our brain very similar to the one that occurs when we ourselves do the behavior. Watching you sew on a button creates an image in my mind very similar to what occurs when I sew on a button myself. Scientists think there are several reasons for this. Mirror neurons help us empathize. In fact, the word "empathy" originally meant the ability to directly imitate a behavior. Today we use it to refer to the ability to feel what someone else feels. When my brain mirrors what you do, I understand your perspective.

Mirror neurons, then, are neural structures that help us empathize and imitate. Interestingly, this imitation is outside conscious control. We don't know we are doing it. According to psychologists John Bargh and Tanya Chartrand,[21,22] people are not comfortable with this notion because we like to believe that we are autonomous. We will strongly deny being manipulated unconsciously. You can see how this applies to the media. For example, when we watch someone hit another person on TV, our mirror neurons respond as if we had done it ourselves. In fact, the response is so powerful that there is evidence the muscles we would use to strike out actually are affected. Unconsciously, we are now more inclined to do that behavior, and at the same time, we are not aware of this stimulus toward aggression. Here again is an explanation of why people deny media effects—they sometimes threaten our sense of autonomy, on the one hand, and, on the other hand, sometimes we are genuinely unaware of what's going on inside our brains as we watch other people's behavior via the media.

Recall also the research, cited earlier, that shows how people are persuaded by factual content that is embedded in fictional stories. We become transported into the world of the story, we become emotionally attached to the characters—sometimes identifying with them—and we do not critically process the messages that are embedded in the story. Exposure to an attitude or idea of a fictional character can change our minds about using condoms or the health benefits of exercising or any other attitude or idea. I want to point out that persuasion through fiction is powerful by its very nature. We are processing emotionally and uncritically, suspending our disbelief, and we may, as theorists note, be persuaded involuntarily. Over time, we forget where we learned the persuasive information, but hold on to the beliefs, whether true or false.[23,24]

WE REALLY DON'T KNOW WHY WE DO WHAT WE DO

This argument wouldn't be complete without telling you about one of my favorite psychology studies of all times.[25] It is an all-time favorite of mine because—like the research on unconscious imitation—it tells us something fascinating about the human mind that I think many people simply won't or can't believe about themselves. In this now-classic research, psychologists put people in a room and gave them a problem to solve. Two strings were attached to the ceiling and the task at hand was to tie the strings together. But you couldn't reach one string if you were standing and holding the other. What to do? A variety of objects were in the room, including a pair of pliers. The solution was to tie the pliers to one string and to swing them, then to go grab the other string and grab the swinging pliers, thus enabling you to tie the strings together. Half the people in this study were given a hint: a man stood in the room with them swinging a metal nut on a string like a pendulum (which was supposed to suggest that they use the pliers as a weight on a pendulum). The other half did not get the hint. Results indicated that those who got the hint of the swinging pendulum were much more likely to solve the problem. Keep in mind that no one was told directly that the man swinging the pendulum was supposed to be a hint.

So far, so good—next, the researchers asked the participants how they solved the problem. Here's where it gets fascinating. Turns out that pretty much no one said that the hint helped him or her solve the problem, even though we know from the evidence that it did help. Were these people liars or cheats? No. They just didn't realize that they were given a hint and they didn't realize that the hint had materially helped them solve the problem. Why not? Psychologists think it is because often, simply put, people do not know why they do what they do. And what do we do when we don't understand the causes of our own behavior? Well, it turns out that we make up reasons that sound good to us.

Let's take another example. In another study,[26] subjects were given different pairs of pantyhose and were asked which pair they thought were the best. Subjects made their choices, then were asked to explain why they liked their favorite more than the others. They gave lots of reasons: their favorites were softer, stronger, silkier, and so on. The catch is that the pairs of pantyhose were all the same: same brand, size, fabric. It turns out that most people preferred the rightmost pair of pantyhose, even though it was identical in every way to the other pairs of pantyhose. This is because of a general preference people show for the rightmost item in a group of items. But did anyone say, "I like these pantyhose because they were the furthest to the right on the table"? No. They didn't realize that was the reason for their preference and when asked for reasons that they did what they did, they simply made up what sounded like rational reasons. Too bad these supposedly rational reasons were totally bogus.

These studies illustrate how we can be completely unaware of the factors that influence us. They also illustrate how we can be convinced of our motives even when our explanations are patently false. We don't always know why we do what we do, but we are perfectly happy to make up reasons that sound good and to believe them as if they were the gospel truth.

Another important factor in understanding the things that influence us can be illustrated by the public conversation that followed the death of Princess Diana. Many refused to believe that Diana's death resulted from a simple car crash. Some suggested that her death was the result of a conspiracy. Why did people think this way? Social psychology provides us with one reason: people tend to believe that a cause and an effect should be similar in magnitude. So, a major event like Princess Diana's death cannot logically be caused by something minor like a simple, everyday car accident. Likewise, racial prejudice or an eating disorder can't be caused by something as innocuous as television shows or magazine pictures. Trivial things don't result in meaningful consequences. I wish it were true. But since it isn't, we have to understand this and teach our schoolchildren to understand it as well.

Also, to the extent that we can mentally reverse an outcome, we feel more strongly about it. Any time we can say "if only" about something bad that happened, we are more distressed. "If only" he hadn't played so many violent video games, maybe he wouldn't have hurt that other child. "If only" he had concentrated on learning to play music or baseball, things might have been different. Compound the trivial cause with the "if only" negative event, and we have an especially maddening situation. "If only" he hadn't played so many violent video games. ... Playing games—what a trivial cause for an important negative outcome like harming someone else. I can understand why we don't want to believe it. I can also understand why those who want to sell us something can have such an easy time convincing us that bad habits don't result in bad consequences.

I took an entire course in graduate school called *Human Inference and Social Judgment*[27] that was all about the psychology of how people make decisions and how we understand our own motives and decisions. In the class, we read about countless research studies on these topics. What I learned vividly from all this research is that people often make irrational decisions but are just as passionate about these wrongheaded decisions as they would be about wise decisions. Turns out, according to our current understanding, the best decision-making involves both the head and the heart. However, we are still vulnerable to making poor decisions, and these vulnerabilities are very predictable. The renowned social psychologist Phillip Zimbardo once wisely said[28] that there are more people who profit from understanding human psychology than there are using psychology to better the human condition. My hope is that reading this book will help you deal effectively with those who are using what we know about psychology against you for their profit and your loss. I also hope this book will make you more aware of what media have benefited you and will inspire you to continue to seek out those media that make your life better.

Fandom, Fantasy, and Reality

One way that fantasy contributes to reality is through fandom. Via fandom we explore a new world from a new perspective. When we take in our favorite shows and films through the eyes of its characters, we vicariously have experiences, make friends, ponder philosophies, and connect with heroes and anti-heroes in a way that's similar to how we do it with real-world relationships. As I'll talk about later, the connection of a fan to a favorite character is much like when a live person links with an on-screen computer avatar.

Fictional stories are different from real life because they are sharper, neater, and perhaps more dramatic. And story characters are lower maintenance than real people and, dare we say it, more attractive sometimes as well. Our favorite stories become part of us—part of who we are and where we've been. Whether we are embarrassed to admit it or proud to be a part of them, fictional stories play an important role in our lives.

ON FANS AND FANDOMS

How would you complete this sentence? "I am a big fan of _____."
Fandoms can center on television shows (Trekkers), film (*Star Wars*), video game franchises (*Call of Duty*), musical groups (the Beatles) and genres (rap), and literary characters (Sherlock Holmes), among other things. You can be a fan of a company (Apple), an author (Stephen King), an actor (Brad Pitt, Angelina Jolie), a super couple (Brangelina), a director (Peter Jackson), or a genre (Sci Fi), among other things.

A fan is an enthusiast and someone who knows a lot about the object of his or her affections. Being "in the know" can mean knowing all the characters and plot lines in the *Star Wars* saga, also called knowing "the text" or "the canon." In today's digital parlance, being a fan can also connote being a "follower" in the sense of keeping up with the latest happenings related to your franchise. *Star Wars* fans may follow the latest *Star Wars*–related news and post about it on social media. If you are a big fan of Harry Potter, you might challenge your friends to a game of Harry Potter trivia. But you could also be more of an enthusiast than someone who claims to know all the details about your franchise. Maybe you like to dress up in period costume and attend a *Downton Abbey* season premier party, but you can't remember the name of Daisy's husband's father. In other words, there are different ways of being a fan.

Media psychologists also differentiate fans from audiences, with fans being more actively engaged than mere audience members. In fact, a key part of being a fan is its instrumentality: fans can influence what happens in the world of their favorite franchise. For example, fans have been known to successfully lobby to keep a television show on the air (*Star Trek: The Original Series* and *Community*), and to influence everything from storylines to the hiring and firing of actors or coaches. In today's world of interactive digital media, fans have a more meaningful and powerful connection with those who work in the business end of their favorite franchises.[1–4]

However scholars may see it, the main thing about being a fan is, of course, that it's fun! Fans love watching their favorite shows, waiting for the next big game or movie sequel, and voicing opinions on social media about the latest happenings in the world of their favorite franchise. For example, one fan posted a message on Twitter about actress Carrie Fisher being asked to lose weight for the latest *Star Wars* film, saying, "#carriefisher: every inch #StarWarsroyalty at any size."

PERSONAL FANHOOD

I propose that there are two *fan styles*: I'll call them the *personal fan* and the *participatory fan*. Someone who experiences a show or sport mostly by himself is a personal fan. Personal fanhood is largely internal and centers on the private thoughts, feelings, and behaviors of the fan in relation to the fan object. Let's say that one summer, you discover the show *Biography*. You start watching biographies of interesting people: actors, entrepreneurs, gangsters, and athletes. Many of the biographies you watch really interest you and make you think. Through your experience with the show, you better understand some philosophies of life and some decision-making strategies that you decide to make a part of how you live your life.

I'd say that you are a fan of *Biography*. Watching the show is enjoyable and so is actively learning from the life lessons that are central to the show's narrative. In this example, your fanhood is mostly personal. The show is important to you, but it's mostly something that you don't really "do anything about" as far as the outside world is concerned. Maybe you talk with your friends about some things you learned from the show: how an actor overcame alcoholism, how a writer learned to persevere despite rejection, or why some people's marriages break up. You might even say you love *Biography*, but it doesn't make you want to dress like the host of the show and go to a convention full of people who also love *Biography*. Those behaviors are the domain of the participatory fan. More on participatory fanhood, after we explore what's going on under the hood of personal fanhood.

Deep Dive into the Fan Mind

Psychologists and other scholars want to know what's going on beyond the surface of the fan experience. One of the major reasons to care so much about the psychology of fanhood is that in our current culture, viewing videos, films, and television shows now garners most of our attention. I think it's a big deal that when we have a choice about how to spend our hours and days, we're most likely to look at screens. When I say "big deal," I don't mean that we should primarily react with fear or predictions of doom. I mean that clearly the topic is worth pursuing. I want to know lots more about the psychology of our infatuation with mediated stories. For starters, I want to know more about "why." Why are we so in love with these experiences? What's happening psychologically when we engage with a character and a story?

IDENTIFICATION AND NARRATIVE PERUSASION
Believe it or not, the psychological study of narrative—of our connection with characters and stories—is still in its infancy. Scholars propose that at the heart of entertainment is a connection to characters. Vorderer, Steen, and Chan[5] define entertainment as involving ". . . the exploration of relationships through simulations that permit individuals to identify with substitute agents and thus create the subjective experience of relationships." It follows then that fanhood is a kind of experience simulator. Fans experience narrative fiction (in other words, films, television shows, videos, etc.) "as if" they were happening to them. More on this later.

When thinking about how we connect with characters and fictional stories, one factor that has often been studied is that of character identification. When researchers ask people how deeply they identify with a character, sometimes the answer has tended to focus on a somewhat superficial definition of identification: similarity. Similarity is the degree to which we see the character as "like me," the premise being that I can understand other people who are like

me. We have also studied "wishful identification," also known as "idealization" or the degree to which we wish we were the character we watch, and
"imaginal identification," which refers to imagining that we are the character
while we watch the story.

Scholars have noted that there are, in fact, many definitions of character identification.[6,7] Maybe there are too many at this point, but it is still
early in this line of research. Personally, I am glad that we have moved
beyond assuming that identification with a character means that you are
"like them" as in the same race, age, sex, socioeconomic status, or even species. I don't know about you, but I can identify with lots of characters who
are not "like me" in those ways. For example, I identify with Elastigirl in
the *Incredibles* (a stretchy cartoon superheroine), with Morgan Freeman in
Bruce Almighty (a Black man playing God), and with a wooly mammoth
(played by Ray Romano) in *Ice Age*. It's really not about how much they are
"like me" superficially—it's their humanity that pulls me in (yes, I used the
word "humanity" to refer to a shape shifter, God, and a wooly mammoth, and
I stand behind that). It's their universal experiences and struggles that make
us want to take the journey with them. And anyway, what would the world
of film be like if it were populated by lots of characters who were superficially "like me"? Who wants to watch a bunch of movies about middle-aged,
White, female professors? (Working title: *Real Professors*; Episode One: *The
Tenure Clock*). OK, one or two would be cool, but then it's right back to lady
superheroes and wooly mammoths.

Dara Greenwood's research[8] offers one demonstration of the way that other
definitions of identification may be stronger than similarity. She asked college women who were familiar with female action heroes about their experience with these heroes and their own real-world aggression. Results indicated
that the main character in the show *Buffy the Vampire Slayer* was the favorite
female action heroine of these college-aged women. In terms of identification,
Greenwood found that behavioral identification (thinking you act similarly to
Buffy) did not predict college women's aggressive behavior. However, idealization (wanting to be more like Buffy) did predict aggression, such that the more
the college women wanted to be like Buffy (or Xena, etc.), the more aggressive
they were in real life.

Igartua[9] created a scale to measure character identification, focusing on
three facets of identification: (1) emotional empathy (understanding how the
character feels), (2) cognitive empathy (seeing the action from the character's
perspective), and (3) merging (feeling that you have become the character).
These definitions of identification are much more satisfying than mere demographic similarity. The idea that a fan is empathizing and merging with the
character she watches describes the experience in a much more satisfying way.

It is also much clearer how these kinds of identification fit with other research that explores our connection with fiction.

Transportation, Engagement, and Experience Taking

As mentioned earlier, one key way that we now understand the personal fan experience is through the process called transportation.[10-13] When a fan is transported, she is lost in the world of the story, and her self and surroundings have become distant. Transportation is similar to other psychological constructs such as engagement, immersion, and flow.[14-18]

One reason that scholars study identification, transportation, engagement, and the like is because they are all factors theorized to act as mechanisms of narrative persuasion. "Narrative persuasion" is the term given to the fact that we change our attitudes and beliefs to reflect what we've witnessed in a fictional story. In other words, the more you are lost in a story and attached to the characters, the more you lose your sense of self, the greater the odds are that you will start to believe in the ideas you hear in the story world. One mechanism for narrative persuasion is that being transported into a story world reduces counter-arguing, meaning that we accept the premises that the character accepts and we don't mentally resist those ideas. In fact, some think that instead of merely not resisting the story world or suspending disbelief, it's more likely that a fan who is lost in the story world accepts the premise of that world implicitly. On the other hand, fans, especially those who actively engage with other fans and with the producers of their favorite franchise, can also be more meta-analytic and more critical. They complain when a show makes a mistake, in their view. They ask for more from the producers, sometimes in the form of more believable and sometimes in the form of more canonically correct content.[14-20]

This conversation is related to the terms "affirmational" and "transformational" fandom, coined by "obsession_inc" in the essay "affirmational fandom versus transformational fandom" (http://obsession-inc.dreamwidth. org/82589.html). In a nutshell, the affirmational fan seeks to affirm what the producers present as the canon, while the transformational fan seeks to play a role in transforming the canon, such as through writing fan fiction in which the story veers away from the canon. The author believes that men are more prone to affirmational, while women are more prone to transformational fandom.

Using "engagement" as an umbrella term for "involvement" (a.k.a., "transportation"), Brockmeyer and colleagues[15] discuss the relationship between video game engagement and the related concepts of immersion, presence, flow, and absorption. They say that "immersion" and "presence" both generally refer to the feeling of being present in the game environment. "Flow" carries with it the connotation of enjoying being lost in the game as well as having the concept of time seem to shift. Flow can be seen as a merger with the game environment. Finally, absorption and dissociation are altered states of consciousness in which the game player goes deeper and deeper into the game world.

To bring this point home, Brockmeyer and colleagues had college men who self-identified as gamers play video games in the laboratory. Then they had accomplices go into the room where the gamers were playing and try to engage them in conversation. The accomplices asked things like, "Excuse me, did you drop your keys?" The more engaged players took longer to rouse out of the world of the game they had entered than the less engaged players did. The take-away from this study, for me, is that playing a favorite game or watching a favorite movie is a lot about "going there" and "being" that person. In other words, personal fanhood is very personal. Being in the story world feels like our experience, not someone else's experience. This is news because sometimes in our culture, we construe watching a story or playing a game as being inactive and disengaged. While that is sometimes the case, if we stop there, we are ignoring a large part of the fan experience.

WHERE? I MEAN WHO?

Bourdage[21] discusses the question of "where" the fan is theoretically when he is absorbed in the world of his favorite narrative. Think about a time when you were watching a show or movie or playing a video game that was highly engaging. "Where" did you feel you were? "Who" did you feel you were? Some say that when we're engaged with fiction "where" we are is both in the room where we watch and in the time and space of the narrative world. Scannell[22] calls these factors "doubled spatiality" (the *where* of narrative engagement) and "doubled temporality" (the *when* of it).

Other than asking "where" or "when," we can ask "who"? *Who* are we when we go deeply inside a story, connecting with the character and with the world? Kauffman and Libby[23] talk about the merger between a person and a character that takes place when the person is absorbed in a story. They call this merger "experience taking," defined as "the imaginative process of spontaneously assuming the identity of a character in a narrative and simulating that character's thoughts, emotions, behaviors, goals, and traits as if they were one's own." These scholars describe experience taking as a sort of identity shift in which there is an inverse relationship between our sense of self and the degree that we take on the experiences of the character. So, a fan who is deeply engaged in watching a favorite character in his story world feels that he is there—that he has merged with that character. Fans feel what the character feels. So, this is why we cry at sad movies and scream at scary ones: because we are experiencing the story's action as the character does.

Sometimes we hear in the press that watching television or film is "mindless entertainment." And if you watch someone stare at a screen, it can appear to be a mindless and impersonal enterprise. Yet, I assure you that the fan experience is quite the opposite. "Getting lost" in the world of the story means that fans experience the story world as if it were happening to them. Using Vorderer and colleagues' language, transported fans are in an experience simulator. Using Kauffman and Libby's language, fans are engaging in "experience taking." Whatever phraseology you use, we can conclude that rather than being a brainless activity, being a fan engages the brain. Simulated experience includes changing thoughts, attitudes, emotions, and even behaviors of fans. If you are experiencing something as if it were happening to you, it follows that the experience is a very personal one.

It's worth noting that I'm talking about fans here, so I am speaking of what happens when someone is deeply engaged, deeply connected. In real life, there are stories that we connect with and stories that we don't. There are times when a story disappoints us, when we start to remember that it is a show and so we're "bumped" psychologically out of our engagement. Sometimes we go deep into the story world. Sometimes, the story does not grab us and we stay at a superficial distance.

Until now I have been talking about our connections in terms of there being one fan and one character. But really we all know that a fan can connect with multiple characters. We can switch affiliations, imagining we are one character and then another. We can spend some time in a deep connection with a character in a story and then step back and think about the actor as a person, then perhaps about the role or the show's production. The connections we make are varied and sophisticated.

When we step back and think about a character from a distance, when we think about the actor who plays him, that's another way of connecting to the character and the story. Have you ever described for a friend why you love a certain scene in a favorite film? I'll tell you about one that I love in order to illustrate a point. In *Harry Potter and the Deathly Hallows*, there is a scene where two characters who are best friends, Harry and Hermione, are on a long and emotionally draining journey. Each of them must take turns wearing a charmed necklace that drags them down emotionally. In turn, the one who is not under the spell tries to support the one who is suffering. There's a scene where Hermione is wearing the necklace, feeling low. Harry pulls her to her feet and dances with her to the radio, bringing a smile to her face. As they dance and hold each other, you can see their mutual affection and strength. I love that scene because it shows such beautiful characteristics of friendship and bravery. I also love how brilliantly the two actors, Daniel Radcliffe and Emma Watson, play the scene. I mention this because it's an example of the kind of zooming we do when we engage with favorite narratives. We zoom in and we "are" one character. Snap! We're in the other character's shoes. Zoom again, and we slide back to examine what we think, first about the character and next about the actor playing the role. We can also pan out to the author's perspective, the film director, other fans—the perspectives we can scan through are rich and varied.

My colleague Lisa Swain once commented that one of the reasons we can grow so attached to a character is that characters do not put demands on us like the real people in our lives do. I think that's a great insight. I also think we can love story worlds and characters because they are drawn so clearly as compared with the real lives we inhabit. Think about the differences between real life and fiction. In fiction, as compared to real life, characters are on a clear journey within a satisfying story arc. Attractive, talented actors who are experts at portraying emotion play characters. This description does not necessarily apply to people we encounter in our everyday lives (sorry, real people!). The things characters say are well crafted by professional writers—dialogue is clear and compelling. You are aware of the characters' motivations—you see them from the inside as well as from the outside. You do not watch the characters during the mundane moments of their ordinary lives, but only through extraordinary circumstance. In other words, story characters and worlds usually beat real life by a mile—and it's not a fair fight. Of course we fall in love with fictional characters and their story worlds—they are extraordinary people on extraordinary journeys who ask nothing of us and give quite a bit in return.

FANDOM, FANTASY, AND REALITY

OK, now here's where I, as the author, want to get a big megaphone and yell to the world, "Hey, this is really important!" As a media psychologist, for years I have been asking myself why we spend most of our free time engaged with fictional stories and characters. Why do we watch so much TV, so many videos and films? Why do we read fiction? Why are our eyeballs so often trained at a screen? Well, right here is the answer I've been looking for, and it's very different from what many people seem to think. One of the major motivations for me to write this book was the regular experience I have had with people telling me, as a media psychologist, that adults know the difference between fantasy and reality and therefore are completely unmoved and uninfluenced by films, shows, advertisements, music—by any form of media. I have long felt frustrated that there is something really major missing from that picture, and here it is, right before our eyes. Essentially, this thing we're missing is that what looks like nothing is something. What looks like watching is more like experiencing. What looks impersonal is personal. These things are a big part of why we appear addicted to media.

As I explained in Chapter 1, I think we sometimes feel silly about our love for media and maybe a little worried about its various implications. I can't tell you how many times, upon hearing about research on the effects of media, that people from all walks of life have told me that media does not influence them. It reminds me of Robert Palmer's song "Addicted to Love," when he sings:

> You like to think that you're immune to the stuff
> It's closer to the truth to say you can't get enough
> You know you're gonna have to face it
> You're addicted to love.

Rather than being immune to the charms of media, it's closer to the truth to say we can't get enough. But I don't think we fully realize why or what it all means. I've talked to you about various scholarly approaches to understanding the process. Next, let's explore these questions through metaphor.

METAPHORS FOR NARRATIVE ENGAGEMENT

If you were to look at a fan while she watches her favorite franchise or reads her favorite author, it may not look like much is going on. But to the devoted fan, highly engaged in the story world, a lot is going on psychologically. If you were to examine her brain with, say, an fMRI (functional magnetic resonance imaging), her neurons would be firing away, making new memories and new connections. Her emotions would likely be kicked into gear. Her mirror neurons would be helping her feel like she was really there, engaged in the action of the story.

Just as people are highly attracted to stories, we are also highly attracted to metaphors. Stories and metaphors help us understand our worlds more readily than data or tersely stated facts. With that in mind, let me offer some metaphors for what's happening to a fan when she is engaged with a favorite story.

Movie Metaphors for Narrative Engagement

How would you describe the journey you take when you are highly engaged with a film or show? One apt metaphor for this experience is something I'll call the *avatar metaphor*. The word "avatar" has a number of meanings. In

Hinduism, it refers to a heavenly deity's Earthly incarnation. In the world of technology, "avatar" refers to an alter ego or on-screen representation of a person. What these definitions have in common is that a consciousness is traveling into another body so that that mind now temporarily inhabits another body and experiences the world through that body.

Horse and Rider

In speaking about avatars, we're addressing an age-old philosophical issue called the mind-body problem. We're asking what and where is "mind," and how does it relate to body. Consciousness researchers sometimes answer this question by using the metaphor of the horse and rider. In this metaphor, the consciousness is the rider and the body is the horse, such that "who we are" is the rider and that we could, theoretically, ride other horses.

The specific definition of "avatar" that is most relevant to the study of narrative is as follows (dictionary.com; avatar, def. 5): "(science fiction): a hybrid creature, composed of human and alien DNA and remotely controlled by the mind of a genetically matched human being." In James Cameron's epic film *Avatar*, the term takes on this meaning. In the film, the main character, Jake Sully, is unable to walk. But while Jake's body stays behind, his consciousness connects to an avatar—one who is half human and half Na'vi—a giant, blue, humanoid race that inhabits the planet Pandora. Jake binds to his avatar through a kind of medical terminal where his brain is hooked up to electrodes that then connected to the avatar. Jake's body stays behind, but his mind connects to the avatar and he thinks and feels as if he were the avatar. If we go back to our consciousness metaphor, the rider (mind) has changed horses (bodies).

If you think about our previous discussion about experience taking, double spatiality, immersion, and the like, you can see that these psychological terms have much in common with the avatar experience. When we engage with a story, when we're transported into the story world, we leave our own personal identity behind and become the avatar. Referring back to the discussion of mirror neurons in Chapter 1, when we watch someone else—and that someone else can be a character in a story—that character is our avatar. As the character thinks, feels, and acts, our brain reflects those experiences to us and even sends signals to the body to reflect the action we see on the screen. What we see with our eyes is mirrored in our brain.

When Jake is connected to the avatar, his brain is active, but his body is still. Jake's sense of himself as a human fades as he experiences life through the avatar. The Na'vi live a kind of natural, ideal life that keeps them spiritually connected to the land, not unlike Native American peoples. Jake makes strong bonds in the Na'vi world, eventually finding a mate and deciding that he wants to stay and live life as the avatar.

"The Bond" as Metaphor Within a Metaphor

In the film *Avatar*, Cameron gives us another metaphor for the connection between horse and rider—this time almost literally. The Na'vi and the avatars have a sort of neural chord called a "queue" that resembles a hair braid. They use these queues to make a neural connection called *tsaheylu* in the Na'vi language, or "making the bond." These neural connections are intimate and can take the form of a romantic bond or a special connection between the Na'vi and the creatures they ride (such as the direhorse) or fly (such as the mountain banshee).

In the context of engagement with character and story, "the bond" represents the neural bond between viewer and story world. It is not a physical neuron-to-neuron connection. But it is a connection in the sense that what happens on screen is mirrored in your brain via mirror neurons. (Maybe our brains came equipped with Bluetooth?) And in that sense it is a kind of neuronal connection. When you immerse yourself in a story world, your mind lights up to reflect what is happening there. What looks like a couch potato to the outside world can be a highly engaged mind who has "made the bond" with the story world and therefore, like the game players in the engagement research, would be hard to rouse out of that world. Awakening the fan from the story world is like breaking *tsaheylu*—the bond between rider and horse.

The Avatar Effect

In speaking about his vision for *Avatar*, James Cameron told the LA Times:[24]

> You've got to compete head on with these other epic words of fantasy and fiction, the Tolkiens and the *Star Wars* and the *Star Treks*. People want a persistent alternate reality to invest themselves in and they want the detail that makes it rich and worth their time. *They want to live somewhere else* [emphasis added].

We now know that Cameron's desire to create a compelling alternate reality worked exceptionally well. Some might say it worked too well.

About the same time it was becoming clear that *Avatar* might become the highest grossing film of all time (it did), news organizations started reporting on a fan phenomenon called the "*Avatar* effect." The *Avatar* effect is the pattern of depression and suicidal thoughts occurring among fans of James Cameron's *Avatar* because of their inability to experience the life they saw depicted in the film. A Swedish game designer described how he experienced the *Avatar* effect to CNN:

> I was depressed because I really wanted to live in Pandora, which seemed like such a perfect place, but I was also depressed and disgusted with the sight of our world, what we have done to Earth. I so much wanted to escape reality.[25]

This young man, and apparently thousands like him around the world, loved the idyllic world depicted in *Avatar*. They felt so connected to the philosophy, the values, the look, and the physicality that they experienced in the film that they preferred the story world to their own. Again, I mention that it would be difficult or impossible for the real world to be as well orchestrated and clear as the world of narrative. Furthermore, the money and effort that goes into creating a fantasy world makes it look effortless, but, as we know, it is a beautiful illusion.

From the outside, it's easy to condemn fans who experienced the *Avatar* effect as crazy, laughing at them for their folly. But I hope after reading this discussion you see that kind of thinking as simplistic and uninformed. Condemning these fans would be making a mistake that social psychologists call the fundamental attribution error—the idea that people do what they do because of who they are, which ignores the power of the situation they were in. Yes, not all people who saw *Avatar* experienced a full-blown *Avatar* effect. But thousands around the world did. Personality and individual differences do play a role in people's responses, but we can't ignore the situation and the shared experience.

Many other people probably experienced a less devastating version of the *Avatar* effect. I imagine that, instead of having full-blown clinical symptoms, many of us simply felt a deep attraction to the narrative world and its characters. Given that *Avatar* is the highest grossing film in history, by definition, we know that the story world was highly compelling to thousands of people around the world.

Have you ever watched a movie and carried with you afterward the lingering effects of the emotions the movie excited in you? Have you ever, even for a moment, come out of a deep connection to a film, book, or game, and realized that you were sad that you were not still a part of that story world? I am betting most of us have. This is why we buy favorite books and films and TV shows—because we want to relive them again and again.

I cannot tell you how many times I have watched the BBC miniseries of Jane Austen's *Pride and Prejudice*[26]—dozens. I read the book for the first time when I was 16 years old. I know how it ends. I watch it again and again to feel what the characters feel, to go where they go, and to feel the satisfaction of the resolution. Jennifer Ehle (who plays Elizabeth Bennett) is my avatar, and when Colin Firth (Mr. Darcy) smiles at her, it makes me so happy. And here's proof that I am not the only one who enjoys reliving those scenes. Recently someone in the United Kingdom erected a giant statue of Firth as Mr. Darcy in *Pride and Prejudice.* The statue commemorates a scene where Darcy emerges from a swim, having tried to forget his burning love for Miss Elizabeth Bennett. So, now there is a giant Colin Firth, dressed in period costume, emerging from a lake in England somewhere, because many of us love sharing that moment (and also, to bastardize an aphorism, because a lovesick, wet Colin Firth is a joy forever). The scene is burned into our brains and underlined with emotion—not so much because of what Colin and Jennifer experienced themselves (though they seem like swell people and I hope they had a good time, too), but because of what we experienced when they were our avatars.

The Matrix Revisited

Another way you can construe the *Avatar* metaphor is to call it a kind of virtual reality. You can change the capital A (representing the movie *Avatar*) to a lower-case a, representing a connection, virtual or otherwise, to another spatiality and another temporality. This kind of virtual reality was represented in the film franchise *The Matrix*. *The Matrix* series addresses a number of issues that are relevant to our discussion, such as what is real and what is unreal, and the relationship between the mind (self?) and the body. If our consciousness is experiencing life as another entity in another space and time, then the question "where are we" becomes more complicated than what meets the eye.

Avatars in the Psychologist's Laboratory

In the last decade or so, psychologists have started to study what happens in the human mind when we form a connection with an avatar—a virtual representation of ourselves. Jim Blascovich, Jeremy Bailenson, Nick Yee, and their colleagues have identified what they call the Proteus effect—the idea that after having an avatar experience, people will tend to mimic or conform to their avatar's experience.[27,28]

The Proteus effect describes a phenomenon wherein the behaviour of an individual operating under a digital persona, adapts to conform to that persona. This is an effect associated with digital self-representation. (en. wikipedia.org/wiki/Proteus_effect)

For example, in one study,[28] researchers assigned participants to avatars who varied in terms of physical attractiveness. After these experiences, researchers measured some behaviors of the participants that are related to self-confidence: namely, self-disclosure and interpersonal distance. They discovered that having a more attractive avatar in a virtual world had a measurable influence on how confidently people acted afterward. Those who had more attractive avatars in the virtual world behaved more confidently afterward in real life than those who were assigned less attractive avatars. Other research showed more avatar mimicry. If we watch our avatar eat candy, we may eat more candy later in the day. If we watch our avatar exercise, we may exercise more later ourselves. If you are interested in this research into avatars and virtual reality, do yourself a favor and read *Infinite Reality* by Jim Blascovich and Jeremy Bailenson.[29] It will blow your mind.

How does this relate to the fan experience? I propose that when we watch a favorite character or player on a screen and we are deeply immersed in the character and story world, that we are experiencing a type of Proteus effect—that afterward we will be more likely to "be" like that character. And that is why research shows that our attitudes and behaviors shift to be in line with the story we are exposed to.

WHO ARE WE? WHERE ARE WE? REVISITED

Both the Avatar effect and the Proteus effect suggest the deep connections between fan and story that can develop, and how fans are changed by their engagement with the story world. One fear the public sometimes voices about our media consumption is that we are going to stare more often into screens than we should, therefore abandoning face-to-face (a.k.a. "real") relationships. For example, in an episode of *Star Trek: The Next Generation* called *Hollow Pursuits*,[30] a character named Barclay is spending too much time in the holodeck—a virtual reality space. He begins to say that the characters he encounters there are more real to him and more important than his real-life friends and colleagues. In the end, his friend convinces him that he is needed in the real world, and he agrees. As the ship's counselor, Deanna Troy, tells Barclay, "There's nothing wrong with a healthy fantasy life, as long as you don't let it take over."

This is an important question that deserves more space than I can give it in this chapter, but it's worth pausing for a moment to consider. My belief is that we underestimate our deep connection to our favorite mediated worlds. I do not believe that means that watching screens is evil and should be stopped. As a matter of fact, I also believe that we sometimes underestimate the value of our connection to mediated stories. In the end, what we need are educated citizens who understand the psychology of mediated experiences. More on that in the last chapter of the book.

SOME PRELIMINARY CONCLUSIONS

Question: Why do we love our favorite stories, whether on film and television or in books? Why are we big fans of popular stories? One answer: Because the experience of those favorite stories is very personal. When we love a show or a book, we are leaving ourselves behind and are entering the world of the story as our favorite character or characters. Kauffman and Libby quote S. I. Hayakawa,[31] who writes, "In a very real sense, people who have read good literature have lived more than people who cannot or will not read. It is not true that we have only one life to lead; if we can read, we can live as many more lives and as many kind of lives as we wish." This applies to film and television and other kinds of storytelling as well. We love projecting ourselves into narratives because we are traveling to another place and time—to another temporality and spatiality. It's in our human nature to travel and to learn from the journey.

So, one answer to the question, "How does fantasy become reality?" is that we experience fantasy (fiction) "as if" we were there. It is real to us. This is also one explanation of why being a fan is so compelling. Personal fanhood is founded on this type of deep engagement, this "experience taking." If I can say that I love Harry Potter, it is because I have been Harry Potter. I have attended Hogwarts School of Witchcraft and Wizardry, made friends with Ron and Hermione, and flown on a broomstick. I have battled Voldemort and won!

Also, my values, attitudes, and ideals have been influenced from the times that I *was* Harry Potter. As discussed in Chapter 1, we can make meaning from fiction when we are engrossed in the story world and we appreciate how, though fictional, the story has its own reality. The reality comes in part from the story's ability to show us characters, situations, and ideas that "ring true." There are times when we watch television or film just for fun – what Mary Beth Oliver and Anne Bartch[32] call "hedonic enjoyment." There are other times, such as when we watch a complex television drama, that we experience mixed emotions. It is from these latter experiences, what Oliver and Bartch call the experience of "eudaimonic appreciation," that we emerge from the fan experience having assessed our own values and beliefs. Eudaimonic appreciation happens in response to thought-provoking media such as complex fictional drama.

My colleagues Kristin Hopper-Losenicky, Cynthia Vinney, Lisa Swain, Jerri Lynn Hogg and I[33] studied how fans of *Mad Men* experience this eudaimonic appreciation. Being that *Mad Men* is a complex drama, evoking complex thoughts and emotions, there is not a lot of hedonic fun happening while watching that show. But fans love it just the same, as underlined by it scoring a place on the lists of top fandoms. Why do they love it so? It's that eudaimonic appreciation factor – a complex drama like *Mad Men* helps fans process what's important to them in everyday life, what their values are, what constitutes a life well lived. Thought-provoking drama can even help us clarify what we believe the meaning of life is. Doesn't sound like our usual stereotype of "watching TV," does it?

In addition to intellectual and emotional stimulation that is evoked through complex narrative, there's another facet that makes consumption of this sort of media personal. We can derive how this works from Keith Oatley's research on written fiction[34]. Oatley claimed that fiction may be "twice as true as fact." This is because fiction intensifies and clarifies real life. It allows us to bring our own unresolved emotions to bear on the story world and resolve them in a space that is, in ways, easier to work with than our own life space. What Oatley said about written narrative is also true of audio-visual narrative like film and television that evoke feelings of eudaimonic appreciation. Not only do we take a journey "as" another person or creature (in the sense of connecting with an avatar), but somehow we simultaneously hold in mind who we are and bring our own experiences and emotions to bear.

Why would we do this, and why would we enjoy it so much? I think one strong possibility comes to us from the application of the work of Matthew Lieberman. In Lieberman's book *Social*, he tells us that when we are not busy doing something specific with our brains, our thinking will default back to thinking about social things. This is because being social is so central to our ability to survive and thrive. I apply this to our experience with deeply engaging film and television. One reason that I think we devote so much time to it is not that we're seriously misguided, but that we're using the social aspects of these storyworlds to hone our own social expertise, which is terribly adaptive. Think of complex storyworlds as a kind of simulation of social life. And recall that, if we apply Oatley's work here – we can actually achieve some depth of feeling and understanding that is hard to achieve in our daily social lives. One might then extrapolate that a person who engages deeply with her social world and with the social world of fiction emerges from both as a more fully realized social creature. And this, I think, is what we in media psychology and we in the world at large have not fully understood about the human connection to fandom and to media use more broadly.

Fans love their franchise with a fervor not assigned to something impersonal because their connection to the story is decidedly personal. As a fan, Harry Potter and his friends in that story world are part of my identity; he is part of my sense of self. His world is my world. Therefore I will be insulted if you insult Harry or those stories. That is what's going on under the hood of personal fandom. Now what happens when you share the love? That's the story of participatory fandom.

PARTICIPATORY FANDOM

To be a participatory fan, you need to start by being a personal fan. You love a show or team or movie franchise and you want to share this love with other people. A friend of mine said that her son is a big fan of the Cleveland Browns. He moved to Denver and found a bar where other Browns fans hang out. He wanted to share the experience—watch the game together, wear the jerseys, talk about the plays, eat, drink, and be merry. Adalian and colleagues[35][para 1] call participatory fandom "Capital F Fandom," which goes beyond liking a franchise to becoming an

> . . . all-consuming, a jumping-off point for a deep dive into fan fiction, convention-attending, recap-writing, role-playing, costume-making, language-learning, and more. There is a passion to this kind of Fandom that binds enthusiasts in the manner of people who share a secret—this secret just happens to be shared with millions of others.

Participatory fans share what Jenkins calls "popular mythology." Fans who go to a public celebration with other fans, such as a convention, a theme park, or a digital space like a fan site, do it so that they can share their enthusiasm with other fans. It may be that they want to talk about plot twists, celebrate the show's inclusive philosophy, or share exciting gossip about what's coming next in the franchise. Fans want to be with other people who share their interests because it is creative and fun and celebrates something they love. Some fans feel lonely just enjoying their favorite franchise by themselves. They want to pretend with other people to be the characters and to be part of the story world. Fans share ownership of their favorite stories. They believe the story is, at least in part, theirs to play with.

In social psychology, there is a theory of attraction that says that we like others who like what we like because it is affirming. If other people love what we love, then it makes us feel smart or discerning or that we have good taste. Part of the fun of participatory fandom is the social affirmation that sharing the love with others brings us.

Because I am a member of the participatory fandom of *Harry Potter*, I convinced my friend Mindy that we should go to the *Wizarding World of Harry Potter* the season it first opened. I should point out that the *Wizarding World* theme park is in Orlando, Florida, and that Orlando in summer is my idea of hell on Earth. Despite the 99 degree heat, Mindy and I and her two teenaged girls, Emily and Gwen, spent hour upon hour in the Orlando sun because we are all mad for Harry Potter. I recall that one fan's mother actually passed out on the pavement while we waited in line to watch a skit in Ollivander's wand shop, followed by the chance to buy our very own wands. And still, the fans who remained conscious played on in the sun. We drank butterbeer together in the *3 Broomsticks* pub. (Believe it or not, I ran into my Aunt Debbie and my cousins Will and Kelsey in the 3 Broomsticks. Maybe Pottermania is genetic?) My favorite attraction at the park was the trip through Hogwarts castle, which ended with a fantasy ride where fans fly through the air on a broomstick in the role of Harry on a new adventure.

And the Pottermania lives on. As I write, a highly anticipated addition to the *Wizarding World of Harry Potter* is on the verge of opening in Orlando, and fans are clamoring to know when. The *Orlando Sentinel* promises: "A signature attraction will be *Harry Potter and the Escape from Gringotts*, which Universal has described as 'an entirely new type of ride that propels guests into the story like never before,' "[36] Yes, that's what we want—to be propelled inside the story world.

If you are a producer, it pays to know that fans want to be part of the story. But it is not always easy for producers and fans to share a story when not everyone has the same ideas about what should happen next.[37] Fans are both enthusiasts and critics. Fans and producers, both claiming ownership in the franchise, are locked in a relationship together, not unlike divorced parents sharing children. The interactive era of digital media has added to the complexity of the relationship. Pearson [², p. 84] writes, "The digital revolution has had a profound impact upon fandom, empowering and disempowering, blurring the lines between producers and consumers, creating symbiotic relationships between powerful corporations and individual fans, and giving rise to new forms of cultural production."

Fans can vocally disagree with producers on everything from plot twists to series cancellations. To producers, fans can sometimes seem demanding and hard to satisfy. To fans, it can feel like the producers cannot take care of the franchise as well as they could. Perhaps it would help both parties to realize what a challenging situation everyone is in because the rules of engagement have changed so rapidly as digital culture rockets us all into an unknown future. One thing is certain: producers need fans and fans need producers.

POPULAR AND ENDURING ENTERTAINMENT FANDOMS

Let's move on now to discussing the fandoms themselves. What are some of the most enduring fandoms, and why do they endure while others fade? Because there is growing academic and popular interest in the phenomenon of fandom, Intellect Press launched a book series called *Fan Phenomenon*, describing the series as "prompted by a growing appetite for books that tap into the fascination we have with what constitutes an iconic or cultish phenomenon and how a particular person, TV show or film character/film infiltrates their way into the public consciousness." The publishers of *Fan Phenomenon* offered a list of enduring fandoms that it was seeking to cover in the book series:[38]

Buffy the Vampire Slayer / Star Trek / X-Files / James Bond / Harry Potter / Star Wars / Doctor Who / The Big Lebowski / Sherlock Holmes / Marilyn Monroe / Rocky Horror Picture Show / Lord of the Rings / The Matrix / Zombies / James Dean / Quentin Tarantino / Anime / Batman / Superman / Jane Austen / Disney.

Before analyzing these choices, let's see if there is consensus about particular fandoms by checking some other sources. Another time-honored source of information about pop culture is *New York Magazine*'s culture section, which is named *Vulture* after the habit in the city of referring to those taking in a show, film, or concert as "culture vultures." Vulture.com published a list titled "The 25 Most Devoted Fan Bases." The stated basis for making the list was (1) the sustained fervor of the fans rather than the sheer number of fans, and (2) the stipulation that the phenomenon needed to be current. The list appears in Table 2.1.

Finally, Mashable posted a list of the current top 10 biggest Internet fandoms, which overlaps with the other two lists in interesting ways. Mashable's list is presented in Table 2.2.

Before you get angry that your favorite object of affection is not included on one of the lists, remember that each list is one slice of the fandom pie. The *Intellect* list is one of enduring fandoms, the *Vulture* list focuses only on what the authors define as current fervors, and the *Mashable* ranks only current Internet phenoms. Their choices do not negate your love of, say, *Monty Python*, Selina Gomez, or *Supernatural*.

Table 2.1. THE 25 MOST FERVENT FAN BASES, ACCORDING TO VULTURE.COM (2012)

Rank	Franchise	Facebook	Fan Nickname(s) of Followers
1	Game of Thrones	4.2 million	Brotherhood without Banners
2	Star Wars	8.85 million	Warsies
3	Twilight	35.2 million	Twi-hards, Twilighters
4	Harry Potter	50.7 million	Potterheads, Potterites
5	Justin Bieber	46.8 million	Beliebers
6	Lord of the Rings	10.4 million	Tolkienites (book), Ringers (film)
7	Hunger Games	7.8 million	Tributes
8	Lady Gaga	53 million	Little Monsters
9	Doctor Who	2.7 million	Whovians
10	Arrested Development	1.6 million	None
11	Tyler Perry	8.1 million	None
12	Joss Whedon	93K fansite	Whedonites
13	Community	1.3 million	Human Beings
14	Star Trek	5.5 million	Trekkies, Trekkers
15	Oprah	7.7 million	None
16	True Blood	10.7 million	Truebies
17	Bruce Springsteen	2.4 million	Bruce Tramps
18	Neil Gaiman	1.7 million	Gaimanites
19	Insane Clown Posse	1 million	Juggalos and Juggalettes
20	Kevin Smith	907,000	None
21	Phish	578,000	Phans
22	Stephen Colbert	2.7 million	Colbert Nation
23	L'il B	269,000	None
24	Real Housewives	varies by city	None
25	Mad Men	2.2 million	None

It is interesting, however, to examine the overlap of the classic and the current. Doing so, we find that the *Intellect* and *Vulture* lists have five franchises in common: *Star Trek, Harry Potter, Star Wars, Doctor Who*, and *Lord of the Rings*. This overlap is not surprising when you consider that the history of the devoted fandom has its roots in science fiction and fantasy. When I think of modern fandom, *Star Trek* is the first that comes to mind. One reason is the story, now famous, of how the fans rescued *Star Trek: The Original Series* from cancellation with a letter-writing campaign. The *Star Trek* phenomenon spans decades and genres. The recent reboot features new actors in the roles played by the original cast in the 1960s.

The *Intellect* and *Mashable* lists have three commonalities: *Doctor Who*, Sherlock Holmes (Benedict Cumberbatch plays Holmes in the BBC show *Sherlock*), and zombies (*Mashable* cites the *Walking Dead*). Finally, the *Mashable* and *Vulture* lists have the following in common: *Game of Thrones*,

Table 2.2. THE TOP TEN INTERNET FANDOMS,
ACCORDING TO MASHABLE.COM (2014)

Rank	Fandom
1	Beyoncé
2	*Game of Thrones*
3	*The Walking Dead*
4	*Doctor Who*
5	*Breaking Bad*
6	*Benedict Cumberbatch*
7	*Downton Abbey*
8	*Hunger Games*
9	*House of Cards*
10	*Mad Men*

Hunger Games, Mad Men, and *Doctor Who*. The only franchise mentioned on all three lists is *Doctor Who*. (Pause for the elation of *Doctor Who* fans everywhere.) Jenkins, discussing the history of fan gatherings, mentions that, in the early days, fan gatherings that celebrated individual franchises were likely to center on *Star Wars* and *Star Trek*, and today those same types of gatherings are more likely to focus on *Harry Potter*.[4] His perspective is consistent with the information on our fandom lists. At the same time, it's true that cons like Comic-Con host a diversity of fandoms.

Media convergence is the term we use to describe the idea that today the message may be the same, whether we watch it on our television set, iPad, iPhone, or computer. I can watch a YouTube video on my smart TV and I can watch a TV show on my smartphone. So, it's less about the device than the content.

Into this context, where messages cross the now permeable boundaries between devices, steps a new kind of fandom. This is the fandom of the new media age, where a person can gain a following in new platforms, surpassing the old gatekeepers. As an example, I'll tell you about a self-made star with a large following who began on the Internet with user-created content. His name is Toby Turner and he also goes by the nickname Tobuscus.

Toby Turner gained fans via a number of YouTube channels, especially for his YouTube show *Cute, Win, Fail*, which was an interactive program where fans could vote on which of the videos of the week was the best in each of the three categories. His notoriety also came from his "literal video" versions of video game trailers in which he would sing to the music of video game trailers stating what was happening in a humorous way. If you want to know more about Toby Turner, I suggest going to knowyourmeme.com and searching for his name (or nickname) or just going to TobyTurner.com.

As an example of the nature of this new kind of fandom, Toby Turner created a YouTube video, which he called "Viral Song" (search for it on YouTube). "Viral Song," in its meta-analytic splendor, is about creating a viral video. Toby's tips for creating a viral video include featuring cats, "hot, hot ladies," and something educational (so that parents will let their kids watch it). Toby's educational content? He repeatedly sings: "Did you know that cashews come from a fruit?" My then 13-year-old son used to go around singing "did you know that cashews come from a fruit?" over and over. [Talk about an earworm!]

I mention Toby Turner because he represents a new kind of self-made celebrity whose popularity came from his YouTube channel. I saw for myself that Toby was wildly popular with my son's friends, who loved imitating the Tobuscus voice and his catch phrases like "Bless your face," and "intro darkness, then redness, then whiteness." As of this writing, "Viral Song" had over 15.5 million views on YouTube. Another of Toby's posts, a literal video interpretation of the trailer for the video game *Assassin's Creed: Brotherhood*, currently has about 40 million views. "Swing My Sword"—about the video game Minecraft—currently has 50 million views. Toby Turner is a new kind of self-made star. He speaks to his fans directly, calling them "audience" in his videos.

Interestingly, when I Google "Toby Turner," the top searches that Google generates are "appearances," "girlfriend," and "net worth," suggesting that fans are most interested in who he's dating, where they can see him in person, and how much money he makes. Searching further for Toby Turner and "net worth" leads me to an article called "Top 15 Richest YouTubers Who Make Money Sharing Viral Videos,"[39] which identifies Toby as the fifth richest YouTuber behind "BlueXephos," "PewDiePie," "Smosh," and "Jenna Marbles." Don't feel bad if you do not know who these are. I wouldn't either if I didn't have a teenaged son at home. We live in a world full of new media choices that are morphing as we speak into something that is yet again different. Parents may feel clueless about where their kids' favorite content lives, let alone the difficulty in monitoring or setting rules about media use. On the other hand, kids may have different dreams about fame and fortune, including new and creative ways to reach an audience. We live in a world where one's 15 minutes of fame (or is it now 15 million views?) may live on YouTube, Twitter, or some yet unknown platform.

THE SOCIAL MEANING OF FANDOM

Friends have told me that in the 1960s, when it originally aired, being a teen *Star Trek* fan might end in public shaming, or worse. (Think black eye, swirly, or wedgie.) Famously, actor William Shatner performed a skit on *Saturday Night Live* in which he mocked the geeky fans of *Star Trek*, telling them to "get a life" and move out of their parents' basements. There was so much interest and backlash from that skit, that Shatner later wrote a book called *Get a Life* that was a love letter to the fans and an exploration of all the things fans delight in about *Star Trek*.

The current scholarship notes that the social standing of fans has improved in many ways in recent years. For example, Stanfil[40] writes: "It has become something of a truism in media studies that fans are now free of the old stereotypes to which they were formerly subject and have been mainstreamed as a model for the new ideal active media consumer." Others note that female fans, or fan girls, may experience more shame and marginalization than male fans do. For example, in their book *Fangasm: Supernatural Fan Girls*, fan studies scholars Katherine Larsen and Lynn Zubernis[41] write about their experiences with shame and misunderstanding as female fans of a sci fi show with two young, attractive male leads. Zubernis and Larsen do also note the positive social aspects of the fangirl experience. By the way, I'd be remiss if I didn't note that there's a term for a scholar who studies fanhood and is also a fan: "acafan" (for academic/fan).

Matt Hills's view seems to encompass both ideas—that fandom still has remnants of social exclusion, but it now also implies that if you are not a fan of something, then something is wrong with you. (What do you mean, you haven't watched *Breaking Bad* or *Game of Thrones*?) He suggests that there is now a "co-existence of negative and positive fan representations."[42] This era seems to be characterized by the idea that you should be "into" the popular media, but that you should not be too obsessed with it, or you risk becoming a crazy fan who has lost all sense of reality.

One of the tenets of the fandom studies classic, Jenkins's *Convergence Culture*,[43] is that the role of the fan has changed and is becoming more active vis-à-vis the media producer. As fans have now come to expect some interaction between the story producers and the consumers, companies are wooing fans[4,44]. *Comic-Con*, as the name implies, started out as a comic book convention with less than 200 attendees. Today the event, held in San Diego, hosts upwards of 150,000 attendees who stand in long lines and camp out in order to experience the excitement of seeing their favorites in person. Comic-Con has changed from a grassroots event to a giant venue for corporations to garner support for a new franchise, though some grassroots elements still remain.

This conversation about the changing social role of fandom raises the issues of agency and authenticity. An authentic love of the story world drew fans to their fandoms, sometimes despite being socially ostracized. Now that corporations have more fully embraced the aspects of fandom that benefit them financially, the question hanging in the air is, who legitimized fandom and why? Is the mainstreaming of fandom a realized dream of corporations or of fans, or both? To what extent is the love of a franchise too artificially generated today?

Some fans feel this commercialization of fanhood keenly. For instance, a *Doctor Who* fan from the early days (*Doctor Who* is more than 50 years old) when the show ran on a shoestring budget may feel a kind of resentment to the mainstreaming of the *Doctor Who* fan phenomenon today. Perhaps he feels that being a fan when it wasn't so cool is much more authentic than being a fan in the era when the show is mainstream and *Doctor Who* toys are available at major retailers.

There are many nuances to this discussion of the social role of fanhood that space prevents me from ironing out here. For now, let us move on to some examples of how fans celebrate their favorite franchises by playing with other fans in public. Some of these have been mentioned already and some have not. Please note that this is only a cursory introduction to some of the many fan behaviors, and cannot be exhaustive.

COSPLAY

Cosplay is short for "costume play," and it refers to the practice of attending fan events dressed as a favorite character or story element. Because I have friends who love cosplay, I can save Oxford University Press the hassle and cost of obtaining rights to print other people's friends in costumes. With that money-saving plan in mind, I'll begin with a picture of my husband dressed as a Klingon (a character from Star Trek, for those who didn't know) (see Figure 2.1). This picture illustrates the time, energy, and care that go into cosplay. Fans do it because it is fun, but it is also a challenge to make the most authentic costume. There are cosplay contests at many fan conventions. Pictured in Figure 2.2 is our friend, actress Alana Jordan, at Comic-Con. Cosplay is a way of simultaneously being a beloved character and playing with others who understand and share your love of the story world in question.

FAN FIC

"Fan fic" is short for "fan fiction," and it is just that: fans write fictional stories or create art set in the story world and using the story characters. Fan fic is free and is distributed via the Internet. Some of the popular fan fic sites are *Archive of Our Own* (a.k.a. AO3) and FanFiction.net (see http://ebookfriendly.

Figure 2.1 Cosplay: 1) My husband Lee (a) being transformed into a Klingon by makeup artist Lee Drew and (b) dressed as a Klingon from Star Trek: The Next Generation.

com/fan-fiction-websites/). The television franchises that currently have the greatest number of fan fic offerings on FanFiction.net are *Glee* (105K), *Supernatural* (96K), *Doctor Who* (63K), *Buffy the Vampire Slayer* (48K), and BBC's *Sherlock* (47K).

One of my students, Cynthia Vinney, and I recently researched fan fic written about the show *Mad Men*. She found that half of the fan fic was about a heterosexual relationship, either canonical (e.g., between characters Peggy and Pete) or extra-textual (e.g., between characters Joan and Lane). The most fan fic was written about the show's female lead, Peggy Olsen, followed by the male lead, Don Draper. Given the fact that most fan fic is written by women, it may be that writing about the female lead helps fans explore their connection with Peggy. A theme in the Peggy fan fic is the further exploration of ideas started on the show, such as taking a show event (such as a failed relationship) and exploring how it could have turned out differently.

One popular genre of fan fic is called "slash." Slash is fan fic that creates ships (short for relationships) between characters that are different than they are

Figure 2.2 Cosplay 2: Our friend, the actress Alana Jordan doing Cosplay as (a) Batgirl and (b) a Ghost Buster.

in the canon of the show and depict a same-sex relationship. Vinney's study, described above, found that about 20 percent of Mad Men fan fic was slash. A famous example of a ship is the Kirk/Spock or K/S ship. (The word slash refers to the slash mark between the names of the characters in the ship, such as K/S. K/S fan fiction can be found at ksarchive.com.) In K/S slash, fans create art and stories about a homoerotic relationship between Kirk and Spock. Fans also look for hints in the canon for such a relationship, such as moments when the two characters gaze into each others' eyes or share other intimacies.

Another popular ship, known as JohnLock, is one proposing a romantic relationship between John Watson and Sherlock Holmes. JohnLock slash became more common with the popularity of the BBC's *Sherlock* franchise, starring Benedict Cumberbach as Holmes and Martin Freeman as Watson. You can find fan fic writers who ship JohnLock on Facebook, Reddit, Tumbler, and Pinterest, among other social media sites.

What attracts fans to writing fan fic? There are many motivations. One motivation brings us back to the discussion about who owns the story. If a fan wants to have control over a story, then she can do that by writing about the characters and choosing what new relationships she wants to form and how she wants the plot to twist. Another theory about fan fic comes from my colleague Alyxis Smith, who writes about the JohnLock ship. Lexi believes that the reason fans are so drawn to slash is that the explicit sexuality of the genre allows fans to express the deep intimacy they see between the story characters. Indeed, one of the compelling factors that draws us in to a Star Trek or a Sherlock is the bond between the main story characters. Fans can argue that the relationship between Kirk and Spock is at the heart of what draws them into the *Star Trek* universe.

The same can be said for the relationship between Holmes and Watson. When my husband Lee was 29 he starred in an off-Broadway play called *Holmes & Watson* (he was also the playwright). To Lee, the premise of Holmes and Watson revolved around a missing piece of the puzzle in a relationship that has captivated fans for decades. Lee felt that Holmes had never adequately expressed what Watson means to him, and this generated the story in Lee's play. The JohnLock fanhood is devoted to the relationship between Holmes and Watson and wants to see it expressed. Go on Tumblr or other social media sites and you'll see the level of intensity of that devotion.

THE TAKE AWAY

> Fiction is a lie that helps us realize the truth.
> —adapted from a quote by Picasso

Pablo Picasso said, "Art is a lie that helps us realize the truth." Let me adapt this sentiment for narrative and say, "Fiction is a lie that helps us realize the truth." I hope that one thing you take away from this chapter is that we have a deep connection to our favorite franchises, whether they are books, television, film, or video games—and that this deep connection comes from the fact that we are not merely a passive audience, we are the rider of the horse—the body connected to the avatar, living out the experiences we see played before us on screens. Fanhood is deeply personal. When we see people peering into screens, and when we calculate how many hours we do that as a culture, we should understand that there is a lot more going on there than meets the eye.

Old and New Media
in Everyday Life

From TV to Social Media

Not long ago, at a conference, a presenter told a story about his teenaged daughter who had been calling him frantically all morning. The daughter had planned to go to a concert that night, but while she was dressing that morning, she had dropped her cell phone in the toilet. When her attempts to dry the phone with her hair dryer had failed, she freaked out. Her problem, according to her dad, was that she could not fathom how she could go out without a cell phone. Her bemused father finally talked her down by suggesting she borrow her sister's phone, but remained intrigued by the idea that for his daughter, leaving home without a cell phone simply did not compute.

There is no job as hard as parenthood. (Can I get an AMEN?) Today, as technologies evolve at breakneck speeds, both parents and children struggle with the issues, and at the same time revel in the fun and excitement, that these new technologies bring. The current media landscape certainly brings with it both challenges and opportunities.

It's been just over 40 years since the first cellular phone call was made. Today in the United States, about 90 percent of adults and about 80 percent of teenagers have a cell phone. Nearly half of adults said they have slept with their cell phones by their beds. About 30 percent of adults say they can't imagine living without their cell phones. About two-thirds of adults say they have tried to answer what turned out to be a phantom cell phone ring[1]. These phantom rings or vibrations have been called variously (and hilariously) *fauxcellarm* (false alarm), *ringxiety* (ring anxiety), and *hypovibrochondria*. In what is perhaps even stranger media news, many adults report using their cell phones during sex! But these revelations seem innocently comic when put beside the stats on texting and driving, for instance. We now know that texting while driving has been responsible for a sharp uptick in the number of serious accidents in the United States. And we also know that, although teens know that texting and driving isn't safe, many say they will do it anyway. This is perhaps a new incarnation of an old problem, not unlike teens who engage in other risky behavior such as smoking or unprotected sex.

Suffice it to say that our collective relationship with media is one that is often wrought with perplexity. Media are changing around us at an unprecedented speed. Some of us feel mostly excited about this; others feel mostly anxious, and still others don't quite know how to feel. Sometimes we just stand there like a deer in the headlights and watch it all fly by.

We have many questions about what the modern media landscape means for us as individuals and as a society. Some common concerns focus on how the rise of social media may mean poorer social skills, especially among youth. On the other hand, high technology brings with it high hopes. This feeling of hope makes sense given that we have seen so many technological dreams become realities in recent years. My advice to you is this: never trust anyone who tells you that media are all bad. Also, never trust anyone who tells you that media are all good. Media bring both risks and opportunities. A poor or simplistic view of media can end up hurting you. A rich and nuanced understanding of media can enhance your life. Throughout these pages, I intend to continue to talk about media use in a realistic and nuanced way.

As mentioned in Chapter 1, one of the opportunities I see for excellent use of media is to understand and deeply experience the meaning that we can make from truly great stories, whether they are stories on film, on television, in books, or in video games. I bet you, like me, have had moments when a story brought you to tears, made you feel alive, or made you see the world in a whole new way.

As touched on earlier, Mary Beth Oliver and Anne Bartsch have explored the difference between "enjoying" a film and "appreciating" one. Sometimes, some of our favorite films are critically acclaimed stories that generate some deep negative emotions alongside some positive ones. For example, you may feel odd saying that you "enjoyed" *Saving Private Ryan* or *Schindler's List*. The word "enjoy" is perhaps more apt for something that is more fun than challenging. A film like *Sharknado*, for example, is, I think, actually made to be more like an amusement park ride than an impetus to contemplate the meaning of life. For those who are unfamiliar, IMDb describes *Sharknado* thus: "When a freak hurricane swamps Los Angeles, nature's deadliest killer rules sea, land, and air as thousands of sharks terrorize the waterlogged populace." [Not to be a spoilsport, but doesn't that mean this film should have been called *Sharkicane*?]

Although meaningful films like *Glory* and *The Shawshank Redemption* are among my favorite films of all times, I admit that some nights I wouldn't mind just firing up something like *Sharknado* on the old TV and taking that amusement park ride. I also admit that, though I've watched many a difficult film, there are some that I haven't seen yet, primarily because it's not always easy to find the time and the right headspace to approach a really emotionally challenging film. According to uses and gratifications theory, we actively seek out media in order to fulfill needs. Different people have different needs, and a person's needs vary over time. Some people find it comforting to listen to sad songs or romantic songs when they have just ended a relationship, while others quickly change the station or the song in order to avoid what are, to them, painful reminders. Music evokes emotion, and we use that fact to enhance or regulate our feelings. Films, which, of course, also contain music and story, send multiple messages and can be viewed at different depths. One of the motives for turning on television or video is for companionship. Another is simply habit. Many homes have the television on nearly constantly, in part because some people find the background noise comforting and the images pleasantly distracting.

Sometimes we want to watch *It's a Wonderful Life* to remind ourselves that life well lived means, not having wealth or power, but loving the people around you. Other times, we might feel stressed out by dramatic scenes in our own lives and we might deal with this stress by playing beautiful music, a fun and easy video game, or watching a silly movie. I think we can all enjoy some *Sharknado* moments, some *Bejeweled* moments, and also some *Life Is Beautiful* moments. What would be cool, at least to me, is if we seek to more fully understand how we use media and to make the choices that help us live a good and fulfilling life. This doesn't mean that we watch only educational TV, listen to only classical music, and generally be a bunch of humorless nanny goats. I mentioned some of my favorite meaningful films. I also am a big fan of such classics as *Anchorman* (starring Will Ferrell and Christina Applegate) and *Due Date* (starring Zach Galifanakis and Robert Downey, Jr.). The latter two are laugh-out-loud, fun films. That's not to say, by the way, that you can't take away something meaningful from a comedy. You can. And it's also not to say, either, that all serious films are meaningful. They're not. I'll make some media choices that you might not make, and you'll make some media choices that I may not make. What's important to me is that we're honest with ourselves and we understand, as best we can, the role of media in our lives, including why and how much we use it and when to turn it off.

SOCIAL LEARNING AND MASS MEDIA

As social animals, we grow up comparing ourselves to others to get feedback about a host of social variables. Am I as smart or as talented as the other kids my age? What is considered cool? What do the people around me think I should do, think, and be? We probably do not question it as we grow up, but we're not as independent as we think we are. Quite the contrary, really. We are absolutely social creatures, designed to judge our successes and failures and to make our choices all in the context of other people. Social psychologists call these processes "social comparison." Just like whether I am a good runner depends on how fast my peers can run, I judge other social variables based on how I think my peers will react and on how my peers actually treat me.

You might be thinking that people are a bunch of conformists. What about the rebels? Well, even nonconformists are heavily influenced by society. If you think about it, a nonconformist is someone who goes against the grain, who defies the status quo. Well, to defy something, you must know about it, care about it, and keep track of it. If, for example, it is the fashion to wear sports apparel—football jerseys, rugby shirts, tennis shoes—and a rebel decides to wear leather and chains to be different, then he is doing just that: actively deciding to watch what others are doing and doing something essentially just to be different, to stand out, to give the impression to others that he refuses to conform. In a twisted way, then, even nonconformity is a sort of conforming social behavior. True enough, there are some people who are less affected by social influence than others. The great humanist psychologist Abraham Maslow wrote about a few individuals he called "self-actualized"—those high-achieving, highly evolved people who seemed to walk their own paths without worrying what other people thought about it.

But the rest of us vastly outnumber those who are genuinely immune to such influence—the true independents. And as developing children, we are even less likely to show this kind of social immunity. If viewed through the lens of biology, this makes an extraordinary amount of sense. We are social creatures. We live together, we mate and reproduce and help each other survive and thrive. As the esteemed social psychologist Elliot Aronson[2] put it, we are "social animals." Although the notion of conformity is decidedly un-cool—perhaps especially for Americans—following social rules and "sticking with the group" is often efficient and adaptive.

There are implications, for our society as well as our kids, that life—even social life—has largely gone digital. Much of our kids' socialization is influenced by or supported by various forms of media. This explains why it is crucial to understand how kids learn social lessons from the media (e.g., watching celebrities), how they are affected by socializing through the media (e.g., social networking sites and text messaging), and also to scrutinize what the most common media messages are.

Sex and violence in the mass media are the topics that have generated the most interest, controversy, and research. It is understandable that we would be drawn to tackling some of the most blatant and potentially harmful effects of media first. But I think we have largely missed, as a culture, some of the subtler issues, including issues of social learning from the media. For example, many people reject the notion that watching TV can change our feelings toward a person, group, or idea. But just like real social interactions, these mediated pseudo-interactions teach kids social lessons. Before undertaking a more in-depth analysis of these social issues, I want to put this in the context of the current statistics of American children's media use.

LIFE ON EARTH—TODAY IT MEANS STARING AT SCREENS

Earlier, I referred to some current media use statistics. These kinds of statistics vary from study to study for a variety of reasons, including the nature of the specific questions asked in a given study and the people who were questioned or observed, so I'll offer some more statistics for your consideration. According to Potter's 2008 report,[3] the average American watches TV about four and a half hours per day and spends over two hours a day with the computer (not counting computer time at work). And research indicates that these numbers are rising steadily. College students have a unique set of media habits. American college students spend about three and a half hours a day on the computer doing activities like e-mailing and instant messaging; they spend another seven and a half hours a day with other forms of media, including TV, books, and music.

Kids and Media in America[4] is a detailed profile of American kids' media use. Authors Roberts and Foehr found that American children use media an average of 6.5 hours per day, not counting media use for school or media multitasking (e.g., looking at a Web site while simultaneously watching TV), with older children consuming media on average about seven to eight hours per day. American kids most often watch TV alone or with peers, rarely with parental supervision. Only 5 percent of American children use media for an hour or less on any given day. About half of American children aged 8 to 18 say they live in *constant TV homes*—homes where the TV is on constantly whether or not anyone is watching it. Two-thirds of these children also say that the television is usually on during mealtimes.

TV viewing is the most common media activity of most American children, on average taking three to four and a half hours of a child's day. One would think that these statistics mean that children enjoy watching TV immensely. But there's a fascinating paradox about TV watching. When you ask children about their enjoyment of TV, you get some interesting responses. Most say that TV is not all that stimulating and, in fact, they often watch TV simply to kill time. Furthermore, research shows[5] that heavy TV viewers say they enjoy watching TV *less* than light TV viewers. Research also shows that most kids say they watch more TV than they *want* to watch. I think these statistics show that media is attention-grabbing and that it sucks us in, even more than we really want to be sucked in. That's because the primary motive for producing media is to attract an audience for advertisers, so media producers make media that they believe will be most likely to grab their audience's attention.

I wonder if maybe we hear so many statistics that we get a little numb and are not able to fully appreciate what they mean. So, let's put this in context. The brilliant psychologist Csikszentmihalyi[6] has written about how we human beings spend our days, including work and free time, and how we feel about these different activities. Roughly speaking, daily life is divided into three equal eight-hour periods dedicated to sleeping, working, and leisure time. Considering that we have eight hours a day to do more or less whatever we choose, let's put those media use statistics in that context. Out of eight hours of leisure time, the average American spends about four and a half hours watching television and another two on the computer. New research out of Ball State University[7] in Muncie, Indiana, confirms that media use is, by *far*, the most common waking activity. In fact, these researchers found that average Americans spend about nine hours per day using media. According to the Ball State study, 30 percent of a person's waking day involved media use as a sole activity, and another 39 percent included media use combined with another activity. Taken together then, about 70 percent of our waking time is spent using media in one form or the other. As Csikszentmihayli notes, one also has to consider that there are a number of maintenance activities in one's day, including personal grooming and activities such as driving to work and grocery shopping. Given that people sleep, eat, work, and perform maintenance activities, if you combine that information with the media use statistics reported here, I would argue that almost *all* of the time we have a choice about how to spend our time, we choose to plug into media.

Let me repeat that: almost every time we have a choice about what to do with our lives, we choose to stare into a screen. Be it the television, computer, smart phone, or tablet, *our lives are spent staring into electronic screens.* Now, I don't know where you are right now, but I am imagining you sitting somewhere calmly reading this information and I don't know if I am communicating to you how un-calm I feel about it sometimes. I wonder if we are too complacently plugged into *The Matrix*, without sufficient knowledge of its power over us. Other times, I am literally in awe of how powerful the technology I own is, in a good way, and the things I can enjoy or accomplish with it.

In the 1960s, Marshall McLuhan understood this and wrote a masterpiece that is eerily relevant today, despite the changes in technology. If you've never read *The Medium Is the Message*, you should. Even if you expect the intellectual depth of the work, its artistry may surprise you. McLuhan's words were directed mostly toward television and the general increase in communication speed, but they apply to our modern technology explosion as well: "All media work us over completely. They are so pervasive in their personal, political, economic, aesthetic, psychological, ethical, moral, and social consequences, that they leave no part of us untouched, unaffected, unaltered. The medium is the message. Any understanding of social and cultural change is impossible without a knowledge of the way media work as environments."[8]

We watch reality shows that purport to track people living their daily lives. It occurs to me sometimes that watching people live their daily lives in America today would largely mean filming them as they stare at the TV or computer. We really need to think about this. It's ironic, in fact, that we're strangely drawn to watching other people supposedly living their real lives, while we spend all our time—well, watching.

I know that some might read my reaction to Americans' heavy media use statistics as the sick ramblings of a humorless, finger-wagging granny. (Read the following in your best finger-wagging granny voice:) "You kiddies with your iPads and your Instagram and your *Grand Theft Auto*! You're turning into a bunch of slack-jawed zombies!" Well, I'm not trying to be anyone's granny, but I do confess I want to make people think. (I'm a professor. Isn't that in my job description?) It seems to me that if most of us are plugged into electronic media virtually every time we can be that there are things we should consider. I offer up the following list of questions as conversation starters about mass media's role in our lives and the lives of our children.

1. If virtually every time we can choose what to do with our free time we choose mass media, what, if anything, aren't we experiencing enough?
2. Are there media that you use that improve your life? What media? In what ways?
3. Have you ever noticed someone who was manipulated by something he (or she) saw in the media? Do you think he knew he was being manipulated? Why or why not?
4. If you could design the ideal media diet for your (real or hypothetical) child or for yourself, what would it look like? What free time activities do you think would make for the happiest, healthiest, most interesting, and fulfilling lifestyle? (And, of course, you can actually do this.)

5. Will there ever again be a human society whose free time is not dominated by the use of media? Would we ever choose to have such a society? Why or why not?

NEW MEDIA, NEW QUESTIONS

Media psychology is still a new and still-emerging field. All of us are stakeholders when it comes to the role of media in everyday life because the way we use media affects us all. I like to keep my ear to the ground in order to keep up with what are the most burning questions on people's minds about media use. Here's a list of some of those burning questions I've noticed lately, in no particular order.

Burning Questions about New Media in Everyday Life

Which media platforms will stand the test of time, and which will be quickly supplanted by the "next big thing"? Why?

What are the latest media that my kids are using, and what should I know about them?

Why are selfies so popular, and what does it mean about us that we seem so into them?

What is the "next big thing" in media? What kind of media will we use 5, 10, or 20 years from now?

How do we deal with all the new privacy issues that emerged due to the explosion of media use, such as social media and smartphones?

Because we are turning more and more to social media, will our social skills suffer?

Are media addictive? If they are, what should we do about it?

How do we deal with the information overload inherent in the media-saturated culture?

What's going to happen to journalism, in print and in other forms, given the new media landscape?

The speed at which scholarly research is published is like an old-fashioned freight train chugging down the tracks, while the speed of technological growth is like a high-speed train flying from city to city. Therefore, it's hard to publish research about a particular topic and keep up with where the public interest is. But here's some of what we do know about new media. I won't answer all of the questions posed above, but will attempt to get at what scientists know about some of these burning questions and their underlying concepts. Also, entire books could easily be written on most of these topics, so just consider this mostly a way of raising these issues rather than an attempt to resolve them.

Right now, media addiction is a topic of some interest in the research world. One of the questions being addressed is whether or not media addiction should be classified as a psychological disorder, like addiction to alcohol or drugs. Especially in Asia, there are media addiction clinics and more of an acceptance that these are needed. Yellowlees and Marks[9] write about problematic Internet use (PIU), saying that it's probably more appropriate to skip classifying it as a mental disorder and to think of it less as a new diagnosis and more as a specific venue for problems, especially for those with a history of addiction and impulse control. Cash and colleagues[10], on the other hand, argue for the inclusion of Internet Addiction Disorder (IAD) in the official manual used for psychological diagnoses, the *Diagnostic and Statistical Manual of Mental Disorders*. In South Korea, there are media addiction clinics and have been for some time.

On the subject of social networking and social skills, new research has started to emerge. Wilson, Gosling, and Graham[11] reviewed the research that had been conducted to date on Facebook and identified five themes in this work. In order from most to least common, the themes were

(1) social interactions (How does Facebook alter social interactions compared to face-to-face interactions?);
(2) user analysis (Who's using Facebook?);
(3) motivations (Why do people use Facebook?);
(4) privacy and disclosure (What are the privacy-related issues related to Facebook use?); and
(5) identity presentation (How are people presenting themselves on Facebook?). As far as social behavior on Facebook, this body of research suggests that Facebook users are drawn to the venue in order to maintain ties with friends, even those who live in a different geographic region. Facebook, it turns out, allows people to carry out a primate behavior called social grooming. When you watch primates at the zoo, they literally groom each other (as in removing mites from a friend's hair). Human primates engage in "social grooming," which are mundane behaviors that connect us and solidify bonds. Instead of picking mites from your college roommate's hair, you find her on Facebook and tell her you like her new haircut. This helps keep the bond between the two of you, though you now live apart and rarely see each other in person.

Facebook users also seek out the site to combat loneliness and boredom. Now, a lot has been made of the notion that social media use eats at the very fabric of our humanity because it isolates users at cold computer terminals and discourages face-to-face contact. Is this true? It's still early in this investigation, and an early stage of the use of social media, for that matter. So, the research we have is preliminary, though there are many things to learn from it. Recently, *Psychology Today* online hosted a series of blogs discussing this very topic: whether social media leads to social deficits. Social psychologist Bella DePaulo recounted the details of an experiment in which college students were randomly assigned to either do nothing different (controls) or to post more often on Facebook than they normally do. The students who posted more felt less lonely and more connected, and this happened regardless of what responses they received to their posts. This is indeed intriguing research because, as discussed throughout the book, there is a clear advantage to an experiment over correlational research. When we correlate loneliness with greater Facebook use, we do not know if the Facebook use caused loneliness, caused something else to change that, in turn, caused loneliness, or if the loneliness was caused by another factor. In the study that DePaulo discusses, we know that the increased Facebook use caused social gains and not social deficits.

What about the darker side of social media? One topic of some deliberation is the idea that face-to-face communication will always be different in a variety of ways from social media communication because of the difference in social cues and social consequences. One way in which the latter manifests itself is any time we are able to comment on another person's posts. This could be in the context of peer-to-peer social media interactions or in the context of journalism such as science or news reporting.

The PR Newswire reported in 2010[12] that 45 percent of social media users have "unfriended" or blocked a social media contact due to uncivil behavior. Though social media use is popular with youth, some college students report avoiding social media, particularly Facebook[13]. A study of college students' social media behavior revealed that even though the students had strong technical skills, they felt the costs were greater than the benefits associated with Facebook. Specifically, these students reported feeling that using Facebook was a waste of time, fearing that using the site might lead to addiction, and also worrying about privacy issues. They shied away from posting political views and personal information because they feared the repercussions.

If you are on social media at all, you know that a current topic of conversation is a certain amount of stress and acrimony that results from finding one's social media "friends" on the other side of the political, religious, or philosophical perspective. Election years seem to bring with them a rash of unfriending. These social media kerfuffles highlight some of the ways that face-to-face socializing differs from social media socializing. For one thing, there's a difference in how we make assertions on social media versus in face-to-face encounters. Think about it: you do not walk into a room and make a random declarative statement, as you might do online. It's actually pretty funny to think about how social interactions might look if we did this. Joe might walk into the room and declare, "It's a tough day in parenting land," while Maria might blast Senate Republicans, and Taylor might declare, "Wait, let me take a selfie." These declarations, when they get into hot-button areas, can make us start to wonder why we became friends with our "Facebook friend" or Twitter follower in the first place. For a social psychologist, it's a perfect live laboratory that opens itself to study. For now, we have some questions, some musings, and a few research answers. As I say, it is early, so we will all need to keep checking in to watch and learn in the months and years to come.

Lingering Questions from Legacy Media

Have you ever been disturbed by images you saw in a movie or on television? I have. There is a scene from the movie *The Fisher King* that has stayed with me to this day, where a character played by Robin Williams watches his beloved wife be suddenly and brutally murdered before his eyes. And there is a scene involving the raping of children in *The Prince of Tides* that has stayed with me as well. In fact, scenes that evoke high emotions like intense fear are supposed to be burned into our psyches because of their relevance to our survival. Joanne Cantor has studied fear, anxiety, and other mental disturbances induced by mass media. Cantor and her colleagues have found that it is common for people to experience sleeping and eating disturbances and mental preoccupation with disturbing material, and even to avoid the situations dramatized in the offending media. In one study, over a third of her respondents who reported being frightened by media said the effects of that fear lasted more than a year. And a fourth said that they still felt the emotional ramifications of the fear-inducing media, even though it had been viewed an average of six years earlier.[14]

A random national survey[15] revealed that 62 percent of parents said their child had been scared that something they saw in the media might actually happen to them. In an experiment, children who saw frightening scenes involving house fires or drowning said they worried that something like they saw might happen to them. The children were also less willing to take part in situations related to the fear-inducing scenes they saw in the media. For example, children who had seen a media depiction of a deadly house fire were less likely to want to build a fire in a fireplace. Children who had seen a media depiction of drowning were less willing to go canoeing than children who did not. Of course, these fear reactions make sense. It is adaptive to avoid situations that might harm you. What's interesting from a media psychology perspective is that the children digested the fictional information as realistic and important to apply in their real lives.

Cantor also notes that children are frightened by different aspects of media stories at different developmental stages, which is helpful for parents to understand when helping children make media choices. Three- to eight-year-old children are more likely than older children to be frightened by things that look strange or by sudden movement. As older children come to understand more social nuances, they tend to focus more on threats of injury and destruction. Adolescents are sensitive to social fears and can start to understand more global, political, and economic threats. So while smaller children might be frightened by ghosts and ghouls, older children would be frightened by potential harm and teens by broader social fears. Cantor gives a great example of this. Since a sizable proportion of parents she surveyed mentioned that their children feared the *Incredible Hulk*, she investigated further how these fears differed by age. She discovered that the younger children were frightened by scenes in which Doctor Banner transformed into the Hulk because they found it physically strange and grotesque. The older children, however, were not as frightened by the transformation because they understood that in the context of the story Banner had good intentions and that when he transformed he fought evil. The effectiveness of coping strategies also differs by age. Younger children cope better with fear-inducing media by being distracted, by covering their eyes, or by hugging a toy or blanket. Older children do better with cognitive strategies like telling themselves the situation is not real or that it probably will never happen to them personally.

Cantor offers advice for parents based on research. Her tips include limiting TV viewing, especially before bedtime; not allowing children to have TVs in their bedrooms; watching what your children watch in order to familiarize yourself with the content; and also being aware of what you watch and how much of it your children see incidentally. For anyone who wants to know more about mass media and fear reactions, I recommend Cantor's book *Mommy, I'm Scared: How TV and Movies Frighten Children and What We Can Do to Protect Them*.

MEDIA LITERACY 101

Given that most of us are growing up spending a great deal of time with mass media, and given the media's power to influence us and the common misunderstandings about media power, some education is clearly in order. I suggest that media literacy be made part of our school curricula. But perhaps a definition of the term "media literacy" is in order. Being media literate means understanding the messages being transmitted by mass media and how those messages affect our culture and its members. One of the basic tenets of media literacy is that literate members of a society are more powerful and more liberated.

I also like the perspective of Dorothy and Jerome Singer[16]: that being media literate can also be thought of as being a *critical viewer*. Let's extend that notion to include the newer forms of media (audio and video podcasts, social networking, etc.) and call it being *critical users* of media. This new model means moving away from passively accepting all media messages as harmless entertainment and moving toward an active model in which we assume that media influence us. What we're currently doing as a society of relatively passive users is similar to taking a politician's rhetoric at face value, trusting that he or she has our best interests in mind, instead of critically analyzing the politician's behaviors, motivations, and persuasive efforts. To extend the analogy, an informed voter understands the persuasive elements of a political campaign and then chooses to vote for the candidate or not, but she is making an educated choice, not a naïve one. In our current media-saturated culture, we need to move from a society of naïve users to one of more sophisticated consumers.

In his book *Media Literacy*, James Potter[17] talks about an issue that's especially relevant to children and adolescents, namely, the way that exposure to lots of mass media messages shapes the way we think about ourselves. He discusses how advertisers expressly try to program how we think about ourselves, specifically wanting consumers to feel uneasy and self-conscious. Why would media executives want their viewers to feel bad about themselves? The answer is that if you feel lacking, you are more motivated to buy some product or service to try to fix yourself. Children and teens are especially vulnerable to such manipulation. Part of the psychology of teenagers, for example, is that they think everyone is looking at them and judging them. Of course, social approval is extremely important to teens, making them a population particularly vulnerable to this type of manipulation.

There are other developmental issues, both maturational and physical, which suggest that teens process media messages in unique ways—ways that definitely affect their evolving self-concepts and their thinking and decision-making. David Walsh's book *Why Do They Act That Way?*[18] elaborates on these issues. As a brief example, adults tend to do their advanced information processing with the frontal cortex, the brain's advanced information-processing center, but teens tend to process information in the amygdala, an area of the brain dedicated to emotional processing. The amygdala is specifically associated with the emotion of anger. This may explain why starting an innocent conversation with a teen sometimes results in tears or screaming. If it helps, keep in mind that when a teen screams, "I hate you," it's really just her amygdala talking. As far as I understand, like the old saying goes, she probably *will* grow out of it.

Now one maturational goal of teen-hood is to move toward being able to successfully separate from one's parents—to become independent. This probably explains why teens prefer to be viewed as young adults and also why they don't want to be seen in public with their parents (in the role of children). Within this context of development, let's now overlay the issue of the digital divide. Kids are now known as digital natives, meaning that they grew up with technology and are likely more comfortable with it. I'd take this further by saying that for a teenager, part of his identity is his media diet—his musical and communication preferences and exploits, for example. On the other hand, parents who've learned new technology are called digital migrants. In recent years, as everyday technology has evolved particularly rapidly, the digital divide has broadened substantially. We could now call it a digital canyon. On the one side are teens, their thumbs flying as they text a friend, while Mom feels good that she knows how to google something, and the neighbor feels left out because he doesn't know all these terms he hears bandied about on TV—like "blog" and "avatar." I actually can't tell you how many colleagues have privately confessed to me that they have no clue how to use an iPod. (My dear colleagues, I am more than happy to give you a free and confidential iPod tutorial. Hint: stop trying to ram your 8-track tape into the thing!) In the end, younger people identify with digital technology, while older people often feel dumb and ignorant (which are, of course, two different things) around technology. I imagine there are also differences in technology use by career and education level as well as other factors. But for parents and kids, one result of the digital canyon separating them is that parents may not feel able to monitor some of their kids' media use. In fact, they may not even know that some of it exists. This situation wasn't the case for other generations of parents and kids.

INCREASING YOUR SOPHISTICATION AS A CRITICAL USER OF MASS MEDIA

Let's consider some specific examples of levels of persuasive information present in media messages. This analysis applies equally to a film, a political flyer you receive in your mailbox, or to the advertisement that appears on your screen as you cruise Facebook. Let's begin with noted communications scholar James Potter's notion that media literacy is multidimensional. A media message is multidimensional in that there are several layers of meaning constructed in any single message. An analogy might be helpful here. Take a face-to-face conversation: two friends are talking about a third friend who they think has a drinking problem. One says to the other, "I'm worried about Carrie. She's going to go to that party tonight and drink, and who knows who she is going to end up going home with." Let's look at the different levels of this communication. Potter identifies four dimensions of mass media communication—the cognitive, emotional, aesthetic, and moral dimensions—and these apply to our conversation as well. On the cognitive level, we have the information that is being shared: an expression of concern for a friend and some reasons for that concern. On the emotional level, we can interpret a variety of feelings felt by the communicator, including worry and anxiety. The aesthetic dimension includes judgments about the communicator's artistry, from her strength as an orator to judging whether what she says is genuine, or whether she is trying to make it appear genuine. Finally, the moral domain relates to values: What judgment is the speaker making about the kind of behavior that is proper for her friend?

Now, moving back to media criticism, one can judge a media message on those four dimensions as well. Let's use as an example something most of us have seen many times: an e-mail advertising a "male enhancement" drug. On the cognitive dimension, a critical user can analyze the factual information in the e-mail on many criteria, including the following: What does the drug promise to do? Is it likely that the drug delivers on these promises? What about the assumption that one would need what the drug offers? Moving to the emotional dimension, as a reader you can analyze how the producers of the e-mail wanted you to feel. Did they hope you would feel anxious about your own personal characteristics and therefore that you would send them money? Did they hope you would get excited about this product changing your life? On the aesthetic level, were there pictures (yikes!), text in ALL CAPS, or other aesthetic features designed to motivate your interest? Did you get the feeling the producers were laughing at consumers while they wrote this ad—or at least thinking about playing to their vulnerabilities? Did the aesthetics make you feel dirty or embarrassed for reading the ad? Finally, on a moral level, what do you think the producers intended for readers to take from the ad? Should one feel that it is "every man for himself" and that to compete with other men in terms of sexual prowess, a man needs this drug? As Potter notes, when we can perceive the values that underlie media messages, "the more sophisticated and reasoned our judgments about those values. It takes a highly media-literate person to perceive moral themes well."

Of course, not all media manipulation is as insidious as the ubiquitous male-enhancement e-mail. Let's take an example of an iconic moment in American media and examine it using Potter's principles of media literacy. In the late 1970s, the miniseries *Roots* aired. Based on the novel *Roots: The Saga of an American Family* by Alex Haley, *Roots* was a story based on Haley's ancestors and their experience as African American slaves. *Roots* received several Emmy awards and is the third most watched TV event in American history, gaining the interest of Americans of all racial backgrounds and drawing their attention to issues of prejudice and discrimination. In a famous scene from the miniseries, a slave named Kunta Kinte (played by LeVar Burton) is whipped brutally for refusing to take the slave name Toby. In that moment in screen history, we can see several messages being sent. There is information (cognitive dimension) that slaves were severely beaten for disobedience, mixed with the emotions engendered by watching this scene, the moral message that such inhumane treatment is reprehensible, and the more general message that when the status quo is morally flawed, one must take action. All of this is delivered in an aesthetic context: the depiction of the skin on Kunta's back as it is lashed relentlessly by the whip, his cries of pain, and the tears in his eyes as he undergoes the experience. Again, a very powerful set of messages has been produced and communicated to the viewer, who interprets all of this. In today's media-rich environment, viewers of the program could also share views through blogs or social networking pages that might discuss some of these elements.

These are some lessons in the critical use of media. Active, critical media users think more deeply about media messages; they don't just absorb them without questioning. Critical users understand the notion that media is produced with an agenda in mind. Often the agenda is simply to capture the audience's attention so that the audience will be there to view the advertising that is associated with that particular TV show, Web site, video podcast, and so on.

I can't tell you how many times, as a media researcher, people have told me that the purpose of media is simply to entertain. As we move toward becoming critical consumers of media, we must reject this notion as the hopelessly naïve premise that it is. The primary reason that people produce media is to make money. From what I've seen, those producers work fiercely to defend their bottom lines. Now that does not mean that there is no meaningful content in media. As discussed earlier, there are plenty of positive and entertaining messages in the media. In addition to analyzing media messages for their potential impact, another one of the marks of a media-literate person is the ability to make active choices about what media to consume. If you think you watch too much TV for your own good or your own comfort, then you can make it a point to watch less, and/or to be more thoughtful about what you do watch. According to the research, you will most likely be happier and healthier for grabbing hold of the wheel yourself and taking charge.

Without adequate skills in media literacy, your natural inclination will be to digest media messages as you would a real-life experience. If a movie plays sad music to evoke a sad feeling, the naïve viewer's reaction is to simply feel sad, rather than analyzing it or being aware that the producers are creating a scene in order to evoke an emotion. Now let's look more deeply at another social psychological issue—a broad analysis of how the media messages common to everyday experience contribute to the formation of culture.

THE SOCIAL CONSTRUCTION OF CULTURE

One of the basic tenets of media literacy is that what we experience via the media plays a large part in creating our culture. To better understand this view, we must begin with a definition of culture. Our culture is our shared reality, created and maintained through common experience and through communication. Culture includes socially constructed meanings, including shared beliefs, values, and rules. A swastika, for example, is a symbol that is understood throughout the world to represent the Nazi movement. The same is true for fantasy objects that were created by the media. If I walked into any elementary school classroom, college dormitory, church, or shopping mall in America with a light saber and showed it to the people who were there, would they understand what it was? I am willing to bet that almost every person I encountered would recognize a light saber as an object from our culture, even though it is a fantasy object created by the media. Taking this concept to another level, there are also *Star Wars* light saber toys for sale, so an American boy may have grown up playing Luke Skywalker versus Darth Vader with his brother using light saber toys. Though Luke and Darth and their light sabers are all fantasies constructed by mass media, they are also all cultural icons—recognizable pieces of our shared culture.

ON POWER AND LIBERATION

Often those who sell media or those who defend media makers' right to include objectionable content say that they want to encourage freedom. Freedom, in this case, refers to the freedom of expression of the media producers. Media makers also tend to support this view of freedom by labeling any media criticism as an attempt at censorship. Is discouraging objectionable content or limiting broadcast hours for this content really censorship, or is this a term that serves those who profit from media sales?

This is an excellent time to talk about "framing." When those who make their money from media call media criticism "censorship," they are "framing" their argument, or hoping that audiences will view it in the way they've defined it. Framing uses powerful, often emotional language to manipulate the impression that the message makes. In this case, media representatives understand that the concept of censorship goes against the American grain. We're a culture built on freedom, and the term "censorship" implies a type of authoritarian denial of liberties that we find repulsive. Using the words "censorship" and "freedom," then, are ways of framing the issue to their advantage. Actually, social psychologists who study persuasion tactics know that this type of framing specifically manipulates those members of society who are *less* knowledgeable. Let's explore why.

John Cacioppo and Richard Petty (no, not *that* Richard Petty) are social psychologists well known for their joint research on the psychology of persuasion. According to Cacioppo and Petty[19], audiences usually take either the "central" or the "peripheral route" to persuasion. In the central route, one considers the content of the message, or the message's arguments. In the peripheral route, one considers more shallow or tangential information. Consider, for instance, that you want to buy some hand sanitizer to send to school in your child's backpack. If you are persuaded to buy *The Germinator* brand hand sanitizer (*The Germinator* terminates germs—patent pending) because you saw a commercial showing a warm, attractive mother giving her child *The Germinator*, then peripheral cues have influenced you. If, however, you read a *Consumer Reports* article that summarized factual information about hand sanitizers (such as the type of germs they kill and the speed at which they work), then central, or meaningful cues, motivated your purchase.

If we go back to the argument about media criticism being censorship, then, we can see that those moved by that argument are more likely to be those reacting to the peripheral cue that "censorship" is a dirty word. A censor removes material that he finds objectionable; therefore, he restricts other people's freedoms and makes ethical choices for them. Media criticism is not censorship, or imposed restrictions. Rather, it involves understanding, questioning, and suggesting possible consequences of media consumption. Those who wish to profit by manipulating consumers use emotional, hot-button words like "censorship" to accomplish their goals. Another tactic they employ is to claim that media research is faulty or that media research does not show that media affect us. Both assertions are unfounded. Ironically, as discussed in Chapter 1, it is *because* people do not want to feel manipulated (censored, restricted, affected by media) that they end up defending those who actually *are* manipulating them—manipulating them for their money. What a perfect situation this is for those who profit from media revenues! Those who are most vulnerable to their manipulations are those who end up being some of their greatest defenders. The only way out of this trap is through increasing our own knowledge and understanding of how media work and how media messages affect us—in other words, when we become more media literate we put both the power and the freedom from manipulation back in our own hands.

"Censorship" is not the only hot-button term used to frame media debates. Another typical attempt at manipulation is to call media critics "alarmists," or to say that we are "trying to scare people." If a doctor informs you that eating an unhealthy diet may put you at higher risk for health problems, is she trying to scare you? No, at least not in any gratuitous sense of the word. When experts give information, it doesn't make them alarmists. Here's a media literacy fact: among children starting school, the more television a child watches, the lower his vocabulary. Do I, as a psychologist, tell you that to scare or alarm you? No. I'm an educator and I tell you that to educate and empower you. Psychologists want people to be healthy. We are fortunate in this country to have freedom of choice, but freedom of choice should not be confused with lack of consequences for those choices. Uninformed choices can lead to debilitating consequences. Free choice doesn't always lead to liberation.

MORE ON FANTASY AND REALITY, OR STORYTELLING REVISITED

In Chapter 1, I spoke about the myth that if people understand media stories to be fantasy—in other words, fiction—they are not affected by the content of those stories. Because of how common this misconception this is, I will spend some more time further elaborating on the role of this "fantasy/reality media myth" and how it relates to storytelling. So get comfortable, and settle in with me for what we might consider an alternative version of TV's *Myth Busters*.

The first step to debunking the fantasy/reality media myth is to think about what the essence of modern media is and what it has replaced, or at least augmented, from our past. The most popular forms of modern media (television, movies, video games) are essentially high-tech forms of storytelling. Noted media scholar George Gerbner[20] spoke often about media taking on the role of storytelling. David Walsh's work[21] emphasizes these points as well. People have always told stories; storytelling is a fundamental element of a social system. A movie, like a book or a play, tells a story about people's life experiences. To understand the social power and influence of mass media, we need to go back and ask ourselves some basic questions about storytelling. Why do we tell each other stories? Who are the storytellers? What are the storyteller's goals? Who are the listeners? How are listeners affected by stories?

Let's examine some classic story forms from the past and relate them to modern storytelling through the mass media. For example, one form of storytelling kept alive through generations is the parable, such as the parables of the Bible. One such story is the parable of the Good Samaritan. This familiar story is one of an injured man in need being refused help by a number of seemingly upright men and being shown kindness from someone who wasn't expected to help. Parables have morals. In this case, one moral of this story is that people who are supposed to be upright do not always act accordingly. Why does Jesus tell this story, and why do others who come after him repeat it? The purpose of the parable is to teach important lessons. Why not just deliver the moral and not tell the story? Because stories have the power to engage the listener and to help the listener more deeply understand. When listening to a story, we identify with the characters and their predicaments. We imagine what we would do in their situations. Stories are metaphors, and people understand metaphors at a deep level.

Now consider another type of story, common throughout human history—the fable. Aesop's fables are a collection of stories designed to teach lessons through metaphor. For example, consider the fable of the Fox and the Grapes. A thirsty fox spies some delicious grapes hanging from a tree and tries to eat the grapes, but cannot reach them. Walking away, the fox says that the grapes were probably sour anyway. What is the moral of the story? It is easy to despise what you cannot have. Again, why tell this story? When we hear the tale of the Fox and the Grapes, we empathize with the fox. We know how it feels to be thirsty. We know how frustrating it is to try to get something you need, only to be denied. We understand what it feels like to want something so badly that you can taste it and then to come away empty-handed. Listening to the story, we put ourselves in the fox's shoes (or in his paws, I suppose), including the feeling of "sour grapes"—of wanting to reject something simply because you know you can't have it. Facing that loss is too painful, so we try to convince ourselves that we no longer want the object of our desire. Once again, it is not enough to simply relate the moral; there is something about telling the story itself that makes the moral that much richer and more meaningful. Simply put, storytelling is a way to share someone else's experience vicariously. We feel what the story characters feel. We live that situation through them. Most of all, for our purposes, the experience has meaning for us, and we are changed by sharing it with the characters.

SOCIAL LEARNING THROUGH MEDIA
IMAGERY AND STORYTELLING

Other than some children's programming, such as *Sesame Street* or *The Magic Schoolbus*, we usually do not think of media as educational. But media are great teachers. What specific kinds of lessons do we learn as we soak in media's typical messages? Let's say we watch a television comedy that showcases a group of friends and their wacky exploits. This is just entertainment, isn't it? What could we be learning while watching this show? There are many social lessons to learn and we are, in fact, astute observers of this information. For example, are members of the group sleeping together? Do they sleep with multiple members of the group? How does their friendship circle react to this? Do they respond with humor? How do they perceive casual sex? What are the consequences? Are there unwanted pregnancies or sexually transmitted diseases? And how do the characters look? Are they attractive, thin, muscular, well dressed? How do they spend their time? What do they think is funny? Whom do they ridicule? What do they value? A new study found that watching TV with sexual content is a risk factor in teen pregnancy. One problem is that the shows do not show realistic consequences of sexual activity.[22]

You see, in many ways, we learn how we should act from watching social interactions on television. We learn what behaviors are reinforced. Psychologists call this vicarious reinforcement. If I see a television character being rewarded for sleeping around, I learn from a distance that young, attractive people value this behavior. I also learn vicariously that there are few negative consequences to promiscuity. Research shows that kids who receive these kinds of media messages actually change their own interpersonal behavior based on what they have witnessed in the media. So people learn values—both what is socially acceptable and what is rewarded—through the media. They also learn expectations of others and consequences of behaviors.

Are media stories fantasy? Well, yes, in that the specific stories and characters are fictional. Does that mean that these stories and images are not real? Not at all. The stories are very real to the viewers in that they represent what the viewer imagines to be the way real people do act or should act and the way real people are rewarded or punished for behaviors. We know that a television actress is playing a role, but we also understand that the story she is acting out has meaning. Why is this? Again, before mass media were so pervasive in our lives, we relied on real, face-to-face social interactions to learn social information. We watched what other people in our village or town did, how they looked, what they valued, and how others reacted to them and their behaviors, and we learned from what we saw. This is the basic idea behind the concept of social learning—we look to others for examples of appropriate social behavior.

One global reason we do this is that it helps our society run more smoothly. When all the group members understand the group values and roles, the group can live and work together more efficiently.

Also, from an evolutionary perspective, learning appropriate social behaviors is adaptive. For example, let's say that sexual promiscuity tends to cause negative outcomes such as sexually transmitted diseases, unwanted pregnancies, and jealousy. To avoid these problems, a society might choose to punish sexual promiscuity for the good of the group at large. Therefore, members of the group must be taught to value and support monogamy or more sexually conservative behaviors. In the past, this social learning took place within a small group of people. With modern media, we've expanded our role models, so to speak, to include anyone we can see through the media. And media do not portray role models with the goal of presenting behaviors that are most adaptive for the social group. Rather, they choose behaviors designed to get our attention (more on this later). The end result is (sometimes unintended) learning to value more extreme behaviors because we are exposed to them more often, and they therefore become more normal to us.

There are many more lessons—both subtle and not so subtle—that we can learn from watching social interactions in the media. We've already discussed the transmission of values through the media. How about the effects of representations of group members, such as women and minorities, through the media? Again, when the media represent images of women, for example, they do so to get the attention of viewers, but they can also present a stereotypical and damaging view of women at the same time. Later in the book, I will discuss the research on the effects of this artificial construction of gender in the media.

PARARELATIONSHIPS, OR "DO I KNOW YOU?"

When we spend more time staring at screens and less time with actual people, one result is the strange feeling of having pseudo-relationships with mass media figures. Communications scholars call these "pararelationships." We might also call them mediated social interactions (with the medium—the television, for example—being the go-between). For example, we may feel like we know Bill Clinton after reading his biography. We might daydream about Jon Stewart of the *Daily Show* laughing at our jokes, or secretly fantasize that our attraction to Johnny Depp or Gwyneth Paltrow might someday be returned. Psychologically speaking, this feeling of having relationships with media figures actually makes some sense. As biological organisms, we weren't designed for this paradoxical social situation where we feel that somehow we get to know people personally from afar. When you've watched an actor laugh, cry, and share secrets through the media, it makes sense that you feel you know that person. After all, your brain wasn't made to tell the difference between watching Gwyneth cry on the screen and watching her cry while sitting beside you. Still, one question we can ask is, what are the consequences of replacing some of our real relationships with mediated pseudo-social interactions? Among other consequences, we spend less time interacting with the real people in our lives and more time watching others live their lives—or pretend to—from afar. We are also exposed to different information, values, beliefs, priorities, and people than we would otherwise encounter, and this exposure can have consequences.

THE SOCIAL PSYCHOLOGY OF SOCIAL NETWORKING SITES

Appearing on the scene in the early years of the 21st century, social networking sites (SNSs) such as MySpace and Facebook are now part of the landscape of how young people interact with each other. If you don't know what a social network site is, it is essentially Web space where individuals can post a personal profile and communicate in a variety of ways with other users. On Facebook, for example, you can write on your friend's "wall," which means you can post a note on an electronic blackboard that the person's other contacts will also see. You can tell all your friends what you are doing right now, updating this as often as you like. You can post information about what music or movies you like, or what political candidate you are backing. Similar sites for younger kids are also emerging, such as WebKinz, where kids buy a stuffed animal and then access a matching character online. While MySpace has 100 million users, Disney's Club Penguin, which media psychologist David Walsh calls "MySpace for the grade school set" now has four million subscribers.[23]

In 2015, *The Pew Internet and American Life Project* reported that 92% of teens (aged 13–17) go online daily[24] . This statistic has remained stable in recent years. What has changed was the 24% of teens who now said they go online "almost constantly," aided by the ubiquity of smartphones. According to a 2007 report, parents thought their kids spent about half as much time online as they actually did. About 75% of teens either have a smartphone or have access to one, with African-American teens being the most likely to have access to a smartphone, at 85%.

In 2007 report, Pew researchers had asked the teens how they socialize with their friends on a daily basis. Teens reported their preferences in this order: landline phone, cell phone, in person, text messaging, instant messaging, sending messages on social networking sites, and—last *and* least—e-mailing. For "multi-channel teens"—those who have cell phones and use other high-tech forms of communication—they preferred cell phones and text messaging, but still ranked e-mailing last. In fact, when this report was released, word hit the press that "e-mail is for old people."

What's interesting to me as a social psychologist is why teens prefer cell phoning and texting to e-mail: because they want to reach their friends right away, wherever they are. It's also interesting that multi-channel teens preferred talking to friends on their cell phone two to one over spending time with friends in person. In fact, talking to friends in person was low on their list of priorities, only ranking higher than e-mailing.

If you think e-mail is for old people, what about Facebook? There has been a buzz suggesting that younger people don't use Facebook. This is not actually true. Facebook is still the most used site on the internet, regardless of age of user. And it is still the most used social media site for teens, by far. The Pew Internet and American Life Project reports that 71% of teens use Facebook, followed by 52% using Instagram, 41% using Snapchat and 33% tweeting on Twitter. The teens also cited Facebook as the social media venue they use most frequently. The report also revealed that Snapchat is more likely to be used by teens in higher income brackets, that girls are more likely than boys to use Instagram and that boys are more likely than girls to play video games. Eighty four percent of boys, compared to 59% of girls say they play video games online or on their phone.

Services such as social networking sites (e.g., Facebook) and photo- and video-sharing sites (e.g., Instagram) have the advantage of letting people carry on a conversation about something with all their friends, albeit not in person. For example, if you post a video on YouTube of your college roommate singing in your dorm room while wearing a towel, then all your friends can make comments that the others will see. According to the Pew survey, almost 90 percent of teens said that when they post photos, people make online comments. With cell phones, you can send out a photo or a video to all your friends simultaneously as well, and you know they're likely to all get it right away, and they can reply to just you or to a whole group of friends. Kids enjoy that kind of immediacy and access to a group of friends simultaneously that these new technologies provide.

I have a profile on Facebook. At first I resisted joining the social networking craze. Frankly, as a college professor, I had the vague apprehension that if I logged on to a social networking site, I would be inundated with compromising photos of my students (illicit drinking photos, images of female students in revealing clothing). I just didn't think I wanted those mental images as I walked into the classroom. I'm not the only teacher who feels this way.

Recently, an eighth grade teacher wrote an article about social networking in which she began by saying that the first time she perused a social media site, she saw profiles of her students who claimed to use hardcore drugs, claimed to be very much older than they actually were, and so on. She realized after working with these sites and talking to her students that kids do the things they've always done, they just do them in new ways now. For example, kids brag about illicit things that they haven't actually done (of course, some have done them). Kids try to claim their individuality by liking the band that's cool to like (so, they're individuals because they're like everyone else—an age-old teen characteristic)—in other words, same stuff, different day.

It's an axiom that the teen years are times when we all do stupid things. There are many ways that as social interactions go digital, those stupid things are more accessible to a wider range of people for a much longer period of time. Simply put, some of these newer technologies make it easier for kids to make mistakes that will end up publicly embarrassing them or otherwise doing them harm. A friend of mine who teaches high school English recently told me that a female student was the talk of the school because she took nude pictures of herself with her cell phone and sent them to her boyfriend's cell phone. You guessed it: the boyfriend promptly put the pictures on his computer and e-mailed them to basically everyone.

Another social psychological aspect of online social networks is that face-to-face social interactions have characteristics that differ in a number of ways from cyber socializing. As mentioned previously, several authors have noted that people can be very mean-spirited online—meaner than that same person would be to your face. Why do you think that is? Well, for one thing, you don't have the immediate facial expressions, body language, tone of voice, and other cues that would be typically done to let someone know when they have gone too far. Also, on a blog or in a chatroom, anonymity can embolden people to say things they wouldn't say if they had to take personal responsibility for them, or if they had to carry on a long-term relationship with that person. A hastily typed comment that makes it to a literally worldwide Web site can take on a gravitas that might be tempting for the perpetrator, and particularly crushing to the receiver.

OMG: MY FIRST MEETING ON SKYPE

There are other ways in which social interactions differ in RL (cybergeek code for real life) as compared to in cyberspace. For example, there are new access points to adult content in cyberspace. As a case in point, I'll tell you about my first meeting on Skype. Skype is an Internet service that allows you to chat (write messages), talk as you would on the telephone, and even send and receive a live video feed from anywhere to anywhere and for free. My friend and colleague Dr. Carlo Fabricatore is the CEO of a video game development company in Rome, Italy. When we began a research collaboration, Carlo suggested we have virtual meetings on Skype. It was a great idea and a great example of how the Internet and new technologies can make so much possible. Carlo was in Italy and I was in the United States, but we could have research meetings almost as if we worked in the same city.

I'd never used Skype before, so I got online, downloaded the required free software, and set up an account. At the appointed time, we both logged on and began talking. There was a lot going on. We were designing some research studies. Also, Carlo, being a very talented person, was speaking about these issues in English—his third language after Italian and Spanish. Furthermore, he is a computer scientist and I am a psychologist, so we bring different perspectives to the table. I was thinking about all of this and was totally unprepared for what happened next. I began getting suggestive chat messages from strange men from different countries. Next, I heard calls ring in with men greeting me. I closed windows and hung up on calls. Carlo, not knowing any of this was going on, continued to talk about research. As if this weren't distracting enough, I was completely unprepared for what happened next: strange men from around the world started to send me pornographic videos. Now you may be wondering what I mean by pornographic videos. Just to make this clear, they were naked videos where the camera was trained right on their penises. So, I'm trying to talk about research with my colleague, and chat windows are opening up with messages like, "Hey, pretty lady, you want to talk dirty?" Meanwhile, I am hearing phone calls engage and men saying, "Hello, hello!" and then videos of penises are popping up on my screen. All the while I am frantically closing windows.

Eventually, I had to explain this to Carlo and we had a good laugh about it. He helped me look through my settings to try to find the problem. I thought I had made it so only my contacts could see my information (a brief profile and photo). It turned out that I had done this, but I had neglected to change one setting. It seems that from a list of choices I had selected "Skype me," which apparently is a euphemism for "send me naked videos." Carlo was very good-natured about it and teased me about solving my "popularity problem." I changed the setting, and we were able to continue our Skype meetings uninterrupted. Who would have ever thought that anyone would have to deal with the issue of trying to have a meeting while pornographic images and messages popped up all over your computer screen? Again, this new form of technology provided us with great opportunities, but also new challenges.

So I end this chapter as I began it, with the notion that there are ample reasons for both excitement (no pun intended) and concern when it comes to navigating in our ever-changing, media-rich world. For those of us who are parents, this is going to mean taking the time to familiarize ourselves with the technology that our kids are using. I know people feel inadequate sometimes when it comes to learning new technologies, but take heart: if our kids can use it easily, believe it or not, we can, too. As with all things, when it comes to new technologies, knowledge is power, and making an effort to be active and involved is always better than choosing to be left behind.

Media Violence

The *Grand Theft Auto* games such as *Grand Theft Auto III, Grand Theft Auto: San Andreas* and *Grand Theft Auto: Vice City* are one of the most widely known video games, making their mark in pop culture due to record-setting sales, critical acclaim in the gaming community, and controversial content. On April 29, 2008, *Rockstar* games released the much-anticipated sequel *Grand Theft Auto IV* to unparalleled critical acclaim as well as to controversy over violent and sexual content, now *de rigeur f*or a title in the series. That week I got an e-mail from Nicole, a former student of mine. She asked me if I knew that they'd named a character after me in *GTA IV,* telling me to go to YouTube and search for "Karin Dilettante."

I got on YouTube and watched the video—a humorous promotion for a hybrid car described as a "seriously bad, morally good, fully customizable luxury V.I.P. style hybrid sedan: the Karin Dilettante."[1] At first I couldn't quite believe it. I asked some of my friends and colleagues who are video game violence experts if they thought this *Grand Theft Auto* car was really named in "honor" of me. They said they thought it was. Come to think of it, naming a car in a violent video game a variation of Karen Dill is a pretty unlikely phenomenon, unless you take into account that a media violence scholar is named Karen Dill. Considering I have publicly critiqued the *Grand Theft Auto* games in various media outlets, in scholarly journals, and in front of Congress—okay, yeah, I see.

Now, if you're not familiar with the term, a "dilettante" is basically an amateur who pretends to be a professional. In other words, a dilettante is someone who thinks she knows what she's talking about, but really doesn't. The word comes from a root meaning to be delighted, and applies especially to a superficial admirer of the arts.

So apparently the guys at *Rockstar* games were teasing me about critiquing their art with my pseudo-knowledge or faux expertise, if you will. I actually

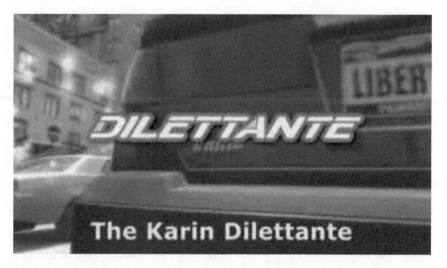

Figure 4.1 A screen shot of my "namesake" the Karin Dilettante—a car in the videogame *Grand Theft Auto IV* by *Rockstar* Games, distributed by *Take Two* Interactive.

think it's a pretty subtle and sly lampoon—in my opinion, quite clever. I don't mind being teased—in fact, I enjoyed it immensely. You might say I was quite *delighted* (or is that *Dill*-lighted?) by the satire.

MEDIA INDUSTRY SPIN: SCHOLARS AS DILETTANTES

But of course, this does beg the question: are media violence experts like myself really dilettantes? Media violence is a controversial topic to be sure, with outspoken, passionate advocates sitting on both sides of the table. In a recent poll of parents of teenagers, about 6,000[2] adults were asked whether media violence exposure (specifically violent video games) affects children's behavior. Fifty-eight percent answered "yes," 31 percent answered "no," and 11 percent didn't know. How would you interpret these results? First, one might note that the majority of the people surveyed believe media violence exposure affects children negatively. But a roughly 60/30/10 breakdown is far from a unanimous interpretation of the evidence. Broadly speaking, there are people who believe media violence exposure harms children and another sizable group believes the opposite. These data were collected on a parenting Web site, so they were probably biased toward more concerned parents. People who clicked on the poll were probably interested in the topic. Why do these people believe what they do? Who is right, if there is a right answer? Is this even the right question?

One very important aspect of a poll like that is it asks people to make a judgment about how other people are affected by mass media. Because of the third person effect, we know that people are more apt to think that others are affected than to think they themselves are. Since most polls ask about people in general, theoretically the numbers would be much stronger than if polls asked people if they personally felt influenced.

Parents and gamers of all ages may be interested in learning about a video game before they buy it. There are a variety of places online to do this. One of the very useful things about having video sharing sites is that we now can pull up video from just about any video game and see what the action is like. Just a few years ago, this wasn't true. Parents can also go to sites like CommonSenseMedia.com and look at the ratings, which include information about age appropriateness and learning potential. Another web site that relates to media violence and children is the American Academy of Pediatrics (aap.org).

Let's take some time here to detail the content that appears in a game like *Grand Theft Auto IV*. What kinds of things do kids hear and see when they play? I think this is a crucial part of the conversation about controversial issues in the media. Content like sex and violence, after all, can be portrayed in an infinite variety of ways. To really understand the issues, you need to know exactly what kids are seeing, and therefore learning about, when they play these games. We should pause for a moment here and acknowledge that parents could not so easily see this content without the Internet and without people who care about these issues providing the content to parents. So these are excellent examples of how media can provide information and community to parents in a way previously unseen.

WHAT'S IN A GAME?

Okay, so let's return to analyzing the specific content of *GTA IV*. For the rating of intense violence, we see characters punching and kicking each other and throwing flaming objects. Moving into the gun violence, we see the main character standing on the street shooting civilians and police officers while cursing his targets, calling them names, and making quips. In one scene he shoots someone point blank in the skull and blood spurts out, the man dies, and the main character curses the man. A promo for *GTA IV* jokes about going out on dates and shooting people, promising, "liquor, guns and fun." For the examples of drug and alcohol use, characters drink or snort cocaine and then kill pedestrians remarking that they didn't like the way the pedestrian was looking at them.

In terms of strong sexual content, *GTA IV* is more graphic than its predecessors. Past versions of *GTA* depicted sex by showing a car rocking from a distance accompanied by sound effects and sexual dialogue. In *GTA IV*, you see the characters' bodies through the car windows—for example, a man on top of a woman clearly having sex or a woman with her head in a man's lap. So, the depictions of sex, although they do not show total nudity, are becoming more explicit. Scenes also show women in thongs and pasties dancing in front of men while the men make crude comments.

Why do thirteen-year-olds say they like the *GTA* games? According to one young player: "Last week, I missed one homework and my teacher yelled at me. When I went home, I started playing [*Grand Theft Auto*] *Vice City*, and did a cheat code to get a tank. I ran over everybody. And I smashed a lot of cars and blew them up. Like, I was mad, and I turned happy afterwards."[3] Very typically, many pooh-pooh the idea that games can affect players and speak in an insulting way about anyone who says otherwise. For example, a news article[4] covering the release of *GTA IV* stated, "Rockstar Games and its GTA franchise are a focal point for critics that fear violence in video games warps the minds of young players and turns them into real-world thugs or killers." Similarly, players are incensed by the notion that game content affects players. In reaction to the discussion of why teens like *GTA* on one site, players posted the following comments.[5] The comment title precedes each quote.

No problems: "I've grown up with the GTA games, and they are no problem what-so-ever! And these cases that have surfaced where a teenager has blamed GTA for him raping a girl, or shooting someone, is the fault of the parents, because they'd rather blame someone else for their kid's mess, and not look at themselves to see what caused the actions!"

Games will not effect [sic] the sane: "I'm 25 years old and have been with the GTA series since the very beginning. Despite all the fun I have causing mayhem in the digital world of GTA, never once did I get the feeling it was ok to do the things I do in the game world in the real world. It really comes down to a person's ability to keep fantasy separate from reality. The GTA games in no way encourage the behavior of it's [sic] characters."

This is about art: "You can find violent material on the very pages of the bible but they will never claim that the bible is influencing our youth negetivly [sic]. This is so hippicritical [sic] i need to stop writing immiediatly [sic] so i can punch a wall. You all need to do a lot more thinking. A 17 year old kid is smarter than you, and thats [sic] just pathetic."

I've read many comments over the years of game players who are angry with anyone who says their games may cause negative behavior. I think these comments are typical of what I've read and I think they merit deeper analysis. First, I understand the frustration of the players and I think it is based on a misunderstanding. The teenagers of the world (especially the boys) play violent video games and they are not morphing into a mob of thousands upon thousands of murderers. The research, however, clearly shows that video game violence exposure increases aggression. Where's the disconnect? The disconnect is primarily that the effects do not typically take the form that the players anticipate—namely, a game play session followed by murder. Keep in mind that psychologists do not measure murder as an outcome in the laboratory—for obvious reasons. What we do measure is aggression—someone harming someone else or believing that they are harming someone else. This can take many forms, including actions like insults, sabotage, or delivering blasts of noise that they believe can permanently damage hearing.

More on these issues shortly, but before I expand on those ideas, I want to address the comment that "this is about art." I think another frustration of the gaming community is that the creativity they admire is not given appropriate respect in the larger community. They are angry that outside the gaming community, the concept that a video game constitutes art is often laughed at. Let me give you an example. A while back, I was a guest on a radio call-in show called *These Days* on KPBS in San Diego. When someone compared the graphics of the latest video game to that of a blockbuster film, the host laughed. Later, a game developer called in and commented that when the host laughed, it hurt him. What happened? The host laughed again.

I felt bad for the caller. I believe a video game can be art and it can be a major technological accomplishment that has value and that the creators can be proud of. But let's be fair here—scientific studies are also important works and some studies could be considered masterpieces. Well-done science also has value, and studies are also conducted with extreme care and with the hope that they will be of value to the world at large. Rather than being dismissive of anyone's work, we can offer respectful critiques. That doesn't mean we must be coldly evaluative. We can have passion about our area of expertise, but it's important also to be open-minded and respectful.

CIVIL DISCOURSE

So, approaching this with an open mind, let's talk about the science behind the social psychology of the mass media—what goes into it and what value it has. I hope along the way that I can clear up some of the myths associated with media violence research and that I can communicate exactly why I believe this research is as valuable as it is—a fact that has sometimes been lost in the media coverage of the social psychological study of media violence. I also believe, as outlined in Chapter 1, that those who are trying to make a profit from media violence have a vested interest in promoting the notion that the science is all wrong. In the end, the little guy who buys the product and supports the wealthy industry execs becomes just a pawn in the game. That person's naïveté about the industry can end up being harmful to him. Think about it this way: when someone has something to sell you and that product is widely regarded by scholars to be harmful, whom should you believe, the scholars or the salesmen? Who is more likely to be using you?

Gamers aren't the only ones lining up to say that the results of media violence research are garbage. *USA Today* published an article[6] summarizing some of my research on the effects of exposure to violent video games. At the end of the article, presumably to be fair and balanced, they interviewed someone with an opposing viewpoint. Jonathan Katz—an outspoken critic of, well, media criticism—was quoted as saying, "If this study was right, there'd be hundreds of bodies lying around. People are pushing an agenda of hysteria on parents."

Okay, let me take these ideas in turn. "If this study was right, there'd be hundreds of bodies lying around." Again, here we see the idea that media violence researchers think that playing a violent video game or watching a violent movie will result in only one thing: murder—lots of murder! As for the "pushing an agenda of hysteria"—that's rhetoric. He's making the argument that if you are critical about media violence that means you are trying to make the unsuspecting citizens of America hysterical.

UNHEALTHY DIETS RESULT IN REAL—IF NOT DRAMATIC—RESULTS

Maybe an analogy would be useful here. Let's say that medical researchers find that fat consumption is related to heart problems. Let's say for argument's sake that the researchers had scientific proof that diets high in fat cause heart problems and this research was written up in *USA Today*. How would it sound if there were a health research critic who was quoted as saying, "If this study were right, people would be dropping dead in McDonald's restaurants all over the country. These doctors are pushing their agenda of health hysteria"? It's really a similar thing. People don't die right after eating cheesecake (thank you, God) or pork rinds or lard, but we understand those things are not heart healthy. What does it mean that they're not heart healthy? It means that the more fat you have in your diet, the greater is your risk of heart problems. Also, the less healthy foods in your diet, like fruit and vegetables, the greater your risk of heart problems.

The same is true for your media diet, and remember, we actually call it media consumption for a reason. You consume media. You take it in and it becomes a part of you. The more you see people hurting each other, disrespecting each other, and treating each other poorly, the more that makes its way into your consciousness. That's especially true with the way aggression is generally portrayed in the media—as cool, gratifying, fun, and without consequences. When my son was in the second grade, he saw one boy from his class beat up another boy in the bathroom at school. When he talked about it, his eyes filled with tears and he told me how bad it had made him feel to see that little boy get hurt. I gently explained that this is one reason why mom speaks out against violence in the media. Real aggression is not cool or fun or glamorous; it's a little boy getting hurt and his friends feeling terrible as they see it happen.

Jeanne Funk and her colleagues[7] understand the importance of children's feelings about violence—like my son's sadness at watching a friend get hurt—in the broad scheme of media violence research. They were interested in discovering whether there was a relationship between feelings of empathy—like my son felt for his friend—and playing violent video games. They measured violence exposure—both real and in the media—empathy and attitudes toward violence, in fourth and fifth grade boys and girls. What they found was intriguing. Of the variables they studied, only video game violence exposure was associated with lower empathy. Watching violent movies and playing violent video games were both associated with stronger pro-violence attitudes. When Funk and her colleagues measured empathy, they asked questions like whether it bothered the child when other children got hurt. When they measured attitudes toward violence, they asked things like whether people with guns and knives are cool. The results of this study have many implications. They certainly show that the more violent video games you play, the less likely you are to be concerned about other people getting hurt and the more likely you are to think that aggression is cool and appropriate. These results are also important because decreased empathy and increased positive attitudes about violence have been linked in previous research to aggressive behavior. Funk and her colleagues also discussed the notion that decreased empathy and increased pro-violence attitudes after media violence exposure also indicate desensitization. In other words, one may not realize one is being affected because negative reactions to media violence become blunted with increased exposure. We can relate this back to the discussion in Chapter 1: one reason people who are exposed to more media do not think it affects them might well be because increased exposure causes desensitization. Furthermore, recent research suggests that increases in aggressive thinking brought about by increased violent video game play is a risk factor for increased aggressive behavior in the long term.

Sins of Commission and Sins of Omission

Let's not forget the other part of the diet analogy, though: the less good stuff you have in your diet, the greater your risk. The more you are watching harm and negativity in the media, the less you are watching anything that uplifts you—also, the less you are doing media-free activities like talking to your friends, playing sports, or drawing. Developmental psychology scholars stress how important it is for children to engage in free play and that such play helps children build skills like managing emotions, delaying gratification, and getting along with others.[8] In fact, media scholars are beginning to talk about the media violence issue in terms of risk factor models. The more negativity and the less positivity in your media diet, the greater your risk for negative outcomes.

Put Down the Fry—Before you Die

When it comes to what we eat, we know what tastes good and we know what's good for us. We also know that what tastes good isn't always good for us. With this knowledge and understanding, we make our choices. To extend the metaphor, we're still arguing that French fries are healthy—that scientists are just alarmists and they want to mess up the fun we have eating French fries. The most controversial topics in media are relational—harming people, presenting an unbalanced view of sex and sexuality, encouraging racial and sexist stereotypes. These are issues that affect us all. They are social issues, not individual ones. That's what makes this everybody's business. My interest is in revealing that the emperor is unclothed. At the individual level and at the level of government and culture, we then make choices about what to do with that information.

MEDIA VIOLENCE MYTHS—ANOTHER KIND OF BIG BANG THEORY?

Before we move on, I want to revisit the myth that media violence exposure causes murder and if it doesn't, then it has no effect. This is just one of many myths about media violence that experts have written a bit about. In *The 11 Myths of Media Violence*,[9] Potter defines a myth as something most people in the culture accept even though the logic is flawed or the evidence does not support it. His number one media violence myth is that people think media violence doesn't affect them, but it does affect others—this is the third person effect that we discussed in Chapter 1. The psychology of the third person effect is actually fascinating. If the result were not a naïveté that makes people vulnerable to being used and makes them more likely to be changed for the worse, I would sit around just being fascinated by it. I think the third person effect represents what Anna and Sigmund Freud would have called a defense mechanism—a way to protect ourselves from the uncomfortable knowledge that we are doing something that doesn't make sense (or at least we are worried that it doesn't make sense). We defend our egos by thinking that we are invulnerable. There's no reason to defend what other people are doing. They can be as stupid or vulnerable as they want and it does not scare us into rejecting what we believe is true—that media violence can be harmful and that others are really vulnerable to its effects. So, we see what people report over and over again—that they think they are not vulnerable to media effects, but that other people are. For example, one study showed that the more violent the video games a person plays, the less likely that person is to think media violence has negative effects.[10] And interestingly, new research demonstrates that those who are most deeply engaged by video games, those who are absorbed and transported by them, also tend to be more aggressive.[11]

Other top experts have argued convincingly about media violence myths. In the book *Media Violence and Children*, Doug Gentile and Craig Anderson[12] outline video game violence research and summarize what scientists have found in this research. They review data from a variety of research designs, including meta-analyses—studies that summarize a large body of past published research—and draw conclusions from the studies. These experts report that the research clearly documents five main findings, as follows. Playing violent video games *(1)* increases the body's physical arousal (for example, heart rate and blood pressure), *(2)* increases aggressive thoughts (thoughts related to harming another person), *(3)* increases aggressive feelings (like hostility), *(4)* increases aggression (behavior intended to harm someone else), and *(5)* decreases helping.

The authors also take on the issue of industry critiques of research, saying that when research threatens the profits of big business.[13]

> there is a tendency for that industry to deny the threatening research and to mount campaigns designed to highlight the weaknesses, obfuscate the legitimate findings, and cast doubt on the quality of the research. The history of the tobacco industry's attempt to ridicule, deny, and obfuscate research linking smoking to lung cancer is the prototype of such efforts. The TV and movie industries have had considerable success in their 40-year campaign against the media violence research community. The same type of effort has now been mounted by the video game industry.

In another chapter of the same volume, Gentile and Sesma[14] outline *Seven Myths about Media Effects: (1)* media effects are simple and direct, *(2)* the effects of media violence are severe, *(3)* media effects are obvious, *(4)* violent media affect everyone in the same way, *(5)* causality means "necessary and sufficient," *(6)* causality means immediacy, and *(7)* effects must be "big" to be important.

Let me highlight and comment on some of these myths. Let's take simple, direct, severe, obvious, and immediate and put them together for a moment. These reflect some of the quotes from real people I mentioned earlier in this chapter. People conceptualize media violence effects as turning kids immediately into murderers or as resulting in piles of bodies lying in the street. We seem to think only in extremes—that if I see the neighbor's kid playing *Grand Theft Auto* and he doesn't turn on the spot and shoot another child, that media violence has no effect on children. This is, very thankfully, not the way the human mind works.

There are, of course, natural restraints against murder. There are social sanctions ranging from disapproval to the death penalty. The great American psychologist B. F. Skinner said that his parents used to hold up the idea of prison as a warning to keep him on good behavior. It's perfectly true that we understand that murder is the ultimate crime and we therefore know there are extreme social sanctions against it. And in the animal kingdom, animals will fight to defend their interests, but there is a strong tendency to prefer fighting *for* something as opposed to fighting to the death. Naturally, this preserves the species and so it is adaptive.

So, please, can we dispense with the notion that playing a violent video game or watching a violent movie will result in the person who is exposed morphing immediately into a robotic death machine? Careful now! Don't swing wildly back to the other extreme. This doesn't mean that media violence has no effects on real aggression. It does. These effects are documented over and over by scientists. It's just that you should understand the effects are subtle (at least more subtle than always and immediately going postal on the nearest human) and long term. They build over time, and the outcomes can take many forms such as harassing a colleague at work, spreading rumors about a roommate, or getting in a fist fight after drinking too much. Make no mistake, a diet high in media violence does predict whether you will end up in jail for violent crime. It predicts whether you will beat your spouse. The negative sides of media violence exposure are definitely there; they just play themselves out in ways that are more subtle than many people apparently expect them to be.

Also important to understand is the idea of "necessary and sufficient." If you've taken a course in logic, you may recall these two words as tools of the trade. Basically, what we mean here when we talk about necessary and sufficient is this: *(1)* everybody who is aggressive wasn't provoked by violent media (duh!), and *(2)* if only violent media were involved, that probably wouldn't be enough to provoke the aggression. This is important, so I'll draw some lines under it: media violence isn't the only cause or even the main cause of violence. Media violence exposure is part of the grand scheme in a person's life. It tends to teach people that violence is an acceptable, socially sanctioned way to solve conflict. It reshapes the brain and makes aggression a more likely outcome. It takes the place of other, more adaptive solutions to life's conflicts. It alters social thinking, for example, to characterize some people as more acceptable targets of violence. Seeing violence on the screen teaches complex ideas about social interactions—about how we should treat other people. Now, let's take a closer look at the science used to investigate media violence effects.

ANALYZING THE QUALITY OF THE SCIENCE OF MEDIA PSYCHOLOGY

Anyone who has gone to college (or primary school, for that matter) has had an education on the fundamentals of science. Let's revisit that education in the context of studying media effects. The most basic premise of science is that it is a fundamental system of logic, designed to answer hypothetical questions while minimizing bias. To perform a scientific investigation, we form a hypothesis—usually based on a broader theory—and then we collect data to see if there is support or evidence for it. All things being equal, if the premise is true, it should be supported by the research. If it is not true, it should not gain support. Over time, if scientists conduct many investigations, a body of evidence emerges that suggests whether the ideas and relationships we study really seem to hold up.

Let me give you several examples and you can see what you think. There are studies, for instance, that demonstrate that children whose school environments are noisy (such as happens with schools in the vicinity of airports) have more difficulty concentrating on their work than students in schools without noise problems. Now, does that mean that children whose schools are near airports are dumb and will never amount to anything? Or is it that they are poor kids and their upbringing is actually causing their school problems? Maybe their parents are to blame because they let them go to school near an airport, therefore making them bad parents? No, those comments are far afield from the actual findings or are outright misinterpretations of the findings. It does, however, mean that, all things being equal, it's harder to concentrate on schoolwork when it's noisy. In the laboratory, scientists simulate such real-world situations by giving people tasks to work on with or without distracting noise levels and measuring their performance. Let's say, as is the case, the scientists discover in their laboratories that noise impairs performance and that these results are reported in the media. What would you think if people got mad about these results, said the scientists were quacks and that they did not believe the findings, got mad about scientists ganging up on noise when there are so many other bad things happening in the world? Well, you see where I'm going with this. Those things actually happen as a reaction to media violence research. My point: one has to be critical of other people's observations about science just as one has to be critical about science itself, or news media, or any other form of authority.

Speaking of education, I was given the gift of an excellent education, and for this reason I feel an obligation to tell the public what I have learned, whether it is controversial or not. I was among the first generation of my very large family to go to college. My education was almost entirely funded by scholarships from University of Missouri-Columbia and the state of Missouri—a fact that I am very aware of and grateful for. While I had to work hard and make the grades, my state government and university supported my education. When I was a sophomore in college, I began working with Craig Anderson, who later directed my dissertation. I consider Craig the consummate social scientist, well versed in everything from research methods, design, and statistics to broad scientific theory. My parents never went to college, but I was trained at the Ph.D. level by one of the finest social scientific minds in the country. I guess America really is the land of opportunity. In that context, it is my firm belief that I owe the larger community the benefits of that education.

I have joked before in print that I have a Ph.D., and I'm not afraid to use it. That joke is essentially true. I understand social science—I understand how the media works and how media messages affect people, and I consider it a fundamental part of my life's work to translate science in the public interest. Whatever those in the media industry may believe, it is not my mission in life to be a killjoy and denigrate video games and people who like them. I like nonviolent video games. I know several people who work for the game industry who are very likable. I am not on a vendetta. But I do have a personal mission to translate science in the public interest; to do anything less would be to fail to give back what I have been given so freely by my state and country.

When I teach the history of psychology, my students write biographies of psychologists. The biography paper assignment is structured so that students present the psychologist's life and career contributions and end the paper with an integrative approach, analyzing how the life experiences and personality of the individual informed the career. This is why I relate my own background, personality, and views along the way in this book. Teaching the history of psychology gives me a broad perspective on the human enterprise that is science. I think the view of any science is incomplete without this comprehensive, human approach because the enterprise of science is made up of scholars operating within the bounds of their own internal mission statements.

Now that you know something of my background and my personal mission as a scientist, let's get into the details of some of the media violence research. I want to point out why I think it is such high-quality research that merits your consideration as you make media choices. Next, I'd like to describe one of the most remarkable research programs in the entire discipline of modern psychology. I am not blowing wind up your collective skirt, gentle readers; you would be hard pressed to find a body of work in the entire discipline that lives up to these standards. Settle in and let me tell you all about it.

Yale child psychologist Leonard Eron began this project circa 1960 with the premise that effective child psychologists should involve themselves in the community. He wanted to investigate the causes of childhood aggression and he began auspiciously by interviewing every third grader (856 to be exact) in Columbia County, New York. He also interviewed 80 percent of their mothers and fathers.[15] Leonard Eron, who died in 2007, was a scientist whose work was a shining example of science at its best. First, it began with a genuine desire to work hard to help children, and it progressed with an unparalleled degree of everything that makes science good: high standards, methods of research that make sense and are uncompromising, and, at the end of the day, findings that matter to a lot of people.

This project that Leonard Eron began evolved into a one of the longest running projects of its kind in the history of psychology—spanning over forty years and known collectively as the Columbia County Longitudinal Study.[16] A longitudinal study is one that follows participants over time, collecting information at different points in time. Along the way, a number of scientists joined Eron on this project, most notably his close colleague L. Rowell Huesmann, now at the University of Michigan at Ann Arbor Institute for Social Research.[17,18]

After the initial interviews with the parents and children in 1960, there were subsequent interviews when the participants were nineteen, thirty, and forty-eight, as well as interviews with 551 of the participants' own children. Let me insert here that if you are a social scientist all these statistics about the Columbia County Longitudinal Study are not only impressive—they may actually inspire the need for a fainting couch. Researchers, as a group, are gluttons for punishment. We enjoy things like design, methodology, and statistics that, at least according to the many students I've known, are quite distasteful to others outside the research world. Some historians of psychology[19] speculate that one reason the modern science of psychology took off in Germany was that Germans are an exacting people—people who enjoy big heaping loads of tedious work. (I myself am of largely German descent, and

may I say I love big heaping loads of tedious work?) The simplest research project is frankly a nightmare to most people, as countless students have told me
over the years. Ninety-nine percent of all humans who have ever lived (and
I am totally making these numbers up) want nothing to do with the amount
of work the most typical research project takes. But the Columbia County
Longitudinal Study—that one required superhuman skills and commitment
from the researchers.

So, after all of that painstaking work, what did Eron, Huesmann, and their
colleagues find? They found that the violent television the kids viewed when
they were eight caused them to be violent later in life. For the sake of detail,
let's look more closely at some of their data analysis. They grouped participants by their scores on preference for violent TV (high, medium, and low
violence preference) and for real-life aggressive behavior (high, medium, and
low aggressive behavior). What they discovered was that regardless of how
aggressive they were as third graders, those who watched more violent TV
as third graders were reliably the young adults (18- and 19-year-olds) who
were the most aggressive. They were also able to ascertain that it was indeed
the violence viewing that caused the aggression—in other words, it was not
simply that kids who like to watch violence also are aggressive but that the
exposure to media violence caused them to be aggressive later in life. They
were able to ascertain this causal connection using advanced statistical modeling techniques. The methods and analyses were sophisticated and powerful.
Furthermore, the scientists did an effective job at translating their high-level
science for public consumption. Though sometimes the scientists who are
smart at the very complex tasks necessary for high-quality research aren't the
strongest at explaining it to laypersons, this was not the case for Huesmann
and Eron and their colleagues. It was stellar science all the way through, from
execution to translation.

Huesmann and Eron's team has also spent decades elaborating on exactly
why and how media violence exposure causes increases in aggression. They
have shown definitively that aggressive behavior is, in part, learned and that
an important part of that learning is how viewing aggression changes how
you think. It quite literally restructures your brain and how you understand
the world.

What reaction did the Columbia County Longitudinal Study receive?
Rowell Huesmann and Eric Dubow tell the story best, describing their colleague Leonard Eron's life work in the *American Psychologist* in 2008:[20]

> The 1970 follow-up was part of the U.S. Surgeon General's initiative on the
> effects of television, and Eron's conclusion from that followup, that media
> violence causes aggression, was published in the *American Psychologist*

. . ... It led to a storm of controversy. Critiques and countercritiques were written.

Mass media interests promoted opposition to the conclusion. Believing strongly in the importance of the public policy role for psychologists, Eron spoke about his work repeatedly in public forums, on radio and TV shows, and in testimony before Congress. His firm but polite demeanor under fire convinced many skeptics of the truth of his conclusions. After hearing Eron's testimony, U.S. Surgeon General Jesse L. Steinfeld testified in March 1972 before the U.S. Senate Commerce Committee that "it is clear to me that the causal relationship between [exposure to] televised violence and antisocial behavior is sufficient to warrant appropriate and immediate remedial action. There comes a time when the data are sufficient to justify action. That time has come."

Huesmann and Eron and their colleagues continued to conduct key studies over the years, including the Cross National Television and Aggression Study. In this version, they began with six- to ten-year-old kids who grew up in the American Midwest and in Finland, Poland, and Israel in the 1970s and 1980s. These participants were first and third graders during the initial interviewing stage. The researchers interviewed them as elementary schoolchildren three times at one-year intervals. Then they caught up with them again fifteen years later when they were young adults. They found that there were correlations between childhood television violence viewing and adult aggression in all the countries. They also found the causal effect of being a heavy TV violence viewer as a child and adult aggression in all the countries except Australia. Huesmann[21] reports:

The boys and girls who were in the top 25% in TV violence viewing at age 6 to 10 behave significantly more violently 15 years later. They are more likely to shove and throw things at their spouses. They are more likely to shove, punch, beat, and choke other people. They are more likely to commit crimes and traffic offenses. They are seriously more aggressive than those who were not watching a lot of TV violence when they were children!

In his book *The Eleven Myths of Media Violence*, James Potter[22] argues that many private citizens and political leaders have believed for a long time that media violence causes harm. This stance is certainly underlined by reviewing some of the now almost fifty years of research produced by Huesmann and Eron and their colleagues, as well as the work of many other fine scholars. One problem, Potter believes, is that those who are concerned simply do not know what to do to solve the problem. Potter cites an impressive series of government-sponsored hearings over the years designed to discuss the problem of media violence. But, he says, what happens after the hearing is over? No specific, powerful, global changes take place and years later we simply end up repeating the process all over again. In fact, Potter argues that when it comes to the public debate over media violence, we have been stalled at essentially the same place for over fifty years!

EXPERTS AGREE: VIOLENCE BREEDS VIOLENCE

Recently a group of the top media violence experts were asked to come together and author a paper summarizing the current consensus among media violence experts. These scholars concurred with Potter that there is general agreement in the scientific community that media violence causes aggression. In fact, these scholars[23] concluded that "the scientific debate over whether media violence increases aggression is essentially over." They reported on the many methods of research used over all the most popular genres of media (TV, movies, video games, etc.)—studies that repeatedly document the same essential message—violence breeds violence.

We already discussed one important research methodology—the longitudinal studies on children's violent TV exposure. Another key type of study that has greatly contributed to our knowledge of media violence effects are the experiments showing that short-term exposure to media violence increases aggression relative to people not exposed to media violence. To be able to appreciate the power of this design, you don't need a Ph.D. in psychology, just an understanding of good logic. Good science is really just good logic. Think about a classic experimental design— there is a treatment group and a control group. For example, let's imagine the treatment group takes a diet pill and the control group takes a placebo (a pill with no medicinal properties). Now let's say there is a box full of pill bottles—half diet pills and half placebos, and the bottles and pills all look alike. Participants are randomly handed a pill bottle. If, at the end of the testing period, the people who took the diet pills lost more weight than the people who took the placebos, logic suggests the diet pills probably cause weight loss. See what I mean? It's just logic. The easiest explanation for the differences between groups is that they took different pills.

Okay, now let's apply this same logic to a basic experiment on media violence. Take 200 people and show half a violent film clip and the other half a nonviolent film clip, and then measure their aggression. If the group who saw the violent film clip are more aggressive, then logic suggests it was probably what they saw in the film that caused them to be more aggressive. When you look at the simplicity and strength of a design like this, it is hard to imagine how people could disagree with the basic premise of what scientists have found. Many studies with strong designs—like the longitudinal studies and experiments described here and more—show that media violence exposure causes aggression. I think that evidence is pretty definitive and that science (again, logic) is one of the best tools we have to try to help us make sense of a complex world.

Examples are always helpful, so let's look at the particulars of some of the media violence experiments. University of Missouri social psychologist Bruce Bartholow and his colleagues[24] asked ninety-two college males to play either *Unreal Tournament* (a violent game in which the player's job is mostly to shoot whoever comes in his path) or *Myst* (a nonviolent game in which players explore and solve puzzles). They told the participants that the study was designed to test how playing video games affects your ability to mentally and physically react quickly and to make decisions. Then they all played a computer game in which a blip appears on the screen and they see how fast they can react by pressing a button. If they were the fastest, they got to punish their opponent by blasting him with an obnoxious noise—they chose how loud and how long the noise blast would be. If they lost, they were the ones who got to hear the noise blast. What Bartholow and his colleagues found was that these college guys punished their opponents more if they'd just been shooting people on a video game screen than if they'd just been playing a game that involved thinking and exploring. The message: practice violence on the video game screen and you will punish a real person more in your real life. Playing at harming someone increases the chances that you would *really* hurt someone. Fantasy creates reality.

Now, in this study, as typically happens in research, the participants really weren't harming anyone—they just thought they were. An actor showed up in the lab and pretended to be the opponent, but he really wasn't forced to take the punishment. What matters, of course, is that the guys thought they were punishing another guy. In fact, any of the guys who said they didn't think anyone was really getting hurt were not included in the data analysis.

Since I've mentioned my dissertation,[25] let me tell you a little bit about it. Craig Anderson and I conducted two studies. In the first study, we were interested in whether playing violent video games predicted real-life aggression. So we tested over 200 college students and discovered that this was the case—the more violent video games you played, the more likely you were to have threatened someone or hit someone, either a schoolmate or a teacher, for example. Playing more violent video games in real life also predicted other kinds of delinquency such as cheating and lying, and it predicted poorer school performance. These relationships were stronger for people with aggressive personalities and for males.

So the first study took a snapshot of the way violent video game players differ from others. But to isolate whether the video game violence causes the aggression, a scientist needs to do a design that will measure that cause, so we designed an experiment to do just that. We wanted to pick a violent game and a nonviolent game and see whether players were more aggressive after playing the violent game. First, we made sure the two games we used were rated by a separate group of students as equally exciting, fast paced, and so on, but different in violent content. Based on these pretests, we selected *Myst* and *Wolfenstein 3D* and randomly assigned male and female students to play one or the other. Those who played the violent game had more aggressive thoughts than those who played the nonviolent game, as measured by a cognitive reaction time task—a test designed basically to measure what thoughts are active in the brain. We measured aggressive behavior using a competitive task, like the one I described above that Bruce Bartholow and his colleagues used. People who'd played the violent video game responded with more aggression toward an opponent than those who had played the nonviolent game. Taken together, these two studies show that those who choose to play violent video games also tend to be more aggressive, and that playing a violent video game causes players to be more aggressive and to think more aggressive thoughts.

Berkowitz and Geen[26] demonstrated how lessons learned in the mass media about violence are evoked and acted upon by viewers. In their study, male participants watched either an aggressive scene in which the aggression was justified, an aggressive scene in which aggression was less justified, or an exciting but nonaggressive control film. Participants were then given an opportunity to administer punishing shocks to an accomplice. For some of the participants, the name Kirk associated the potential victim of the participant's aggression with the aggressive film character. Results indicated that viewing justified aggression increased aggressive behavior. Also, if the victim had the same name as the actor in the aggressive film (Kirk Douglas), he also received more punishment. The latter finding showed that an insubstantive cue like a name can evoke aggression when connected with media violence. So here we see that trivial things associated with a violent film, like the character's name, can trigger aggressive responses. Furthermore, if in the world of fantasy aggression is justified, we take that as real information and act more aggressively because of it.

WHAT EXACTLY ARE WE LEARNING FROM VIOLENT MEDIA?

We've seen that the science shows that when people are exposed to violence in the media, they are more aggressive than others who weren't exposed to that content. We've seen that you can predict with accuracy that if you play more violent video games in real life, you are more aggressive. But what exactly are we learning? There are many ways we are changed by watching violence that is condoned, encouraged, and/or glamorized in the media. Bear in mind that while we may conceptualize the learning of aggression from media as the sign of a low society, in an ironic way it is actually a sign of what astute social learners we are. When we play a video game in which it is cool to blow people away or pummel them to death with a golf club (as in *Grand Theft Auto*) we are learning that the "right people" around us support violence. Young, hip guys who program video games think this type of violence is cool, hip, and exciting. How could violence really be bad if a swanky, professional piece of media like the *Grand Theft Auto* series is produced by the big dogs and finds its way to shelves in clean, shiny stores around the world? We're not dumb when we learn violence from media; we're merely learning a complex social lesson that we are being sold. What would be smarter is if we would understand the whole context of how media is produced and marketed and make more evolved choices about how to spend our time. Now let's examine another study that took a different approach to studying the outcomes of media violence exposure.

Aggression isn't the only possible negative effect of exposing oneself to media violence. For example, media violence exposure might blunt the tendency to help other people. Brad Bushman and Craig Anderson[27] wondered how exposure to video game violence might influence the way people react when they witness a real-life argument between two people. Three hundred twenty college men and women were in the laboratory participating in a study in which they had played either a violent or a nonviolent video game. The researchers had a surprise in store for their participants: they arranged for a fight to (apparently) take place within earshot of the students. In a clever prediction, they thought the people who'd just played a violent game would be less likely to intervene to help the person getting hurt right outside their door. They were right: those who'd just played the violent game were less likely to help and those who did help took longer to do so than those who had played the nonviolent game. They also asked the people in the study to make a judgment as to how serious they thought the fight was and found some interesting results. The people who'd just played the violent game thought the fight was less serious than the other participants did. Furthermore, the researchers found that people who played violent video games regularly were also less likely to help and thought the fight was less serious than those who played fewer violent video games by their own choice. So, the implications of this study are that there are immediate effects of playing a violent video game, and there are also long-term effects such that playing violent video games can make people less helpful and less sensitive to fights happening around them in real life.

In a second study, Bushman and Anderson investigated the effect of watching a violent movie on adult moviegoers' responses to a woman in need of help. An accomplice of the researchers with a bandaged foot dropped her crutches just outside a movie theater and was struggling to pick them up. Moviegoers who had just seen a violent film were 26 percent slower to help her than moviegoers who had just seen a nonviolent film. But what if people who choose to see violent films are just less helpful than those who choose to see nonviolent films? The researchers took this into account, too. The accomplice flipped a coin to decide whether to stage the crutch-dropping scene before or after the movie. There were no differences in helping before the movie based on movie type. In other words, these data suggest that it is not that less helpful people choose violent movies, but rather it was watching violence that caused the moviegoers to be less helpful.

MEDIA VIOLENCE ON THE BRAIN

Because people find it hard to believe that media violence has a real effect on people, it is helpful to look at some of the brain research. Even skeptics would have a hard time explaining the very real changes in the brain that take place after media violence exposure and the consequences of those changes documented by the research. Bruce Bartholow, Brad Bushman and Marc Sestir[28] conducted a series of studies that tell a clear and important story about what happens in the brain as a consequence of media violence exposure and why it matters. Again, many people criticize media violence research either in ignorance or in order to manipulate the public for their own purposes. But consider what a great set of studies these are scientifically and you will realize it's easy to offer a kind of lazy criticism, but it's difficult to produce this kind of truly high-quality science.

Bartholow, Bushman, and Sestir identified young men as heavy or light players of violent video games and investigated whether there were differences in how these men's brains reacted to violence. They found that the brains of violent video game players worked differently from brains exposed to less video game violence. Specifically violent video game players showed reduced sensitivity when looking at real violence. This blunted brain response is called desensitization—meaning that those with this response are less sensitive to the suffering of others. (We discussed Jeanne Funk's work on desensitization in children earlier.) Bartholow and colleagues cleverly ruled out a number of alternative explanations for these findings. For example, the men did not show desensitization to negative, nonviolent images (for example, a baby with a deformity). So, it wasn't the negative quality of the images that violent video game players showed a blunted reaction to. Violent video game players were less sensitive specifically to other people getting hurt. Furthermore, these studies showed that when the men were given a chance to attack someone else in the lab, the heavy violent video game players were more aggressive than the light violent video game players. Bartholow and colleagues also tested whether this response was due to the men's having a prior aggressive personality and found that it was not; it appears to be the game content that accounted for the differences in both aggressive behavior and in desensitization. To sum up this important set of studies, I'd say it tells us that exposing yourself to higher levels of media violence causes your brain to change so that it is less sensitive to other people's suffering and that you are then more willing to inflict harm yourself.

There are other interesting brain studies that support what Bartholow, Bushman, and Sestir found. One of the first relevant studies was published by the British journal *Nature*.[29] The doctors who authored that study found that when we play video games, the brain releases a pleasure chemical called dopamine. This suggests a number of things. For one, it suggests that when we perpetrate violence on the video game screen it is rewarded by a very pleasurable release of endorphins. Players learn that hurting other people is fun and rewarding—it feels very good. These data further suggest that playing video games can be physically addicting. The authors note that dopamine release is implicated in behaviors involving learning, reinforcement, attention, and skills that integrate senses and movements. Another way of saying that is that video games are very powerful teachers. Game developers seek to get players in the zone where they are working hard and learning, but where they also feel motivated toward reaching their goals and getting the high that comes from being successful in the game.

I've heard game developers speak about this and I know they are very aware of the psychology behind what creates this kind of gaming experience. And I think that's great if the game content isn't antisocial. I think if players really understood that their brains are literally changing for the worse when they play violent video games instead of flying into an angry state of denial, they might realize that this is not at all in their own best interest. The research shows that you can tell a teenager that smoking is bad for him and he won't really care. But tell him that smoking makes him look un-cool or makes his breath bad and he will care. You know, sometimes people don't want other people to look out for their health and happiness. Sometimes people just want to smoke their cigarettes or eat their unhealthy diets or fill their hours with unhealthy media and that is their choice. It remains an irony, though, that the people who care about these young people—the people who have their best interests in mind are the ones whom they reject while the people who are using them for profit are the ones they defend.

Okay, back to the brain research. A study funded by the Mind Science Foundation (www.mindscience.org) investigated how children's brains respond when the kids are watching violent versus nonviolent TV.[30] The scientists reported that watching TV violence

> recruits a network of brain regions involved in the regulation of emotion, arousal and attention, episodic memory encoding and retrieval, and motor programming. This pattern of brain activations may explain the behavioral effects observed in many studies, especially the finding that children who are frequent viewers of TV violence are more likely to behave aggressively. Such extensive viewing may result in a large number of aggressive scripts stored in long-term memory in the posterior cingulate, which facilitates rapid recall of aggressive scenes that serve as a guide for overt social behavior.

Furthermore, the researchers explained that although the children were consciously aware that the TV violence they watched was not "real," their brains reacted as if it were real. When it comes to seeing violence, our brains react as if we are undergoing threat. We don't distinguish in that way between fantasy and reality.

REEL-TO-REAL

Again, we're so attracted to media not because stories on TV, in books, movies, or video games are "real" in the sense of nonfiction but because they have a reality to us in the sense of being meaningful. Why do swarms of kids and adults alike flock to their local bookstore when a new *Harry Potter* book comes out? Do they stand there waiting in line for the latest installment in the story because they love stories that aren't real? No—that's dumb. They love the story of *Harry Potter* because he is real to them. Yes, they know he's not sitting in a castle somewhere in England. Yes, they know people can't really shoot lightning bolts out of a magic wand. (If we could, I would do little else.) But J. K. Rowling is one of the richest women in the world because she's made characters and situations that are so human and meaningful to us that we choose to hold them in our mind's eye as real, even though part of us knows they are not real in the mundane sense. I guarantee you, for many people in the world, Harry Potter is more real than their own next-door neighbor.

Let me give you a couple of examples from my own life. Sometimes when life presents me with a challenge, I think of how Professor Dumbledore said to Harry Potter—okay, sorry— nerd alert! Anyway, I was saying, I think of how Professor Dumbledore said to Harry Potter, "Dark and difficult times lie ahead. Soon we must all face the choice between what is right and what is easy." Or I think of a time when Harry's schoolmates shunned him unfairly and how the truth redeemed him in the end. These are inspirations to me because of the real ideas I take away from fiction. The author of a book or a movie or a game paints us a picture of possibilities. What if you were in a situation where your peers did not believe you? How should you act? Could you be brave like Harry Potter? How do young people who are dating feel about each other and treat each other? Is it socially acceptable to cheat on your girlfriend? To hit her? Is it okay to talk trash about your best friend behind her back? All of these scenarios are the social psychology of real life that we've seen played out before our eyes on small screens, big screens, and pages of books and magazines all of our lives. We are always learning about the nuances of social situations—romantic relationships, interacting with your boss or co-workers, feeling lonely or ugly—from watching many, many stories produced and packaged for us by the media.

MORE MIRROR NEURONS

I mentioned research on mirror neurons earlier, but I want to revisit the topic and relate it to media violence. One of the most fascinating scholarly papers on the subject of media violence that I have ever read came not from a psychologist or a communications Ph.D. but from a philosopher. In *Imitation, Media Violence, and Freedom of Speech,* philosopher Susan Hurley says that we think of imitation as childish, but in fact imitation is a relatively complex skill and one that is important for our survival. Imitation requires getting inside the mind of someone else and is a fundamental mechanism in building complex social systems.

Psychologists have studied the importance of imitation in human development. The great American psychologist William James discussed the importance of what he called "ideomotor theory," the idea that "every representation of movement awakes to some degree the movement it represents."[31] Media violence theories include the presence of this kind of instigation to physical imitation. In terms of media and learning, "watching an action sequence speeds up your own performance of the same sequence, even if you cannot explicitly distinguish and recognize that sequence."[31] When a child watches his mom bake a cake or when we as adults watch a chef prepare a meal on television, it is actually part of the process of learning how to do the task through imitation. If the model is rewarded for the behavior, we learn that lesson as well. In our mediated culture (a culture in which we watch social behavior taking place on screens), this might mean seeing TV chef Rachael Ray get a magazine deal or watching her have dinner with a member of Aerosmith on one of her shows. (There's a complex social message for you: Great cooks get to have dinner with Aerosmith. Insert mental guitar riff here!)

A fascinating set of research studies has demonstrated that we uncon-sciously imitate those around us, but that we are not aware of it. Psychologists like Chartrand and Bargh[32] have shown that if we are in the room with a "foot shaker" or a "face rubber" we'll shake our foot or rub our face more as well, but we won't be aware of it. The "chameleon effect" is their finding that we unconsciously and passively imitate the behaviors of those around us. When asked about their imitation of the witnessed behaviors, participants in the study claimed they hadn't even noticed the behaviors in question. This work reminds me of the paper by Nisbett and Wilson I discussed in Chapter 1, in which they demonstrated—among other things—that you can give a person a hint to solve a problem and you can show that she used the hint, but that she will be unaware of it and would even deny it if asked.

As mentioned earlier, neuroscientists have uncovered a brain mechanism for this type of social imitation called "mirror neurons."[33,34] Recently, scien-tists have explained how what we see is pretty dang literally *mirrored* in our minds for the purpose of helping us learn to imitate it. The brain responds very similarly whether you are doing something or watching someone else do it. This makes a great deal of sense since imitation is adaptive—it's one crucial way we learn. Here's where Susan Hurley makes an important connection. She wonders if we can't help but mirror in our minds what we witness, and if wit-nessing violence in the media increases violent behavior, then how can media violence be protected by freedom of speech? Doesn't that come under the cat-egory of yelling fire in a crowded theater? Liberal societies, she argues, protect freedom, so long as it doesn't infringe on others' rights by causing harm.

Recently, top aggression theorist Leonard Berkowitz[35] has emphasized the importance of understanding the role of automaticity in aggression. Berkowitz notes that "many impulsive actions, particularly antisocial ones, are due to failures of restraint after they were initiated involuntarily."[35] It's important to note that Berkowitz also thinks that controlled psychological processes, like teaching aggressive ideas or priming aggressive schemas, are also important links in the chain between media violence exposure and aggression. But he argues that situational cues, such as media violence, that are associated with aggression and negativity can involuntarily initiate or heighten aggressive responses. Regarding mirror neurons, Berkowitz writes, "It is even possible that neuropsychological mechanisms, such as the operation of the mirror neu-rons in the brain, contribute to this susceptibility to observed violence by cre-ating an inclination to imitate what was just witnessed."[35]

DISSENTING OPINIONS

Recently, the Supreme Court considered a California law that restricted the sale of certain video games to minors. The Court decided that video games are protected speech and therefore it is constitutional to sell them to minors. This led some to believe that based on scientific research it had been decided that media violence does not cause aggression or antisocial behavior. In fact, the Court ruled on video games as protected free speech based on the First Amendment, not based on the media violence literature. In fact, Justice Scalia, who wrote the majority opinion, stated that he did not even read the scientific literature.[36] The fact that he did not read the science was not lost on Justice Breyer, who wrote the dissenting opinion and criticized both Scalia and the California Court for not considering the science in making their decisions. We value freedom of speech, and rightly so. Therefore, we generally prefer not to get into arguing about legalities when it comes to what is good for us or bad for us in terms of restricting content. If we did that, the Supreme Court would likely be filled with cases where people found content objectionable. Many people agree that even if they find content objectionable, they would rather leave the choice of what to show children to parents rather than to the government. This logic could extend to what is legal to sell children.

I should note that we have restricted the sale of some things to adults only, such as "girlie" magazines. One might reasonably argue that "girlie" magazines are less offensive than the type of graphic violence presented in some video games. I'll also point out that, given our migration from print and physical media to digital media, these issues are changing rapidly. Today, our kids may be able to access content online that many parents aren't even aware exists. So, it's now less a question of what a child can buy in a store than what a child can find online.

Let's return to the wide-angle view of the public understanding of social science research. My friend Elizabeth teaches remedial English at the local community college. Wanting her students to be able to read and understand research that's relevant to the public, she assigned her students some research articles about the relationship between poverty and quality of life. These articles suggested that wealthy people have access to a myriad of experiences and perks which enhance their quality of life, whereas poor people experience the opposite. Less wealthy Americans are less educated, have more health problems and generally experience lower levels of advancement and enrichment. When Elizabeth's students read these articles, they were offended. They interpreted them as prejudiced against their families – the people on the lower end of the income bracket. What the research said was that income predicts quality of life – that the wealthy generally have a higher quality of life, as defined by a number of indicators. It means that you can predict your quality of life from knowing your income. It doesn't mean that no one makes it out of poverty or that no poor people achieve their dreams. It does mean that it's a lot less likely to happen if you are poor than if you are rich.

I understand why her classes found this offensive. I imagine it launched them into a state of denial and rationalization. And I feel for them. I raise the point here only to draw a parallel between some reactions to the media violence literature and to this literature on wealth and inequality. There are some research findings that we don't want to believe. That may lead us to vilify the researchers or to question the research on any level we can think of. In the end, this becomes an argument about feelings rather than an argument about the facts. I understand why this happens. I'm just suggesting that if we rationalize away research findings that don't suit us, we're not doing ourselves any favors. Instead of killing the messenger of bad news, maybe there's a better way to deal with this.

No reasonable scientist suggests that media violence exposure is the sole cause, the main cause, or even a sufficient cause of violence in the world. The research says something different — that media violence exposure can blunt empathy and increase everyday aggression. The latest research indicates that violent video game playing increases aggressive thoughts, which, in turn, increase aggressive behavior over time. If you don't hate your doctor for telling you that eating trans fats will increase your likelihood of obesity, then don't hate media violence researchers for saying that exposure to media violence increases your likelihood of thinking aggressively and a tendency towards harming others in everyday ways. Like one's diet, eating some things that are "bad for you" now and again won't kill you, but to the extent that you overdo it, you increase your odds of developing health issues. So, my advice is to be mindful of the extent and nature of your exposure to media violence and be thoughtful about it. Don't overstate or understate the research evidence. And, perhaps more important, enjoy looking for the good in your media diet. Good doesn't need to be sappy sweet or even educational, but something that means something to you and enhances who you are.

Representations of Social Groups in Media

Race, Gender, and Beyond

> Most of what we know, or think we know, we have never personally
> experienced. We live in a world erected by stories. Stories socialize us
> into roles of gender, age, class, vocation, and lifestyle, and offer models
> of conformity or targets for rebellion.[1]
>
> —George Gerbner (1999)

In August 2014, feminist vblogger Anita Sarkeesian received death threats
for her online critiques of the portrayal of women in video games. Sadly, these
were not the first death threats that Sarkeesian, who created the *Feminist
Frequency: Conversations with Pop Culture* Web site (and YouTube Channel,
Facebook page, and Twitter feed), has received, nor are they likely to be the last.
After receiving death threats for speaking out about sexism in the media, Sarkeesian
launched a kickstarter to fund her work, which reached its initial goal in 24 hours
and was successfully funded by about 7,000 backers. She is perhaps best known for
her Tropes vs. Women series on the portrayal of women in video games.

A gamer herself, Sarkeesian consistently calls for better from the media
genre she loves. I am happy to say that, even with the harsh backlash she's
received, (a) it hasn't stopped her, and (b) she is getting respect now from
some surprising places. For example, in response to a critique of the portrayal
of women in *Saints Row* in the vblog "Women as background decoration,"
Steve Jaros, creative director at the company that developed *Saints Row*, made
a public mea cupla. Speaking to a magazine popular with gamers called *The*

Escapist, Jaros said, "I think it's fair to be called out on your s**t," and, "I think that it's a sad man that can never be self-reflective."[2]

My response to Mr. Jaros's impressive "the buck stops here" candor is respect and gratitude. Of course, not everyone shares my enthusiasm, as witnessed by some of the comments to this story on gamestop.com. For example "Kujel" posts, "It's disturbing how people take this liar Antia [sic] seriously. ☹" "Flamewolf75" says, "This Feminist movement is literally only a problem in first world countries. These people have become so privileged that they can no longer complain about actual problems, so they decide to make up bullshit to feel relevant in the world again." S14cka adds, "She probably slept with him to say that.?"

Since my research has often argued for respectful representation and social justice in media portrayals, I imagine you don't need me to tell you what I think of these types of comments. I underline them here hoping to encourage a dialogue among those reading this book—from college campuses to living room book groups. What do you make of this? Before you answer, let me rush to add that there are those on this gaming site that add their voices of support. For example, "Warlord_rochi" says, "Accepting critiques like a pro. Nice one." "Picho86" adds, "I really liked his answer. While the subject of whether Saints Row is harmful in its portrayal of women is not a simple one, it is something that is ought to be taken seriously, and I'm glad he does."[2]

To be truly media literate means understanding what the likely psychological reactions are to the way ideas are presented to you on the screens you watch. There is a great deal of opportunity to do social good through the media and a great deal of harm that can be done if we don't understand the psychology of media use.

PROGRESSIVE IMAGERY UPLIFTS, DEGRADING IMAGERY TEARS DOWN, OR UP WITH OBAMA, DOWN WITH THUGS

Let me give you a case in point. My colleague Melinda Burgess and I wanted to demonstrate the difference it makes if we are exposed to stereotypical images of Black men versus progressive images of Black men. We hypothesized that exposure to negative stereotypes would be harmful and exposure to positive images would be beneficial, not to the men in question, but to *other* Black men.

So, we conducted a study[3] in which young White men and women saw either positive or negative media images of African American men. The positive images were of highly esteemed African American figures such as Martin Luther King Jr. and Barack Obama. The negative images were stereotypical African American male video game characters whose portrayals were typical of negative stereotypes of Black men found in video games—powerful, violent thugs. Next, the college students who participated were asked to give feedback about the Web site of an unknown political candidate. All the students saw the exact same Web site, except that half of them saw an image of an African American candidate and the other half saw an image of a White candidate. These images were selected so that the men looked like respectable political leaders, each wearing a suit and speaking from a podium. The students believed they were rating how well the candidate's Web site worked for him, but along the way they rated their feelings toward the candidate himself. They also reported how likely they would be to vote for him, given the chance.

The results were striking. Those who had seen Barack Obama and Martin Luther King transferred that positivity to an African American candidate, liking him more, rating him more highly, and being more likely to vote for him than their peers who rated a White candidate. But for those who had seen the stereotypical Black video game characters, the opposite was true. Evoking this image of the dangerous Black male thug caused college students to rate an unrelated African American candidate significantly lower than their peers rated a White candidate.

If you put out a positive image of a group (women or African American men, for example), this tends to cause positive thinking about that group. You are giving an example that this group can be really good. In contrast, if you put out a negative picture (literally) of a group, this causes people to evaluate unrelated members of that group more poorly. How the media portray members of the group can help or harm other members of that same group.

For all those who thought that what we watch on our screens doesn't matter, that media are just entertainment and no matter what we see, it changes nothing, this study demonstrates that this is not true. How you portray someone—be it by race, gender, religion, sexual orientation, or any factor—makes a difference for other members of that same group. The representation can help or hurt. The reason is that you are telling a story about what members of that group are like and therefore priming that view. This causes people to think in ways that are consistent with the stereotype or the image that you brought up with your representation.

We may not realize it, but very often we learn about other people through what we see in the mass media. This is especially true when the other people we're talking about are different from ourselves and we have little face-to-face contact with members of their group. Who believes—or would want to admit—that he or she learns about other people and ideas primarily through watching TV and movies and playing video games? Nobody, right? And that is part of the problem. As described in Chapter 1, when we fear or reject the influence of mass media, we make ourselves vulnerable to being directly used or manipulated. In the case of media stereotypes—of race, sex, age, sexual orientation, and other social categories—we open ourselves to seeing others through the eyes of the media instead of through our own eyes.

So, what's wrong with learning through the media? As demonstrated above, learning through the media can be positive or negative. Sometimes mass media stories can be informative, even inspirational. Think of a show, reporter, or other source that you trust. It might be *Sesame Street* or Tom Brokaw, *All Things Considered*, or *Scientific American Frontiers with Alan Alda*. For example, I subscribe to a National Public Radio podcast called *Driveway Moments*. NPR characterizes *Driveway Moments* as stories that audience members found so riveting, they kept listening to the story even if they had to sit in their driveways to finish. One of these *Driveway Moments* is from NPR science correspondent Robert Krulwich. Krulwich's report *Going Binocular: Susan's First Snowfall* describes how Susan—a visually impaired woman who had never seen the world in three dimensions (3D)—underwent a treatment that miraculously gave her binocular vision for the first time in her life. Through the interview, Susan relates that snowstorms had always looked more like distant white sheets than like individual flakes dancing around her. I am mesmerized listening to her describe being overwhelmed with the joy of seeing the big flakes of a snow shower falling lazily around her for the first time.

The NPR story of Susan's first 3D experience of a snowfall is an example of mass media communicating social information well. I have never experienced what Susan did; I didn't know about her condition or its treatment or what it would be like to go from 2D to 3D vision. But after listening to the story, I feel like I understand something about the essence of that experience from afar. I've picked up information about a group of people—those with visual impairments—and I've learned something about their struggles and triumphs through NPR's telling of this woman's story. I've also learned more about perception and medical science.

How does a mass-produced, mass-marketed image bias or alter our social understanding about members of different groups? Let me borrow an example from Clint Wilson, Felix Gutierrez, and Lena Chao, the authors of the book *Racism, Sexism and the Media*.[4] They ask us to think about what we know about Native Americans and where we got that information. Unless you are a Native American, or have other direct knowledge, you almost certainly took much of your information from the mass media: Clint Eastwood or John Wayne movies, Disney's *Pocahontas*, and TV news magazine stories about Native Americans, for example. Well, we may not think about it, but when we do this we are learning about Native Americans mostly through the eyes of a select group of White males, which is very different from learning about them from Native Americans themselves. The news media tend to cover Native Americans in one of two ways: as what the authors call "zoo stories," or "problem people stories." Zoo stories are more or less caricatures of Native American culture—like Tonto saying "How!" Problem people stories are those that focus on Native Americans as alcoholics or as impotent drains on society.

Also problematic is the potential harm that negative stereotypes in the media have on the way the targets of the stereotypes view themselves. According to Linda Holtzman,[5] author of *Media Messages: What Film, Television and Popular Music Teach Us about Race, Class, Gender and Sexual Orientation*, Latino men have been variously ignored by the media or characterized as largely poor, uneducated, or buffoons. This type of media image sends the message that other people have a negative view of your group. Portrayals of African Americans in the media have often involved problems with misinformation and distortion. For example, in the film *Mississippi Burning*, the heroes of the film were White. The director claimed that if the heroes had been African American, this would have been unacceptable to predominantly White audiences of the 1980s. According to Holtzman, early films were overtly, even outrageously, racist, such as the 1905 film *The Wooing and Wedding of a Coon*. Films continued to show blatant stereotypes of African Americans, which evolved from hateful images to images of happy slaves and servants. After World War II, the portrayal of African Americans transitioned into more dignified, yet nonthreatening roles, such as the part of Sidney Poitier in *Guess Who's Coming to Dinner*. In the 1960s and 1970s, there was an era of "Blaxploitation" films such as *Shaft*. In the 1980s and 1990s, more complex black characters emerged, and black actors, actresses, producers, and directors gained widespread popularity. While there have been advancements in the role of African Americans in the media, there are still issues including stereotyping, unequal representation, and submission to the White culture. When we see representations of people in the mass media, we form or add to our schemas, which are expectations—either about our own group (the psych term for this is "ingroup") or about groups to which we do not belong ("outgroups"). Schemas are a type of mindset that can evolve into pre-judgments or stereotypes.

RACIAL AND GENDER STEREOTYPING IN VIDEO GAMES

Because it is important to understand how young people learn information about other racial groups and their own through the lens of mass media, my colleagues and I[6] investigated how video game characters represent different racial groups. We chose two types of formats to analyze: video game magazines and video game covers. Both of these provided still images—scenes depicting video game characters from the top games—to analyze. The magazines we analyzed included *Game Informer, GamePro*, and *Electronic Gaming Monthly*, which are three of the top 10 best-selling magazines among teens. By the way, did you know that *Game Informer* and *GamePro* have more subscribers than *Maxim* or *Rolling Stone*? I didn't.

When you analyze hundreds of images, you start to see the trends in how different people are characterized. I think that a big picture perspective is very telling. Like the examples cited above, the people who write and produce video games are predominantly White males, so characterizations of women and non-Whites are largely from the perspective of outgroup members. Our analysis of video game magazine images revealed some intriguing trends in how men of different races were portrayed. Men were very violent on the whole, with African American (73 percent) and Hispanic (80 percent) men proportionately a bit more likely to be portrayed as violent than White men (66 percent). Deeper analysis was even more revealing. White men were the largest group (26 percent as compared to 14 percent of African American men) who were portrayed in ways that glamorize aggression. No Asians were shown this way. While 30 percent of African American men were portrayed playing a sport, only 8 percent of White men were, and no Hispanic or Asian men were. And while a third of Asian men were shown using computers and technology, as were 14 percent of White men, only 3 percent of African American men were portrayed this way. Past research has shown that there are three central traits of the negative African American stereotype: lack of intelligence, athleticism, and rhythm. These findings highlight two of those three central stereotype characteristics.

REPRESENTATION AND CHARACTERIZATION

Let's talk a bit more about representation and why it's important. Representation means that members of different races, sexes, and other social groups should be portrayed proportionally in the media—in a way that is roughly similar to their numbers in the larger social group they represent (like the US population or the US military). Individual television shows, movies, or games need not be representative of the larger population because individual storylines may focus on a particular group—like a movie that tells a story about Latinas. That is why one looks for representation as a larger trend, such as in a genre like TV sitcoms or commercials or bestselling men's magazines.

One of the first scholars to study the influence of mass media on culture, George Gerbner, was widely known for his analysis of television, known as the Cultural Indicators Project (www.disinfo.com). Gerbner—who was a Hungarian refugee—often focused attention on how White males in what he called the "prime of life" were the most typical TV characters. He also noted other discrepancies in representation, such as the fact that men outnumber women three to one in prime-time television. In violent scenes, men are most often the aggressors, and women and non-Whites are disproportionately likely to be the victims of aggression. Gerbner also recognized that men are more likely to be media executives and producers, game developers, and even narrators.

We can ask how well a certain group like women or men of color were represented in a genre. Then we can ask whether that representation was respectful—whether it showed positive or realistic and nuanced portrayals. When you underrepresent a group as a trend within a genre, you are telling a subtle story about race, gender, sexual orientation, and other traits. You are saying that these people don't matter as much, that they are not "regular" or "normal" people—that they are not the people we want to tell stories about and get to know, for example.

Scholars call the stories we tell about a person a "characterization" or "portrayal." I think these are informative and appropriate terms. Characterization suggests that you are sketching the character or moral value of a person. Portrayal implies that you are framing the person—telling that person's story your way—so both terms work well. Not to confuse, but we can also use the word "represent" to mean characterize or portray. Represent can mean that a character acts as an image of other characters like him. This is similar to the idea that one character can be a stand-in for other characters of the same race, sex, age, or other demographic, which is of course why representation is important.

Speaking of representation of women in the media, a gauge that has received notoriety in the past few years is the Bechdel test (bechdeltest.com). To meet the standards of the Bechdel test, a film need only meet three very simple criteria: (1) the film has at least two female characters, (2) the characters must talk to each other, and (3) they must talk about something other than a male. Easy, right? Not so. See bechdeltest.com for ratings for hundreds of films.

REPRESENTATIONS OF BLACK MEN IN GAMES

In our investigation of video game covers, we found several characterizations of different racial groups. African American men were again clearly stereotyped. For example, we defined "thug" as someone who engaged in criminal behavior absent clear and present danger and "vigilante" as a criminal response to a threat. While 23 percent of African American men were portrayed as thugs, only 3 percent of White men were. In a reversal, no non-Whites were portrayed as vigilantes, while 3 percent of Whites were. Nineteen percent of Whites wore protective

Figure 5.1 Our research on portrayals of African American men in video games reveals that they are disproportionately represented as thugs and criminals and dangerous aggressors, and as athletes, while they are less likely to be portrayed as soldiers or as using computers. (Screen shot from *Grand Theft Auto: San Andreas*—from Take Two Interactive and Rockstar Games.)

armor, while no African Americans did. Seventy-five percent of Asian men were martial artists, compared to 6 percent and 5 percent of White and African American men, respectively. Thirty-two percent of African American men were portrayed as athletes, compared to 5 percent of White men. While 7 percent of White male video game characters were soldiers, not a single African American, Hispanic, or Asian man was portrayed this way, which is in stark contrast to the 33 percent of the US military who are non-White. These characterizations tell a story about African American men. The story is that African American men are likely to be either thugs or athletes, not soldiers. The image from *Grand Theft Auto: San Andreas* shown in Figure 5.1 is representative of that characterization of African American men as violent street criminals.

SEEING STEREOTYPES CHANGES HOW YOU THINK

These negative characterizations engender negative effects. In an experiment, my colleagues and I[3] exposed White participants to video games with White and African American male characters and then asked them to respond as quickly as possible to violent objects (e.g., a sword) and nonviolent objects (e.g., a cell phone) flashed on a screen. Results showed that participants responded faster to the violent objects after seeing African American male video game characters and faster to the nonviolent objects after seeing White male video game characters. These results show that the negative stereotype of African American men as violent was brought to mind by the African American male video game characters. This was true regardless of whether the game was violent or not. Just the presence of an African American male video game character *primed* (brought to mind) the concept of violence.

DIGESTING IMAGES OF SOCIALLY CONSTRUCTED STEREOTYPES

I thought it was crucial to unpack these video game images for a number of reasons. Media imagery is a source of powerful social storytelling and one that we've just begun to understand. Visual imagery plays an important role in socialization, specifically in how we extract and apply meaning from everyday experience, and therefore in how we construct social realities. I like the way Ostman[7] put it: "Visual communication contains a trove of emotionally-laden, non-logical connotations" that become part of the viewer's social schemas. And Cowan[8] said: "Given the popular culture's devotion to visual media, the socialization process may be influenced strongly by exposure to visual materials." The old saying is "a picture is worth a thousand words" and I think this is true when it comes to learning about people from the images of mass media. It's amazing the amount of nuanced social information that can be portrayed in an image. Not only do we remember images better than words, but we also can get away with telling a story about social groups (women, African American men) with a picture when we couldn't get away with saying the same thing with words.

EXACTLY HOW FANTASY IMAGES BECOME OUR REALITIES

Morgan Slusher and Craig Anderson[9] explored the extent to which people distinguish between their own real experiences with stereotypes and times when they just imagined stereotypes. In one study, the authors found that when people are asked to imagine members of groups such as lawyers or clergymen, they tend to imagine them as their social stereotypes. For example, when imagining a lawyer shopping for a car, one imagines a wealthy man shopping for a Mercedes rather than a guy in jeans shopping for a used pickup truck. In a second study, the researchers told male and female college students that they were going to participate in a study of visual imagery to test their visual imagination skills. Participants imagined scenes that were either stereotypical or not stereotypical and they were also given open-ended situations in which they could generate stereotypes or not. Findings indicated that participants weren't able to distinguish between stereotypes they were exposed to and stereotypes they just imagined. Slusher and Anderson[10] put it like this:

> When people imagine a picture, they come to believe that they have actually seen that picture more often. We suggest that when people imagine other people, particularly those who belong to an identifiable social group, they incorporate their stereotypes into their imaginations. As a result, people may come to believe that they have seen this "picture" more often (i.e., the picture of an individual fitting their own stereotype). If this occurs, people are providing their own *imaginal confirmation* of their previously established stereotypes.

Imaginal confirmation means that we may actually confuse *seeing* an African American man behave like a criminal and *imagining* it. Isn't that amazing? This is another way of saying that we confirm our own stereotypes—and without even knowing it. The participants in the study failed at "reality monitoring," at knowing when they had really experienced a stereotype or when they had just imagined it. Now, when you apply this to how an African American man is represented in the mass media, you can easily see that we would confuse seeing a real person behave stereotypically and seeing just an image of it on a video game cover, for example. We're not likely to sufficiently differentiate between seeing a thuggish African American man in *Grand Theft Auto* with having seen a real person like this on the street. In an important sense, our minds treat media imagery like this is as if it were real. Therefore, when you degrade someone in the media, you are degrading the real members of that person's social group. Our brains don't fully recognize the difference.

Recall, too, the research suggesting that when we are transported by fictional stories, we are more easily persuaded by their content. This transportation theory, I think, can also be used to explain the persuasive power of mass media images. When you get lost in a story, you become uncritical of the persuasive messages embedded in the story, accepting them involuntarily.[11] Persuasive messages can be verbal, such as a description of a character who holds racist views, but they can also be communicated through an image, such as when an African American man in a video game is portrayed as a street criminal. Since we don't differentiate between stereotypes we've just imagined and those we've seen confirmed in real life,[12] then surely we don't differentiate between real people who confirm a stereotype and fictional characters who do. Again we see how media characters portrayed in a stereotypical manner persuade us that the stereotype is true.

(DIS)LIKE AND (DIS)RESPECT

Let's examine further why the particular representations of African American men described earlier lead to negative stereotypical thinking.[13] For one thing, creating this vision of the African American man as a member of the "dangerous minority" becomes an iconic representation of what it means to be an African American man. You've told a story about what "these people" are like. Just imagining it makes you think you have seen it in real life. We don't make the fantasy-reality distinction we believe we do. Thus we've learned about other people through mass media storytelling. Once again, crucial here is the fact that we most likely do so without realizing it. In fact, if asked, we'd be likely to deny it.

Patricia Devine and her colleagues[14,15] have shown that racial stereotyping is implicit—in other words, often done automatically or without conscious awareness—and that even people who don't endorse racial stereotypes are aware of what those culturally held stereotypes are. Since media consumption, as discussed earlier, is the main waking activity of the human race right now, I think it's safe to say that most of our stories about race and gender come from the media. Isn't that an astounding notion? Most of our "encounters" with people who are different from us involve our watching produced video on a screen. If specific sources of media, such as video games, are consistently presenting stereotypical views of women and non-Whites, the public should become conscious of this and then act on that knowledge by calling for change from the industry.

STEREOTYPING THEORY: THE IMPORTANCE OF WARMTH AND COMPETENCE

Susan Fiske, Peter Glick, and their colleagues have worked for many years to help us understand stereotypical thinking and its effects.[16-18] These scientists explain that the content of stereotypes falls into two basic domains: warmth and competence. For example, the mentally retarded are regarded as warm (likable and good intentioned) but incompetent (unable to compete with us).

A major conclusion from this research is that perceived competence follows from social status, and perceived warmth follows from the degree to which you feel you compete with a person.[19]

Members of any given group can be high or low on warmth and high or low on competence, and this determines how we feel about members of that group; it determines whether we are prejudiced against them. For example, several samples of students and nonstudents were interviewed and asked what groups are the targets of stereotypical thinking. Results showed that African Americans were the group thought to be the most likely targets of stereotyping; they were mentioned, in fact, by a full 74 percent of respondents, whereas the next most common group that people thought were stereotyped were Hispanics, mentioned by only 45 percent of the sample. Further questioning revealed more detail about the nature of stereotypes. "Rich Blacks" fell into a category of relative competence, but relative low warmth—forming the stereotype that group members have high status but are relatively disliked. Fiske, Glick, and colleagues say this group evokes "envious prejudice"—jealousy and resentment that comes from feelings of injustice but a begrudging acceptance of competence. Also in this "envious prejudice" group were Asians, Jews, and feminists. The authors note that less successful people in otherwise dominant groups—such as poor Whites—are perhaps more likely to feel this type of envious prejudice.

In contrast, "paternalistic stereotypes" are applied to groups not likely to compete for resources or otherwise threaten the ingroup. Examples of warm but incompetent groups are housewives and the elderly. Another group is what these researchers call the "low-low" group—those low in competence and warmth, such as welfare recipients. These groups come closest to generating what the scientists call the "pure antipathy" of "contemptuous prejudice." People feel the following prejudicial emotions toward these groups: anger, contempt, disgust, hate, and resentment. People in the "low-low" group are thought to be an unfair drain on society. Groups that fell into this category included poor African Americans, poor Whites, and migrant workers.[20]

When we look at how groups are represented in the media, it's important to see how they fit in with these types of stereotypes and evoked prejudices. As Glick, Fiske, and colleagues note, attitudes toward African Americans differ greatly depending on whether people stereotype them as wealthy or poor, for example. In our analysis of video game characters, we see that the African American males were evocative of a very specific stereotype—the "dangerous minority," the criminal or thug. This stereotypical person is not warm or likable, and not competent in the sense of successful in socially sanctioned ways. This figure is also a drain on society as a criminal element that is a threat to others. Thus, the stereotypes of African American men as they are represented in video games are particularly likely to evoke the constellation of emotions cited above—anger, contempt, disgust, hate, and resentment. Anger, of course, is associated with aggression, and one outcome of these feelings of antipathy and dislike is aggression against the stereotyped group. Aggression can take many forms, from outright physical violence to much subtler forms of discrimination and derogation.

Scholars have noted that one reason for racial stereotyping in the mass media is that producers want to make their messages clear and often have a short time to do that. So they resort to stereotypes to make a point quickly and to establish characters. Of course, the "concern is that those stereotypic, snapshot depictions present young people with a social reality. Even if a program is judged by children to be fictional (or even scripted and rehearsed), it may still be perceived as socially realistic."[21]

I'm not a successful African American man, but I am a professional woman. That means I fall into that same category as a potential target of envious prejudice, so I understand the feeling. As an example of the behaviors this can evoke, consider the following study by Jennifer Berdahl called *The Sexual Harassment of Uppity Women*.[22] Berdahl hypothesized that sexual harassment is not primarily a crime of passion but rather a crime of aggression motivated by a desire to inflict harm. If it were a crime of passion, so to speak, men would be more likely to sexually harass traditional women—women who would fit Glick and Fiske's warm but incompetent group. If, however, men harass women to inflict punishment, then men should be more likely to harass so-called uppity women—feminists, successful professionals, and women who believe in equality between the sexes. She found that women who had more instrumental personalities—meaning they were typified by the traditionally male qualities of "getting the job done"—had experienced more sexual harassment (such as sexist jokes and sexual advances) than more traditional, less threatening feminine women. So, belonging to a stereotyped group can lead to real harm.

MUSLIM AND MIDDLE EASTERN STEREOTYPES IN THE MEDIA

Enny Das and her colleagues[23] noticed that the news media have lately associated terrorism with Muslims in general, rather than with Muslim extremists. They wondered what the ramifications would be. Das and her colleagues found that exposure to news coverage about terrorism increased death-related thoughts and also increased agreement with a news article that suggested problems with integrating Muslims into society. They also found that prejudice against Arabs went up after exposure to terrorism news for Europeans, but not for Arabs. These researchers suggest that terror management theory offers a theoretical basis for understanding these results. For example, they found that people with higher self-esteem reacted differently than those with lower self-esteem when reminded of death. For individuals with high self-esteem, their levels of prejudice were low whether they had seen news about terrorism or a news story that didn't involve terrorism. But for those with low self-esteem, prejudice against Arabs rose after seeing the terrorism news report relative to the control news report. Again, evoking the specter of one's own mortality can increase protectionist sentiments for some. Therefore, reporters should make clear the distinction between Muslims in general and Muslim extremists. Another important factor is the audience; if they are only processing peripherally or not making critical distinctions themselves, this will alter their perceptions.

In a related set of investigations, researchers from the University of Michigan's Aggression Research Group studied the effects of exposure of American youth to images of Middle Eastern violence in the media.[24] They found that exposure to perceived acts of violence in the mass media was related to increased prejudice against the target groups. Furthermore, these scientists found that identification with a particular group (Arabs or Israelis) predicted more negative stereotypes about the opposing group.

MEDIA REPRESENTATIONS AND SOCIAL POWER

So far we have touched upon the issue of social power, but now I'd like to focus on it in more detail—to talk about the social hierarchy of various groups within our culture; how that hierarchy relates to stereotyping, prejudice, and discrimination; and where media representations fit in. Social power is also called hegemony. Sociologist R. W. Connell[25] writes about hegemonic masculinity and emphasized femininity. Hegemonic masculinity includes a very specific vision of masculinity that is purported to be dominant in the culture. The vision of the dominant male in our culture is a man who is White, heterosexual, young, strong, and Christian. Because this view is one of male dominance, women are always construed as subordinant and subservient to these men—there is no hegemonic femininity. Connell is careful to stress that this is a socially constructed ideal and that in reality most men don't fit the mythic ideal (like John Wayne, for example). Speaking of myth, enter the media, which conform in a very interesting way. Media visions of men and women serve not to report reality but to reflect and support the cultural mythology of hegemonic masculinity. As Connell[26] puts it, although "few men are Bogarts or Stallones, many collaborate in sustaining those images."

And as Slusher and Anderson so skillfully showed us, we don't differentiate well at all between the myths we hold in our mind's eye and what we take to be a real view—in this case, of the sexes. And in fact, either through ignorance or malicious intent, big media can sell us an image of people—be it the hegemonic male or the "dangerous" African American man—that we accept as part of our reality, not realizing how this reality was constructed for us or the degree to which it contains myths.

(MR. AND) "MISS" REPRESENTATION

Ambivalent Sexism Theory[27] also accepts the notion that men are dominant in our culture but with the awareness that there are in fact mixed (ambivalent) feelings about both men and women that society recognizes. These mixed stereotypes are that men are "bad but bold" and women are "wonderful but weak." Stereotypes about men take two forms: hostility toward men (e.g., men are sexual predators) and benevolence toward men (e.g., men are more willing to put themselves in dangerous situations for others). Ambivalence toward women takes two forms, referred to as benevolent sexism (for example, a kind of paternalistic care for the "weaker sex") and hostile sexism (e.g., negative feelings toward women who challenge men, such as feminists, or women who "use their feminine wiles").

You may recognize that these clearly relate to the aforementioned view that encapsulated stereotypical notions as relating to two general dimensions: warmth and competence. Women are warm—they are more likable than men, and men are often seen as arrogant and hostile. But men are dominant because they are instrumental. Their social power is then legitimized because it becomes inevitable—they have the competence needed for success in the culturally important arenas. Women are likable, but likability doesn't get the job done and it doesn't put you on the top of the status hierarchy.

Other theories of prejudice also support the idea that the inherent right to power and the privilege of the dominant social group maintain the status quo of the current social hierarchy. For example, research by John Jost, Mazarin Banaji,[28] and others supports System Justification Theory—the idea that there is a general motive to support the social hierarchy, the status quo. Paradoxically, this motive is often stronger for those who are lower on the social totem pole and is partially responsible for people in disadvantaged groups feeling inferior. Interestingly, in the light of the unconscious nature of many of the effects discussed here, justification of the social status quo is most readily observable at unconscious levels of awareness.

THE CONSEQUENCES OF SOCIAL INEQUALITY

What are the ramifications of these types of social beliefs? Data from an international sample,[29] representing 16 nations, documented an inverse relationship between ambivalent sexism and the United Nations indices of gender inequality. These UN indices of inequality included women's representation in high-status jobs in both business and government, and other measures such as life expectancy, literacy rates, educational attainment, and standard of living. In other words, to the extent that we accept the notion of men as "bad but bold" and women as "wonderful but weak," we support real, material gender inequality. This translates worldwide into seeing women as less likely to attain career and educational goals at the level that men do.

Relating this back to media representations, we can see that it is important that such imagery does not project the "bad but bold" and "wonderful but weak" gender mythology because to the extent that it does, it will support social inequality. And, as we have seen, even those most likely to be negatively affected by such mythologies often are unaware of many important aspects of the situation. They are unaware that mythologies in the media affect them. They are unaware that they are motivated to justify the status quo of their own social inferiority.

MEDIA REPRESENTATIONS OF GENDER

Television and the Macho Man Image

Erica Scharrer[30,31] defines hyper-masculinity and hyper-femininity in ways that are consistent with the theories described earlier. Hyper-masculine men think aggression is "manly" and have hardened attitudes toward sexuality. Hyper-feminine women are submissive to and dependent upon men and display emphasized (hetero)sexuality. Scharrer exposed college men to *The Sopranos*—a show that has both violence and a theme of hyper-masculinity as well as to a nonviolent show and a violent show without a hyper-masculine theme. She found that seeing the *Sopranos* caused its young, male viewers to be relatively more likely to endorse the hyper-masculine beliefs that violence is manly and thrilling.

While being powerful has its appeal, glamorizing violence is far from universally beneficial to its male viewers. In fact, research tells a much different story. Aggressiveness is negatively correlated with intelligence across the life span: if you are more aggressive, you are generally less intelligent. TV violence viewing is also predictive of the likelihood that you will go to jail for a violent crime.[32]

Another important factor is the extent to which viewers identify with or want to be like the characters they watch. This in and of itself implies something fascinating about reality and fantasy—if you want to be like a fictional character, he or she must have a certain reality for you. Longitudinal studies have shown that when a child feels similar to an aggressive character on television, he or she is more likely to imitate that aggression later in life.[33] Furthermore, Dara Greenwood[34] found that when young women idealized (wanted to be like) female action heroes such as *Buffy the Vampire Slayer*, they were more likely to feel and behave aggressively.

Viewing Masculinity, Femininity, and Male-Female Relations Through the Lens of Video Games

Erica Scharrer studied how men and women are portrayed in the advertisements of three top-selling video game magazines. She found that males outnumbered females three to one and that males were depicted as muscular and females as sexy. Fifty-five percent of the ads contained violence. Tracy Dietz, in an earlier study of women in video games,[35] found that females were mostly absent from games, but when they were depicted, it was most likely as weak characters needing rescue by the male hero. This characterization, of course, still exists in video games. Mario is still trying to rescue the Princess from the evil Bowser. However, the latest research shows that the characterizations of females have changed quite a bit.

Kathryn Phillips Thill and I[36] found that most females (roughly 60 percent for each characterization) in the top-selling video game magazines were portrayed as sex objects and as visions of beauty. At the same time, the great majority of men (over 80 percent) were portrayed as powerful aggressors. Furthermore, by what we believe is a conservative estimate, about a third of the men were portrayed as hyper-masculine. We used Scharrer's definition of hyper-masculine and rated characters as such only if they had particularly outsized muscles and fairly extreme emphasized masculinity (e.g., chiseled features and stubble). Interestingly, about 40 percent of female characters were both sexy and aggressive, which is a departure from what Dietz had found nine years earlier. What we see in these characterizations is that the depictions of males and females in video games are the kinds of stylized myths about men and women that we discussed earlier. Men are powerful aggressors. Women's sexuality is emphasized: they are sex objects, and thus their importance as serving men's needs is emphasized. This juxtaposition puts us right back to the theories of sexism that we have discussed. Powerful masculinity is hegemonic. Femininity is stylized, objectified, and subordinated.

Giving "Glamour Shot" a Double Meaning

One of the first things that attracted my attention about video game magazines was that their images of men seemed to highly glamorize violence. This is problematic because, as the National Television Violence Study (NTVS)[37] demonstrated, glamorizing violence makes violence more attractive and thus more likely. The NTVS also noted that television sanitizes violence, depicts it with unrealistic consequences, and often pairs violence with humor. These are antisocial lessons about violence. I noticed that often these violent men in video game magazines were just standing there with their weapons, as if to say, "violence is cool." So we specifically looked for this type of characterization—times when video game characters were not fighting and not using their weapons. They were just standing around doing what I call "posing" with weapons. I also like to think of it as the "aggressive glamour shot."

When you look at this juxtaposition of the female sex object and the male violent hero, we see brought to life for young people blatant examples of a sexist social hierarchy. These characterizations are exactly what the theorists described earlier were writing about when they expressed concerns for how sexism is socialized and what the consequences of a sexist socialization are.

Now, we wondered, to what extent are these blatantly sexist characterizations just being transmitted to avid gamers? Do youth in general know about these sex-role stereotypes? So Kathryn and I asked 18-year-olds about their mental images of male and female video game characters. These were male and female teenagers who were not, as a group, avid gamers. I was actually surprised by how much the results of this very open-ended questioning mirrored the images of characters that we had studied. How did our teenagers describe the typical male video game character? The five most common characterizations, in order, were as follows, starting with the most common answer: powerful (e.g., "strong"), aggressive (e.g., "violent," "deadly"), hostile attitude (e.g., "mean," "cocky," "belligerent"), athlete, and thug (e.g., "gangsta"). The single most common term used to describe a male video game character was "muscular." For female characters, the teens noted these common characteristics: provocative dress (e.g., "tight clothes," "naked"), curvaceous figure (e.g., "big boobs"), thin (e.g., "skinny"), sexual (e.g., "hooker," "slutty," "sexy"), and aggressive (e.g., "likes to kill.") The single most common term used to describe a female video game character was "big boobs."

So, we've seen that among video game characters, there are overt racial and sex-role stereotypes. For example, in one study, my colleagues[38] and I discovered that there were only two female main characters out of 20 video games analyzed: one was African American, the other Israeli. We also analyzed which characters were most likely to be the targets of violence. Of the human male targets, 25 percent were Middle Eastern. Thus, women were grossly underrepresented as heroes, and Middle Easterners were grossly overrepresented as targets of violence. This may well send the message that Middle Easterners are the "kinds of people" whom it is socially acceptable to harm.

DO BLATANT SEX-ROLE STEREOTYPES PROMOTE REAL HARM?

What are the implications of exposure to images that are so blatantly stereotypical? What effect does viewing these stereotypes have on young men and women? It follows that exposure to the pervasive imagery of men as powerful, mean, and violent and women as degraded objects to be used and subjugated has implications for the harmful treatment of women in real-life situations.

My colleagues Brian Brown, Michael Collins, and I[39] investigated these issues. We started by choosing stereotypical images of male and female video game characters that this earlier research had revealed were typical representations in the culture. We selected representative images of women and men from top-selling video games including *Grand Theft Auto: Vice City*, *Grand Theft Auto: San Andreas*, *Dead or Alive Xtreme Beach Volleyball 2*, *BMX XXX*, *Saint's Row*, *Resident Evil*, and *Gears of War*. (See Figures 5.2A and 5.2B for examples of actual images used in the study.)

Now, as we have discussed previously, in an experiment one uses at least two groups for comparison—the experimental group and a control group. In the experimental group, participants saw the stereotypical video game content. We wanted to select a control group of images that would present *both* men and women in roles that were realistic and high in social status and power. We therefore chose real pictures of men and women who were current US congressional representatives. The hope was that we were presenting a vision of men and women as competent and powerful in positive ways. Participants either saw a 10-minute video presentation of the video game images or the images of the congressional representatives.

Figures 5.2A and 5.2B Examples of sex-role stereotyped images from video games (5.2A) and of professional men and women (5.2B) used in Dill, Brown, and Collins (2008). The image in Figure 5.2A is a screen shot from *BMX XXX* (*2002*, Acclaim Entertainment). Figure 5.2B is a photo of Senator Mary Landrieu (D-LA) (www. landrieusenate.gov). After viewing stereotypical images like the one in A, young men were more tolerant of sexual harassment, compared to those who saw the professional, respectful images (such as B).

We wanted to measure the differential effects of this exposure on a real-world outcome in which women experience harm because of their gender. We decided to study sexual harassment because it is so commonly experienced and because, as described earlier, it is not a sexual crime but a crime intended to harm the victims (as the "uppity" women study demonstrated). Would stereotype exposure lead to greater support of harassment of women? Would men react differently from women to these images? To find answers to these questions, we thought it was important to use a realistic example of harassment, so we chose the author Naomi Wolf's personal account of her experience as a young college student being sexually harassed by her male professor (excerpted from *The Silent Treatment* by Naomi Wolf—from NewYorkMetro.com). One reason we chose this story is because we believed it was not on either extreme (e.g., a story of a rape or of a mild flirtation). Thus we thought that perceptions of the story could vary fairly widely. All participants read this story and then were asked some probing questions about their views. For example, they were asked to judge, if the story is true, whether this means the professor is guilty of sexual harassment and then how harshly he should be punished for his behavior. Further, they rated the extent to which they blamed the female student for the professor's behavior and then how deeply they felt the experience affected her, how seriously she should be taken, and how sorry they felt for her. Taken together, all these judgments indicate the participant's sensitivity toward and tolerance of sexual harassment.

The results were very interesting. While men and those who had viewed the video game characters were more tolerant of sexual harassment, further differences emerged. We found a significant three-to-one contrast. Do you remember the game from children's TV in which the characters sang, "three of these things are not like the other"? That's what a three-to-one contrast shows—that one group responded differently from the other three. In this case, what we found was that the men who saw the stereotypical images of men (as powerful) and women (as sex objects) behaved differently from the other three groups. They were significantly more tolerant of sexual harassment than any other group. So seeing stereotypes of men as powerful and dominant and women as demeaned and objectified caused these men to be less likely to see an event like this as even being sexual harassment. Further, this group reported that they would be more lenient to the perpetrator of sexual harassment. This has implications for male bosses who receive complaints from female employees; if they are more exposed to these media stereotypes of gender, this study suggests that they would be less helpful to their female subordinate and potentially could cause her harm by failing to appropriately punish the transgressor.

ARE STEREOTYPES IN THE MEDIA
"JUST HARMLESS ENTERTAINMENT"?

Scientists at the University of Maryland's Center for Children, Relationships and Culture[40] wondered what young people thought about the idea that stereotypes in the media are "just harmless entertainment." They showed students stereotypical video game content such as women as sex objects and violent men. Male adolescents were more likely to view both violence and gender stereotypes as harmless entertainment, though they did disapprove more of the stereotypical content. Also, people who played more video games—mostly males—were the least likely to think that exposure to violence and stereotypes in video games could actually change people's behavior. This was a general finding as well: most of the adolescents didn't think people were affected by exposure to media violence or media stereotypes. The more someone uses media with negative content, the more they are likely to say that the content does not affect them. Again, we see what is either naïve or self-protective thinking. In other words, those who use more media are either less informed about its effects or more likely to rationalize an increased use that at some level they know is harmful.

LET'S HOPE YOUR BOSS DOESN'T
WATCH JERRY SPRINGER

Sensationalistic talk shows such as *The Jerry Springer Show* are now common in our media culture. We have probably all laughed at the extreme guests on some of these shows. But does viewing this kind of content cause harm, or is it harmless fun? A team of researchers[41] studied how watching promiscuous women on *The Jerry Springer Show* affected viewers. Participants saw a clip from the Springer show, featuring either a promiscuous or a nonpromiscuous woman. Later in the study, they read a sexual harassment scenario. They were asked to rate this unrelated woman in the sexual harassment story as to how promiscuous they thought she was. Results showed that those who had seen the promiscuous women on the Springer show applied this stereotype to the unrelated woman who had been sexually harassed. In other words, being exposed to stereotypical, degrading images in the media of promiscuous women affected how people rated other, unrelated women. It taught stereotypical thinking—in this case, "women are just like that." In this particular case, the viewers of the stereotypical content also believed that the sexual harassment victim had experienced less trauma and that she was more to blame for her own harassment. In the end, what we learn from this once again is that stereotypes in the media do really matter. They are not, in fact, "just harmless entertainment." They change our view of the world around us.

TEACHING DEGRADATION THROUGH THE MEDIA

Pornography research has stressed the idea that when it comes to sexual video material, it is not explicit sexual content that is harmful, but it is degradation that matters. When women are depicted in pornography in degraded and sub-missive roles, viewers become less supportive of equality between the sexes and more lenient in assigning punishment to a rapist. Media degradation of women can also reinforce the ideas that women are sex objects and/or sexually promiscuous and can undermine reactions of empathy to real women.

Researchers from the University of Massachusetts[42] invited participants to take part in two short studies: a censorship study and a study about legal decision-making. In fact, this was all part of one investigation: the researchers were interested in how seeing degraded women would influence participants' views on rape. The scientists constructed a 22-minute video compilation of scenes from the movies *9½ Weeks* and *Showgirls* that was rated to degrade women. They defined degradation as depicting women as objects to be exploited and manipulated sexually. The film clips they used included a striptease and a scene with a blindfolded woman. These scenes contained male dominance and power and female availability and submission, and also emphasized male—but not female—sexual gratification. First, participants watched either the deroga-tory scenes or a control video from an animation festival. Next, in what they thought was the legal decision-making study, they read a magazine account of either a date rape or a stranger rape. Results showed that the men who had seen the degrading media images of women showed significantly different reactions to the date rape account. These men were more likely to say that the victim of the date rape enjoyed it and that she secretly got what she wanted. Again, we see that men can learn lessons about women through exposure to media stereotypes.

It's important to note that these movie scenes did not even contain violence against women, but they still supported what are called "rape myths"—false stereotypes and cultural beliefs about rape, such as the notion that women deserve rape or that they secretly want to be raped.

MORE ON MEDIA, RAPE MYTHS, AND SOCIAL LEARNING

In another study,[43] men and women were exposed to magazine advertisements containing either objectified or progressive images of women or containing no people at all (the control condition). Interestingly, men and women reacted differently to the objectified versus progressive women in the ads. Whereas seeing the derogatory images of women caused men to become more likely to endorse rape myths, it caused women in the experimental group to be less likely than control participants to support rape myths. The authors noted that incidence rates of rape were higher in states that had higher circulation rates of pornography and—in a seeming paradox—were higher in states where women's power and status were higher. The authors interpreted this as indicating a backlash against women's rise to social power in the form of violence against women. Again, we see that stereotyping in the media raises issues of status and power of men versus women in the real world.

In a classic study, Edward Donnerstein and Leonard Berkowitz[44] angered some men by giving them electric shocks; others were not shocked. Then the men saw a film. Some saw a neutral film; some saw a nonviolent, sexually explicit film. The most theoretically interesting conditions in the study involved two rape scenes. In one rape scene, the victim protested; in another version, she initially protested, but then appeared to enjoy the attack. This was the "rape myth" video—a rape scene that brought to life the idea that women secretly want to be raped. While the angered men tended to react aggressively in general, there were interesting differences in the behavior of the nonangered men, which varied depending on what type of film they had seen. Only the men who had seen the "rape myth" scene were more likely subsequently to be aggressive toward a real woman in the laboratory.

Once again, we see that people learn ideas in the media that can change their behavior. Media messages do matter. In fact, not only do they matter, but they are powerful teachers. Again, when you take into consideration the power of the media coupled with the strong tendency of people to be ignorant of or to deny that power, there is a lot of room for harm. Here we see that so strongly because the harm we are talking about is aggression against women. Violence breeds violence. Degradation breeds degradation.

MUSIC AND DEGRADATION

One more example: a group of researchers[45] conducted a national longitudinal sample of over 1,400 teenagers. They were interested in whether listening to music with sexually degrading lyrics affected the teens' attitudes and behavior. The researchers selected 16 artists whose music represented a variety of genres. They classified the sexual content of the lyrics on these artists' latest recordings. Here is one example of a sexually degrading lyric, from Ja Rule's *Living it Up*: "Half the ho's hate me, half them love me / The ones that hate me / Only hate me 'cause they ain't fucked me / And they say I'm lucky / Do you think I've got time / To fuck all these ho's?" (By the way, have you noticed that if your kids are in the car with you, this is the song that will be blasting from the car next to you at a stoplight?) Results showed that teens who listened to the degrading music lyrics more often were more likely to initiate sexual intercourse or more advanced sexual behaviors during the two-year course of the study. Of course, such activity is related to sexually transmitted disease rates as well as teen pregnancy. These teens themselves had a tendency to see early sexual behavior as problematic and to wish they had waited longer to have sex.

POSITIVE IMAGES OF GENDER
AND RACE IN THE MEDIA

After that conversation, I imagine you are ready for some good news. I know I am. And there are, thankfully, positive examples of gender and race in the media. There are media messages that can influence us for the better. A film like *Akeelah and the Bee*, for example, shows the struggles of an African American girl to find her own positive voice and identity and to believe in herself. The depiction of Akeelah is respectful and nuanced. Viewers identify with the universal elements of her characterization. That underlines an important element in respectful characterization—telling stories with universal elements erases boundaries. It doesn't matter if Akeelah looks like you or comes from your neighborhood, you see her humanity. You understand what she's going through and you like her. Such characterization transcends social class and is unifying.

Since 2004, *Time* magazine has ranked the 100 most influential people in the world. The list is diverse and is based on the power of the person's influence—for better or worse. On the cover of the 2008 *Time 100* are men and women of many colors. Notable Americans include Oprah Winfrey and Barack Obama. Oprah is categorized among the "heroes and pioneers," while Obama is on the "leaders and revolutionaries" list. Oprah, as a media pioneer and notable public servant, is surely one of the great examples of positive media images of African American women. She represents what can happen even against the odds and thus she is an inspiration.

Similarly, seeing Barack Obama through the eye of the camera has moved people across the country and around the world. Interestingly, he was ranked higher than John McCain, Hillary Clinton, and George W. Bush on *Time's* 2008 "leaders and revolutionaries" list. Obama's mother was white and his father Kenyan, so he is of mixed race. Like Oprah's story, Obama has taught us that media exposure to truly inspirational people of color can change things. Running on a message of change, Obama's rise to the top as the first African American president was helped by his media exposure.

BUILDING A HEALTHIER MEDIA CULTURE FOR ALL

Respectful depictions and multicultural interactions in the media are very uplifting and healthy for all of us. When children from different backgrounds play well together on children's shows such as *Sesame Street*, and when they are each presented as equally valid human beings, it sends important messages. It is the premise that was used in casting a group of racially diverse men and women for the TV series *Star Trek* in the 1960s. It's the reason—as mentioned earlier—that Martin Luther King Jr. reportedly told actress Nichelle Nichols, who played Lieutenant Uhuru on the show, that she could not quit because she was a role model to so many African American girls. Just as degrading characterizations cause damage, respectful characterizations are powerfully good.

Let me leave you with what I think is a very fine example of representations of race and gender in the media. PBS's station WGBH in Boston, funded in part by the National Science Foundation and Arby's restaurants, produced a show that debuted in 2006 called *Fetch! with Ruff Ruffman*. The show—a reality game show hosted by comical cartoon dog Ruff Ruffman—features a cast of real kids that changes each year. The tween-aged cast is half girls and half boys and is racially diverse. Furthermore, the kids look like real kids, in T-shirts, ponytails, jeans, and tennis shoes; there are no Hollywood wannabes there. Every week the kids are given a variety of challenges, including taking quizzes, solving puzzles and problems of all sorts, and exploring different jobs. They have been asked to shovel manure on a farm, solve mysteries in a castle, do stand-up comedy or forecast the weather on TV, make chocolates, and track animal scat and pitch makeshift tents in the wilderness. It is a competition, but the show also teaches cooperation. Here is part of the show's educational philosophy from www.pbskids.org/fetch:

> FETCH! shows that reality programs can help kids learn how to tackle problems, overcome fears, brainstorm, and collaborate. Reality programs allow viewers to see that real expertise often takes time to develop and that learning is about the journey, not the destination. And, rather than be an impetus for anti-social behavior, they can create a positive environment for modeling pro-social skills and resolving conflicts between kids.

The show also encourages what it calls "habits of mind"—problem-solving tools including "curiosity, perseverance, risk-taking and creative and critical thinking."[46] With other shows using stereotypes as a lazy storytelling strategy, being mean-spirited and sometimes antisocial, a show that encourages growth in so many ways is absolutely amazing. It does what all shows should do regarding social categories like race and sex—it simply lets people be real people and it encourages these real kids to grow in healthy, challenging ways. I wish more programs were created with the kind of consciousness that PBS's *Fetch! with Ruff Ruffman* has.

When media producers treat race and gender respectfully—when they treat *people* respectfully—they can do some good, rather than simply using their audience for all they think we're worth.

> Racially prejudicial stereotyping is debilitative in a society, especially one as diverse as the United States. Not only does the stereotyping work against the groups' recognizing and understanding the common humanity of all people, it also provides succeeding generations of all racial groups—White and non-White—with distorted self-images. The coupling of biased portrayals with the social and psychological power of mass entertainment threatens the maturation of American society into a model of multicultural tolerance and unity.[47]

At this time in history, our nation is becoming more culturally diverse. We have witnessed the election of the country's first African American president and we have seen positive reactions to Obama's election both here and around the world. We know that so many have been inspired by President Obama and his family and embrace the progress they represent. Now, more than ever, we need to be aware of the power of mass media images of gender and race—both for the bad and for the good—in the process of socialization. Media producers will give us respectful representations of diverse groups if we as an audience decide that we will accept no less. How well we understand and address media representations of race and gender will have consequences for the future of our evolving society.

Advertising, Consumerism, and Health

One of the most influential psychologists in history, John B. Watson, was a radical behaviorist. Behaviorism holds that people and animals learn through basic, observable principles, such as by associating one experience with another or by learning through the consequences of actions. For example, Pavlov trained his dog to drool when hearing the sound of a bell because a dinner bell always sounded when dinner was served. B. F. Skinner trained animals to play the piano and to play ping pong—even to guide missiles for the US military—by manipulating the consequences of their behavior. Famously, J. B. Watson taught "little Albert"—a toddler—to fear white, fluffy things. How? He gave Albert a white, fluffy toy or animal and then made a scary sound, which caused Albert to cry. After that treatment, just seeing the toy or animal would make little Albert cry.

What else did Watson, famous for warping the mind of a toddler, contribute to psychology? Basically, he found a way to make the rest of us pretty neurotic, too, because he was one of the first psychologists to actively influence advertising. It's an interesting story, actually. John B. Watson had a pretty warped childhood himself. His father, from whom he later became estranged, was a drinker and a carouser. His mother was "insufferably religious"[1] and his nanny instilled in him a lifelong fear of the dark by telling him the devil was in the dark and might come and take little John to hell. He had trouble dealing with his emotions and publicly endorsed an unsentimental method of parenting that favored shaking hands over hugs and kisses. His own children and grandchildren were apparently scarred by what many would consider an emotionally blunted upbringing, and his son William committed suicide. His scholarly career soared early, but was cut short when he had a first-marriage-ending affair with his graduate student Rosalie Raynor, who had assisted him in the "little Albert" research. Banished from academia, he reinvented himself and became an advertising executive, making four times his professorial salary.[2]

Advertisers have programmed many of us into a shopping habit.[3]
                                                             —James Potter

Apparently operating under the same ethical code implemented during his academic career, Watson recommended to advertisers that they could make a fortune by manipulating basic human motivations and emotions to their advantage, and often, of course, to the consumer's disadvantage. One of his basic ideas, used with gusto and impunity by advertisers today, was to convince people that their possessions were inferior and consequently that they needed new possessions. In other words, he helped create the modern consumer mentality: one does not buy an item out of need but out of a psychological desire to compare favorably to others' material possessions, or out of a general neuroticism based on the notion that buying will satisfy deep motivations. That's where the social psychology meets the basic behaviorist psychology. Advertisers manipulate our desires, and often these desires are social, like the desires to be liked, to be attractive, or to do what everybody else is doing.

Let's take a look at an example of advertising using behaviorism with a social twist. Everyone knows that hot rod magazines often show what on the hood of the car? Right: a sexy woman in a bikini. Now this is crazy from any rational perspective. So why use bikini models in the ads? From a behaviorist perspective, the car is associated with the sexy woman. When you think of the car, it excites the kinds of feelings you get when thinking about the sexy woman. Using another learning principle, a guy shopping for a muscle car might now believe that if he buys one, it will attract a hot woman. So in a funny way, buying a car now becomes a more social decision, rather than a decision that is purely about transportation.

Since social motives are powerful and fundamental to human nature, ads often exploit social motivation. You buy mouthwash because you don't want to turn off coworkers or potential dates. You associate a fresh pot of coffee with a commercial featuring a warm, happy family. The coffee's brand and look now make you feel the pleasure associated with a warm, happy family, and you may buy that kind of coffee hoping unconsciously to draw that social situation to yourself. I suggest to my students that when you want to buy a product, do a very simple thing: think about what you get when you buy it. If you want to drink coffee and you like the taste of a certain brand, then buy it. But if you buy based on the mythology of the commercial, you are really not getting that when you buy. If you buy an expensive perfume based on an elegant ad, you probably want to ask yourself if you really like how it smells, if you can afford it, and if you even like wearing perfume at all. Companies sell sneakers by making commercials showing the wearer having fun with his friends. The message: these sneakers are fun! These sneakers will make you look cool to the kids at school! Again, you have to think through what you are getting, as well as how you are being manipulated. Always be wary of the original plan that John B. Watson suggested to advertising executives: make people think they need new stuff. Do you need another pair of sneakers, or has a company manipulated you to give your money to them?

On the positive side, there are companies marketing products or services that consumers will really enjoy and that will arguably make our lives better. For me, the ethical line is where an ad ceases to tell us what the product can do for us and crosses into the territory where we'll buy something for the wrong reasons. This includes the cases where the advertisers know that the product is not good for us, but want us to buy it anyway. There are certainly products that I'd rather not live without and that live up to their ads. The computer I'm writing this book on comes to mind as an example. (Hi to Steve Jobs up in heaven!) There's an ethical line between capturing the imagination of the audience and attempting to manipulate them. I gave the story of J. B. Watson as an example of an early influence in the advertising business who came at it explicitly to try to sell people things they did not need.

TWO VIEWS ON MATERIAL THINGS: CARETAKING VERSUS CONSUMING

At a largely unconscious level, advertising sells values, like the value of acquiring new material possessions. My grandparents on my mother's side—Grandma and Grandpa Leonard—had a different point of view about how to handle your property. They were great believers that hard-earned belongings merited care and that what you cared for would and should last. They were proud that they knew how to take proper care of things; it meant that they were skilled, responsible, and not wasteful. They had a clock, for instance, that the whole family admired, and they kept it clean and in excellent working order. When they died, my aunt inherited the clock as a prized possession. I grew up loving that clock—a beautiful and unique polished cherry wood mantel clock whose pendulum was a lovely blonde girl in a blue dress on a swing.

My Grandma Annie, my father's mother, had another perspective on the value of possessions. As Grandma Annie got on in years, she acquired the habit of marking her possessions with a family member's name. When my Uncle Tom asked her, "Mom, why does this thing have my name taped on the bottom?" Grandma would reply, "Because I'm leaving it to you when I die."

This would cause eruptions of merriment all around because on my dad's side of the family, we are all, shall I say, delightfully irreverent?

But in all seriousness, I tell these family stories because we are encouraged by mass media to be a throwaway culture, and I do not know how many people today grow up with the mentality of keeping and caring for possessions. The younger generations have grown up in a consumer-oriented society in which buying is akin to a sport and having "old" things is something of an embarrassment inasmuch as it indicates that you are not well off enough to afford new ones. Another aspect of a throwaway society is that products themselves tend to be made to last only a short period of time, both satisfying and perpetuating the consumer culture.

Now, I'm not suggesting that I am not a product of the age in which I grew up. I think it's a big mistake to project the image that expertise makes me immune to the psychological mechanisms I study. It doesn't. I like to randomly blurt out confessions during my talks just so the audience doesn't think I'm peddling some myths of my own. Psychologists are human. For instance, right now my Facebook page contains images of shoes I have searched for on Amazon. com. And I have to admit that when I see those cute shoes on my screen I sort of salivate and think—I deserve a new pair of shoes, right? Like everyone, life presents me with conflicting motives, and I make choices. I'm not immune to the concepts I study, but I am a kind of freak about them. My son, for example, could tell you all about commercials trying to sell you something from a very tender age. Everyone knows that psychologists warp their children.

This example brings up another fact about the evolution of marketing: the idea that now these sorts of pop-up ads represent one of the digital approaches to marketing. They know what we write about and what we search for online and they try to sell us those things. Some say that this is very convenient for us and it takes away all those ads (for Craftsman power tools?) that wouldn't work on me and replaces them with something I might really want. Others say that this is privacy infringement. I admit, it is kind of creepy when you write an e-mail to your best friend and mention a product, and then that product appears in an ad on your gmail account. It does smell of Big Brother.

> I don't care where the eyeballs come from. I care about the eyeballs.
> —ANDY MARKOWITZ, *director, Digital Marketing,*
> *Kraft Foods, speaking at an advertising summit*[4]

If we were alien scientists whose job it was to understand Earthling behavior, I think we would wonder a lot about why Earthlings spend so much time staring into screens. Why do they spend more time watching other Earthlings pretending to do stuff instead of doing real stuff themselves? And why watch each other on video instead of live? Yep, I'm pretty sure I would shriek and gesture wildly with my tentacles at my fellow alien scientists trying to come up with a good theory for that one.

It's all very simple. Advertisers are well aware that the more our eyeballs look at their ads, the more money they make. Seeing an ad makes us more likely to buy the product, but we are mostly unaware that this is true. If you ask people, they will say that ads do not affect them, and yet we know they do. Ads are powerful. The psychology that hooks us in to devoting most of our free time to media is very powerful. The biggest reason we spend an incredible amount of time staring into screens and at other forms of mass media is that we are being manipulated by big business to do so.

Business manipulates us to get our money. This is a basic tenet of media education. It's so simple. We know it, I think, at a cognitive level. If you ask us to think about it, we could tell you that ads work—they sell products. The third-person effect, though, protects our egos by making us believe that other people are manipulated—not us! Of course, that makes us more vulnerable to manipulation. We even defend the manipulators, becoming media apologists, not unlike a victim of abuse defending her abuser. What a perfect prescription for exploitation!

A group of researchers[5] studied how different people react when a brand they identify with is threatened. They had participants read an editorial criticizing Facebook. They also primed their self-concepts. They found that for those participants who liked Facebook (no pun intended) and who had low self-esteem, they reacted to the threat to their brand by liking Facebook *more* after the threat. In other words, if they drew some of their own self-esteem through association with a brand, they defended the brand as if they were defending themselves. In the face of evidence like this, it's hard to argue that we don't take products or their advertisements both seriously and personally.

ADVERTISING AND AGENDA SETTING

Some argue that advertisers, and indeed all media, do not influence what we think as much as they tell us what to think about. This is called the agenda-setting theory because media are said to set the agenda for viewers like a leader sets the agenda for a meeting. When an advertiser emphasizes a product or its attributes or a brand, this suggests what value it has and how other people view it. Sutherland and Galloway suggest that advertisers do more agenda setting than persuading. They write:

Products that are advertised heavily have a status conferred upon them—i.e., they are felt by customers to be "the most popular" products.

The media are assumed to carry that which is more important, more in demand, more notorious. Just as "the ordinary person" does not appear on TV, neither does "the ordinary product." The fact of something being included in the media is not seen by the reader or viewer as giving that thing status, but as strong presumptive evidence that the thing has status—otherwise it would not be in the media.[6]

We see in this explanation a social message that underlies repeated advertising of a product, value, or brand. Namely, other people must like it, want it, value it, and in some cases agree with the underlying values or messages. Indeed, consumers believe that advertised products are superior to products that aren't advertised, for example, that a brand-name clothing detergent is superior to a no-name brand. I think that when we impute social status onto ideas projected in an advertisement or in other forms of media, this presumes that the media have done more than set the agenda. They have persuaded us of the social status and worth of the product, habit, value, or other idea they communicated.

Advertisements do set an agenda. For example, the many commercials for hair removal products, such as waxes, appliances, and creams for legs, face, and the so-called bikini area, imply that women need to be hair-free in all of these areas, and that one will not be socially acceptable if one does not purchase such products or services. The products that are advertised most frequently are believed to be superior and to be used and liked by more people. A woman may digest different kinds of social messages from these ads, such as which products a person of her age and social position should prefer and use. Again, I think this means that the ads have gone beyond setting an agenda to persuading consumers of a product's social value.

LEVELS OF MANIPULATION

John B. Watson advised making people believe their things are inferior so that they would buy new things. That is a blatant and intentional type of manipulation. You want people to believe something that both isn't true and isn't in their own best interest to believe. There are other forms of manipulation that cause intentional harm. For example, I sometimes notice advertisements that appear designed to shame women into feeling bad about themselves, thus motivating them to buy what the ad sells. Some ads present "before and after" photos of women, and the "before" photo will give a more average size, such as size 12 or even 10. The "after" photo will give a very small size, like a size 2. The message this sends very clearly to most of the viewers—since again, the average American woman is about a size 14—is that *their* size is considered fat.

This is a very straightforward case of implied social comparison. It also implies that an appropriate goal would be for average American women to be quite small. This isn't realistic or even necessarily the healthiest goal.

Other manipulation that occurs via the mass media appears to me to be less intentional. This manipulation is less like a direct attack and more like collateral damage. If producers follow the general premise that they want to do whatever encourages people to tune in, then they create media that grab attention. These attention-grabbing elements may teach unintended lessons. For example, we regularly see highly attractive people in the media. Producers may have made that choice because highly attractive people—unsurprisingly—attract attention. It gives us pleasure to look at beautiful people. But then the media become filled with highly attractive people, and people spend more time watching these attractive people. In the end, they see many highly attractive people in the media, and the availability heuristic tells them that it's because there are many highly attractive people around. I now have to adjust my views of my own looks to be less attractive than "all the people I see every day." I now feel that my looks are inferior as a consequence of mass media doing everything they can to get my attention. It's not necessarily intentional, but it doesn't need to be intentional to have a major influence on people. And of course, sometimes it is intentional.

Something similar to what happens with physical appearance happens with material possessions and lifestyles. We define normal or desirable by what we view in the media. Mass media constructs a norm of consumerism. A T-shirt I once saw said, "Whoever dies with the most toys wins." People I see in magazines or on TV have many things, and I make the inference that I need to have them too in order to fit in or to outdo my neighbors. According to the book *Affluenza: The All-Consuming Epidemic*, the average American home in 1955 is equal in size to the average American *garage* in 2000. The advertisers push our buttons and we respond—one reason that so many Americans today are in debt. Advertisers make people anxious and needy for products that promise to make them happy, popular, and attractive. Consumers spend money chasing this elusive dream of social currency, only to wind up very often in debt, thus creating more anxiety and stress.

PRODUCT PLACEMENTS—PRETTY SNEAKY

Have you ever noticed people in a movie, television program, or even on the Internet using a product? Maybe they are drinking a Coke or smoking a Camel. In the TV show *Heroes*, for example, the character Hiro Nakamura mentions repeatedly that the car he and his friend Ando have rented is a Nissan Versa.

These are called passive ads or product placements. These passive ads send subtle social messages: this movie star that I love smokes; therefore, smoking is cool. Or take another message: this perfect family created on the screen before me drinks Coke. I associate Coke with something warm and happy. If I drink Coke I will be like them and I will have the things that they have, including love and warmth. All of this is part of the same equation—behaviorism plus social psychology equals manipulation, as well as the math that matters most: manipulation equals profits.

There is a set of values that says there is nothing wrong with this. America was founded on principles of freedom. Free enterprise and the free market are foundational to how we do business and why we are successful. That's one business perspective on values. What about a sociological, psychological, or even anthropological perspective? Respectively, these disciplines would ask the following: What makes a society strong? What makes people happiest and healthiest? What kind of culture will have a lasting positive impact on human history? In this context, I think any business approach that resembles manipulative profiteering is short-sighted and benefits only those who profit financially from it in the short term. Anyone who cares about humanity from a larger perspective—certainly including spiritual, philosophical, and ideological perspectives—should have problems with the negative, manipulative kind of marketing we see so often today.

ADVERTISING FOOD AND FITNESS

Mass media do create some beautiful illusions. Earlier I mentioned the way thin, sexy stars eat high-calorie foods on camera, creating the illusion that we can all eat that way and look like they do. For me, one commercial takes this to the extreme to the extent that it's probably even making fun of itself. The ad I'm talking about is the one in which Paris Hilton washes a car in a manner described by critics as resembling soft-core porn, and then bites into a huge Hardee's hamburger. There was an ad of this kind circulating when I wrote the first edition of this book, and a new one is out as I write the second edition (see Figure 6.1A1). We have to laugh when we see this ad—I don't think Paris or her girlfriends usually drive-through Hardee's for lunch. A parody ad by Accolo recruiting featured a man who looked more like he's had a few Hardee burgers in his time, the fictitious "Eugene" (see Figure 6.1A2). If you look at the Paris Hilton ad and the parody ad side by side, you get a dose of fantasy versus reality. When you eat a high-fat diet, you generally get fat, but media create illusions that we easily swallow (pardon the pun.) We want to eat like

Figures 6.1A1 and 6.1A2 A 2014 Hardee's commercial described by some critics as soft-core porn, in which Paris Hilton washes herself and a car and then eats a Hardee's hamburger in as sexual a way as humanly possible (6.1A1). In a parody ad (6.1A2), "Eugene" eats the same hamburger with more realistic results on his figure.

Eugene and still look like Paris, so we're vulnerable to the fantasy that media producers sell us.

MEDIA ILLUSIONS: SEEING IS BELIEVING

But there is also a more innocent level here. Since our brains weren't created to process media but to process real social information, I imagine if we see a beautiful person eating rich food and still looking thin, part of us believes it is true because seeing is believing. We're not built to discount what we see, to identify illusions. We're built to do just the opposite—to take in social information as just that. From an evolutionary or biological perspective we are *supposed* to believe what we see, not doubt it. Our thinking makes perfect sense if you look at it that way. We shouldn't feel bad, but, given that most of what we see now is fantasy and not reality, we should get smart about it so that we are not as vulnerable to other people's agendas.

THE CYCLE OF FAT TO FIT TO FAT AGAIN

On a road trip years ago, I checked out a book on tape from the business section of our local library that promised to be about improving your communications skills. As I drove and listened to the tape, I soon became incredulous at what I was hearing. The author suggested that you should listen carefully to what other people say so that you can learn what is the most important thing in the world to them. Why? If you know what's most important to someone, you can exploit that information for your own gain!!! I realized that some people are unscrupulous enough to try to exploit others, but I didn't know they would actually (1) admit it in public, and (2) unashamedly publish a book telling everyone what an awesome idea it is.

It seems that advertisers often take a page out of that guy's book. They think about what we want most and manipulate those motives for all they are worth. It's no secret that people want to be attractive and that attractiveness is basically synonymous with thinness in our culture, especially for women. Thousands of American women were surveyed[7] about what they want most in life. Did they want world peace or a cure for cancer? Did they want money? More than any other goal, these women wanted to lose 10 or 15 pounds. For advertisers, the insecurity and impassioned motivation that makes losing a few pounds the favorite dream of so many means that the same people will spend billions annually trying to grab the illusive brass ring.

And it's clear that the brass ring often isn't health; it's attractiveness. For example, people smoke cigarettes sometimes because they think it helps keep them thin and, of course, cigarette smoking is one of the single worst things you can do for your health. Attractiveness means feeling good about yourself, feeling that other people value you, want you, even envy you—that's what makes something that might sometimes masquerade as a health goal really a social goal. And at the heart, it's all about perception. I say often in my social psychology class that in my field what we're interested in is perception. If a plastic surgeon's patients feel inferior, that's what motivates them, not the relatively factual notion that they are already attractive. They are similar to the domestic violence victim whose husband tells her she is fat and ugly and useless, so she stays with him in part because she believes it. He has altered her reality, like advertisers alter our realities.

In the 1920s, the boyish figure of the flapper dancer was stylish, and buxom women actually bound their breasts to better fit the fashion. Today, teenaged girls ask a surgeon to implant bags of saline under their breasts so that a society attracted to disproportionately large breasts will find them more attractive. Thinking about this rationally, surgically altering one's body to gain self-esteem is a pretty extreme move, but social motives are very powerful, and media help normalize this extreme behavior. With TV shows like *Extreme Makeover* showing how to transform an ugly duckling into a swan, viewers are enticed by the notion that they can transform themselves.

Extreme-ly Misguided

In a college class on gender in society, my colleague sociologist Beth Wright and I showed an episode of *Extreme Makeover* and discussed it with our students. In the episode, a young, perfectly healthy size 10 woman wanted to find love. The solution: *Extreme Makeover*! They showed her in her underwear, pointing out all her "flaws." They gave her pretty extensive liposuction, reducing her to a size 2, and increased her breasts to C cups. She also had plastic surgery all over her face, sessions with a personal trainer, a makeover, new hairdo, and new clothes. Wow, apparently beauty is a lot of work! The "reveal" segment showed her family crying tears of joy over her new look, coupled with a discussion of how she was now going to find a man.

Our class discussed the way the show gives the impression that anyone can become "a beauty" and concluded that the amount of work done to this young woman would cost many thousands of dollars. Therefore, this kind of transformation is actually available only to the wealthy or to those who make it on the show, thus highlighting the unreality of this type of "reality"

TV. Our students also commented about the show's subtle manipulation technique of pathologizing a normal, healthy body. This young woman was not overweight, but she was scrutinized in her bra and panties, while a doctor pointed out all the areas where he could surgically remove fat from her body.

Next, the class watched a segment about a woman who had found her true love. He was a farmer who treated her gently and had even helped rescue her from home foreclosure. He was the salt of the earth. He loved her kids. He loved puppies. He was handy around the house. The problem: he was seriously lacking in the "hottie" department. Our class actually didn't agree that his looks were a problem. He looked like a regular guy to them—OK, his ears were a little big maybe, his teeth a little crooked, but no big deal. Well, this guy wanted to be his fiancée's dream man, so he underwent plastic surgery to have his "love handles" removed (his farmer body was perfectly healthy to start with), and his eyelids lifted, among other things, and endured personal training sessions in which he learned how to punch like a man (according to the show). He got veneers on his teeth, a new hairdo and new clothes. Our class concurred that at the end of all this he was not better off than when he started. He basically looked like a plastic soap opera star, I thought. Worst of all, arguably, were the veneers on his teeth. The class agreed that the show's producers had wanted the quick fix for their big reveal, and had sacrificed real dental work for awkward looking TV-ready veneers. Again, the media were selling cosmetic procedures while pathologizing "real people" looks, encouraging feelings of inadequacy in viewers, and promoting a shallow focus on appearance. The media were also selling the fantasy that attaining these results is easy and accessible. And in both cases, the goal was social—to attain love and admiration.

Advertisers certainly have tapped a vein of gold by harnessing this intense social motive to enhance one's physical appearance. Without being conscious of it, we have allowed advertisers and the mass media in general to set standards for our looks that both make us feel inadequate and neurotic and move us to spend a great deal of our money on an array of products that never take away the bad feelings.

On the other hand, there are certainly products and services that can help you be healthier. Right now, I have a smart watch with a pedometer that helps me reach my fitness goals. And I use an app called myfitness pal that helps me track my nutrition and movement. I find these both very motivating. I actually did not buy either of them because I had seen advertisements. The gym I go to recommended using devices and apps like these to help you with your fitness goals.

FOOD AND FITNESS MARKETING:
SELLING FITNESS AND FATNESS

We all have guilty pleasures. I'll confess to one of mine: I am drawn to women's magazines at the grocery store checkout counter—the more mundane the better. I buy them for escapism and end up reading them as the wife and the mommy—but also as the media psychologist—that I am. I have noticed a trend on the magazine rack at the grocery store—one that I find so amusing it's almost charming. Have you ever noticed this? The covers of some women's magazines regularly feature both weight loss and decadent food. To show you what I mean, I searched for general "women's interest" magazines on Amazon. com and found a favorite "guilty pleasure" magazine of mine that is typically on sale at my grocery store. I had to laugh as I scanned through the recent covers of this magazine because the cover stories fit my expectations to a "t." All three of the available magazine covers showed this "fit but fat" pattern. One issue proclaimed: "Lose six pounds this week," but also, "Eat your way happy." Another cover promised, "Lose ten pounds this week," but also happily reported, "Christmas cookies cure depression" and offered recipes for "8 delicious holiday muffins." The editors of the third apparently missed the humor of simultaneously advertising "Look perfect in jeans" and "Your body can be 10 years thinner" right next to images of Easter cakes and cookies running the entire span of the magazine cover. Next time you are at the grocery store checkout, scan the women's magazines. I'll bet you can find some examples like these.

TEMPTATION FOLLOWED CLOSELY
BY SHAME—AND MORE BUYING

When the good Lord created us, it was not to eat in an environment where so many high-fat, high-calorie foods were so readily available. The Garden of Eden did not have a Kentucky Fried Chicken drive-through and a Krispy Kreme shop. (Probably a good thing, since we seem to have gotten into enough trouble with just the apples.) From what I understand, high-calorie foods taste good because in an environment where food is scarce, it is adaptive to store fat in the body. Fast forward to modern-day restaurants and grocery stores and it's not hard to see that it takes some restraint not to really pack on the body fat. Enter the advertisers, whose job it is to manipulate and exploit our most fundamental desires, and voilà: an all-time high for obesity rates.

I don't think our problem is a rational one. Most people know that it's better to eat fish and broccoli than burgers and fries—we just don't want to. And then late at night we are sitting on the sofa watching TV and a pizza commercial comes on. The pizza is steaming hot. The cheese is bubbly. Our hand is on the phone. Heck, the Domino's commercials even play the sound of the phone dialing to encourage you to take that last step. Do you know the sounds I'm talking about? If you can sing them out now, that's probably a sign that their advertising is effective. We probably don't think much about being manipulated. We don't say, "Dang that Domino's for trying to make me fat!" As I've said, we're pretty unconscious about how our emotions and motives are being manipulated for profit. If you're like my family, someone just says, "Pizza!" in a voice like Homer Simpson's and with eyes glazed over with culinary anticipation like Homer's—and picks up the phone.

Subway turned the tables on these types of advertisements by choosing to emphasize the consequences of overindulging in fast food. Have you seen the ad? A man and woman are at a drive-through ordering, but instead of naming food items, they name the way their bodies will look if they eat them. The man orders love handles and his wife wants thunder thighs and a "badonka donk" butt. Subway's ad line is, "When you get greasy fast food, what are you really getting?" Don't get me wrong—it's still manipulation, just manipulation toward something that is better for you. There are products and services that honestly offer something useful or needed. The difference is all in the awareness: Do you know that you are being manipulated, and can you evaluate which products and services will promote your well-being and happiness and which won't? Can you look beyond the hype to what you are really getting and make a choice based on that? Beyond that are other issues, such as whether you can afford what's being sold. Psychologists who study decision-making know that good decisions involve both rational and emotional components. What's clear, though, is that an uninformed, unconscious decision is a lot less likely to serve you, and more likely to serve the person getting your money.

CHILDREN AND FOOD ADVERTISING

Up until now we have been talking about the effects of advertising on adult consumers. In the past, children were considered off limits to advertisers, but no more. Kids, especially teenagers, are a highly sought-after target group for advertisers, because they tend to have a lot of disposable income—recently estimated at about $200 million annually.[8] In other words, if you don't have to pay the gas bill, you might spend your money buying a video game or driving through Taco Bell late at night. Kids, of course, are even less likely than adults to be critical of advertising. Research has actually shown that kids—especially those below about age seven or eight—can't always tell the difference between what is a commercial and what is not.

The esteemed medical journal *The Lancet* has been published since the early 1800s and has a high impact worldwide on important medical issues. The word "lancet" means a window to let in light, as well as a kind of scalpel to cut out disease, and the journal's founder embraced both meanings of the word—shedding light on medical issues and removing disease from the system. In true *Lancet* style, the journal has taken a strong stand on the issue of food marketing to children,[9,10] reporting that the relatively recent movement to target children with advertising has damaged children's health—both in the United States and in Europe—for a number of reasons. Media marketing to children has contributed to the evolution of children from active and creative to passive consumer. The journal writers note decreased body image and decreased general emotional health, and increased aggression, obesity, and type 2 diabetes.

The advertisers are very conscious of their aggressive marketing strategies toward children. The *Lancet* reported that at a recent convention on marketing to kids called Kidscreen, organizers advertised that they wanted to help marketers find ways to "own" kids, to "own" their minds, and to create "lifelong consumers." Pulling no punches, the *Lancet* called these strategies exploitation and quoted a leading speaker at the Stop Commercial Exploitation of Children Summit who compared these aggressive marketers to pedophiles in their motivation to understand children.

WEIGHTY ISSUES

Beyond the very basic notion that it is not OK to exploit children—or anyone—destroying their health for your own financial gain, both the United States and the European Union are recognizing the very recent explosion in obesity rates and linking the problem with, among other causes, unscrupulous marketing practices. The *Lancet* reported in July 2008[11] that in 23 of 27 European Union countries, more than half of the adult population was overweight or obese. In the United States, the Centers for Disease Control report that the incidence of overweight in children and adolescents increased three to four times in the past three decades, ranging from about 15 percent to 20 percent of American children today.[12] There are multiple causes of this epidemic, most notably the coincidence with marketing unhealthy foods to children coupled with the increase in sedentary lifestyles that is associated with the boom in watching mass media as the most commonplace pastime. Research (and logic) links the sedentary lifestyle associated with mass media viewing with decreased health on a mass level. For example, an intensive longitudinal study in New Zealand[13] assessed 1,000 participants from birth to age 26 and found that those who watched more TV were more likely than those who watch less to be obese and to have poorer overall physical health and fitness.

FANTASIES AND ILLUSIONS
CHANGE HEALTH REALITIES

Both the United States and the European Union have held meetings and made suggestions to food advertisers, with little effect.[14] In the United States in 2005, the Institute of Medicine recommended forming a presidential task force on childhood obesity prevention, but it was not done. Also in 2005, the Federal Trade Commission (FTC) held a workshop with the Department of Health and Human Services to "develop guidelines for the advertising and marketing of food, beverages and sedentary entertainment to children and youth."[15] The recommendation from the workshop was that the industry self-regulate and advertise responsibly. This is arguably asking the fox to guard the henhouse, but the officials wanted to give the industry a chance to do the right thing. What happened next? "Food and advertising industry representatives have resisted efforts to regulate advertising to children, which led to the establishment of a bipartisan congressional Task Force on Media and Childhood Obesity in March of 2007."[16]

Meanwhile, the Federal Trade Commission was investigating how all the top US companies market and advertise food to children and adolescents. The FTC investigated the activities of 44 companies in the year 2006 (the year after self-regulation was suggested), and filed its report in July 2008. According to the FTC report,[17] the advertisers spent $1.6 billion to reach children and adolescents in 2006. The top food products marketed to children and adolescents were carbonated beverages, quick-service restaurants (a.k.a. fast food), and breakfast foods. How did the advertisers and marketers win over the hearts and minds of American kids? One strategy is using beloved celebrities to endorse a product. Another strategy marketers used a lot was "cross-promotions." Cross-promotion means linking a food product with some other thing kids love, like a cartoon character, TV show, movie, or toy. Companies often used cross-promotions for breakfast foods, restaurant food, snacks, candy, and carbonated beverages.

Of course, we all know they do this. Especially if you have children at home, this phenomenon is part of your life. McDonald's associates the funny cartoon movie *Kung Fu Panda* with their chicken nuggets. *Superman*

Returns and *Pirates of the Carribbean* were two big movies of 2006, and the advertisers used these films to promote everything from cereals and fruit snacks to carbonated beverages and lunch kits. They created "limited edition" frozen waffles, candies, cereals, and snacks using images of popular characters as a sales technique. (Limited edition waffles!? Are you supposed to bronze them and put them on the mantel?) Junk food was also advertised using "spokescharacters" such as cartoon M&Ms with different personalities and colors. Of course, every fast-food restaurant has a kids' meal with toys, and these are often associated with the latest movie or hot toy item.

According to the FTC report, the food industry also used more high-tech advertising techniques to reach children, such as Web sites and text messages. For example, kids are sometimes enticed by product packaging to go online and play "free games," which are really advertisements. If you go to www.happymeal.com as of this writing, at the top of the page in smallish print, you will actually see the words, "Hey kids, this is advertising." A newer form of marketing to youth is so-called viral advertising. This is the digital version of word-of-mouth. Viral advertising might include a Web site or a social networking site where kids are invited to send an e-card or a text message to their friend that promotes a product. Advertisers are excited about the notion of getting people to tell each other about their product. If it comes from a friend, it is more persuasive.

ATHLETES ADVERTISING JUNK FOOD

The FTC noted one common marketing strategy that really makes no sense: the use of athletes to advertise junk food. For example, BMX biker Dave Mirra advertises for Slim Jims—the beef jerky. By the way, in a true cross-media ad campaign, Dave Mirra's BMX video game includes a character named Slim Jim, accessible through a cheat code. McDonald's and Coke both paid large sums of money to sponsor the 2008 Summer Olympics in Beijing. Of course, Olympic-level athletes have special diets and I'm thinking these probably don't include lots of Big Macs, fries, and Cokes. Well, maybe for the Sumo wrestlers.

A consistent theme in these marketing schemes is fantasy. Advertisers create an illusion. It's an illusion that top athletes eat junk food diets. It's an illusion that you can eat a junk food diet and stay fit and trim like the actors and celebrities in the ads. We see it and it looks so real, so appealing. We want to do it, too—eat yummy high-calorie foods and still be healthy and slim as a celebrity or an Olympic athlete. But it is a fantasy, and it is one that harshly shapes our realities.

Offering our kids a toy to encourage them to buy a fast-food kids' meal may be a brilliant marketing strategy. It may make companies lots of money, but strategies like this are, in reality, making our kids fat and damaging their physical and psychological well-being. I understand, believe me. I have small children and they both recognized McDonald's Golden Arches as toddlers. They love to get toys in their Happy Meals. Fortunately for me, they both like to play more than eat. My daughter rarely touches French fries, even if they are on her plate. But that's less the result of good parenting than it is simply good fortune. I do have to consider these things and make choices about them. I consider how often my kids eat fast food. When they do, I steer them toward fruit side dishes and milk, and I am glad these are available. I talk to them about nutrition and health. Parents indeed have to make the choices. I think government and media and marketers have roles to play, too. When advertisers draw us in with illusions—and especially when they present these illusions to children who are less equipped to deal with them—they share some responsibility for the consequences.

An assumption of government in a modern, developed nation is that they have a responsibility to protect consumers. And prevention is much more powerful than cure, in many cases. That is probably why the governments of developed nations around the world are stepping in to try to get something done about advertising junk food to kids. They realize it is going to be much more effective if the advertisers stop peddling these illusions than it would be to reason with consumers or to tell them what foods are healthy. Advertising is so powerful that it has the effect of encouraging people to make decisions they know consciously are not in their best interests, like eating junk food. Media imagery is powerfully motivating, and governments everywhere are dealing with the effects and considering ways to get advertisers to be less manipulative.

A recent ad slogan for McDonald's Happy Meals said that a Happy Meal has a full day's supply of happy. Some residents of the Beatles' hometown of Liverpool, England, apparently disagree. London's *Daily Mail* reported in 2008 that the Liverpool town council met and decided to ban Happy Meals because they are contributing to childhood obesity. Locals offered their support, making the following comments:[18]

"We consider it is high time that cash-hungry vultures like McDonald's are challenged over their marketing policies which are directly aimed at promoting unhealthy eating among children."

"In most Happy Meals the toy is sold with a burger containing four or five tablespoons of sugar, along with high-calorie fries and milkshakes."

"The most calorific Happy Meal—cheeseburger, small fries and chocolate milkshake—has 740 kcals, almost half of children's recommended daily allowance of 1600."

"They know that most children won't want carrots and water but put them on the menu to stave off the criticism from health campaigners."

"These fattening meals are being shamelessly promoted through free toys and it is clear that it is going to take legislation to combat the practice."

Yes, kids love toys, they love sugar, and they love fun. But no kid finds it fun to be fat, to feel unhealthy, or to be the object of ridicule from the other kids at school because of his or her weight.

And there are other reasons fast food sells, of course. Parents are busy. When mom and dad come home from working all day, it takes a lot of effort to make dinner and clean up and do all the other household tasks. It's easier for parents to feed the kids fast food, and it may also be harder for parents to resist their kids' demands when they are tired. The more the government and the public demand it, the greater the chance that we'll have healthier choices for fast food. I think it is a step in the right direction that more fast-food restaurants are offering healthier choices. If we continue to work toward improvement, I think we can, as consumers and as governments, ask for and receive food that is quick and easy to get, but healthier. I spend a fair amount of time in airports, and I have noticed that there are consistently restaurants that offer fresh fruit, like bananas. It is very convenient to know that I'll be able to find a healthy snack at the airport. The more restaurants that provide choices like this, especially in a closed system like an airport, the easier it is for consumers to find something healthy to eat.

SELLING THE DREAM: ADVERTISING WEIGHT-LOSS PRODUCTS

Another issue in the cycle of advertising both fatness and fitness is the marketing of diet pills and other "quick fix" weight-loss products and services, such as fad dieting books and foods. Diet pills have been called hope in a bottle. When an advertiser sells diet pills, he is really selling the magic bullet that consumers dream will make them attractive and will win them love and affection. Thus diet pills and fad diets represent the intoxicating dream of the immediate gratification of a fervent desire.

The National Eating Disorder Information Center, or NEDIC (www.nedic.ca), reports that 80 percent of women do not like their body shape and size, that 70 percent of women are chronically dieting, and that 76 percent of respondents to a survey considered themselves too fat, although 45 percent of those were underweight according to a doctor's chart. Perhaps most shocking, one in 10 women surveyed said they would abort a child if they knew it had a tendency to be fat. NEDIC notes that although the diet industry makes $32 billion annually, dieters have a 95 percent failure rate. That is, 95 percent of dieters regain all their lost weight in one to five years. Amid graphics promoting the celebration of "real woman" bodies, NEDIC's slogan proclaims: "It's not our bodies that need changing. It's our attitudes."[19]

In recent years, some diet pills and herbal supplements have even been linked to serious illness and death. And this is even in the context of a fair amount of public acknowledgment that diet pills do not work. For example, in a recent high-profile settlement, the Federal Trade Commission fined the makers of several top-selling diet pills a combined $25 million for making false or unsubstantiated claims of quick and dramatic weight loss.[20] Some even falsely claimed other health benefits, such as decreased risk of Alzheimer's disease and cancer! Among those who paid fines for false advertisement were the makers of TrimSpa, Xenadrine, CortiSlim, and One-A-Day Weight Smart. Consumer's Union[21] reiterated its stance that diet pills can have dangerous effects on health, including heart problems. They cited recent research that reported more than half of consumers think diet pills are safe and also erroneously believe that diet pills are regulated by the Food and Drug Administration (FDA). Diet pills are classified as supplements, like vitamins, so they are not regulated by the FDA.

We are indeed attracted to the quick fix, and marketers prey on this weakness. Sometimes diet pills are boxed, priced, and named like prescription drugs as a marketing effort to give them added credibility. Some are sold in fancy bottles to resemble boutique products. Recent research[22] analyzed how women's magazines in the United States and Korea address the issue of weight loss. Results showed that Korean women's magazines typically promote passive methods of weight loss such as diet pills, diet drinks, aromatherapy, and even so-called diet crèmes (how swanky!). The Korean magazines took on the Western ideal of beauty and thinness that has been constructed, in part, by those who wish to profit from it. The researchers concluded that women who read the magazines may learn that losing weight is easy, quick, effective, and painless. According to the magazines, all it takes is a pill, a drink, or a crème! The authors therefore called for government regulation of these messages and also encouraged the magazine publishers to take responsibility for these false messages.

Of course, as Naomi Wolf explained in the *Beauty Myth*,[23] women's magazines make money through their advertising, and much of that advertising is for beauty products. Sometimes what masquerades as a magazine article is really another advertisement. Have you ever noticed that many women's magazines have "articles" about which mascara to use, what products "work" best on different hair types, what are the hot makeup colors? If you haven't read one of these magazines, browse through one next time you are in the store. When I was younger, I used to wonder naïvely how they decided which products to mention. Now I understand that these are advertisements masquerading as articles. It actually goes further than this deception of ads-as-articles. For example, if an advertiser's company profits from breast augmentation surgery, this will influence whether the magazine runs a health article suggesting problems or concerns about this surgery.[24] Women may think they are buying entertainment, escapism, or even helpful hints. What they are really buying in many cases is essentially one big advertisement. Rather than leaving readers feeling relaxed or entertained, these types of magazines often leave them feeling inadequate or anxious and motivated to buy all kinds of products to "improve" their looks.

One of my lines of research involves teaching people to meditate using free podcasts. Right now I am conducting a study, in collaboration with Catherine Seo, Srivi Ramasubramanian, Willa Miller, and Anna DiStefano. We are exploring what kinds of meditations or other interventions help women feel better about their bodies and themselves. In a previous study I spoke about earlier, we found that you can teach self-compassion meditation via podcast and that listening to these meditations results in increased self-compassion and body satisfaction and decreased body dissatisfaction. It also results in feeling that your value is less about your physical appearance and conformity to media's ideals of the perfect body. In the follow-up study, we are exploring whether one of two different kinds of meditation might help more or less and how this compares to a cognitive intervention. Again, these studies show us one way to combat the feelings of physical inadequacy that sometimes accompany visions of "perfect" bodies in the media.

PUBLIC SERVICE ANNOUNCEMENTS

Happily, ads *can* be used to improve our health and safety. Take for example, public service announcements, or PSAs. We've all seen PSAs such as the Smokey the Bear "only you can prevent forest fires" campaign or the US Department of Agriculture's food pyramid Web site at mypyramid.gov. The nonprofit Ad Council (AdCouncil.org) uses professional advertisers to create ads, and mass media outlets donate time or space for the ads. In a recent study, marketing professor Magdalena Cismaru found that more effective PSAs factor in consumers' perceptions of how difficult it will be for them to make the life changes the PSA suggests.[25] For example, the US Department of Health and Human Services launched the Small Step PSA (www.smallstep.gov) that suggests little things people can do to lose weight and improve their health. Some of the tips include switching from whole milk to skim, eating before grocery shopping, and eating only half of your dessert. The Ad Council also produced TV and magazine ads as part of the campaign. For example, one ad shows a man's love handles gradually getting smaller with these labels, "started shooting hoops with son," "eats healthier and skips desserts," and "considering changing name to Buff Daddy."

The Ad Council's own research found that 55 percent of American children agreed that they would rather watch TV or play video games than play outside, and that 57 percent of parents said that getting their child to eat healthy food is a major battle.[26] To encourage activity in children, the Ad Council produced a PSA encouraging children to take the small step of getting up and playing for an hour a day. Some PSAs have focused on drugs, such as the famous "Just Say No" to drugs PSA or the Ad Council's current anti-steroid campaign. Let's turn now to the ways big business markets drugs to the American consumer.

PRESCRIPTION DRUGS

TrimSpa and Happy Meals are one thing, you might be thinking, but advertising does not affect the serious world of prescription drugs. If you are blissfully unaware of the marketing of prescription drugs to consumers, I hope it is because you are healthy and not in the market for a prescription drug yourself.

In the 1960s, the FDA was given authority over advertising of prescription drugs. At that time, drugs ads were usually to be found in medical journals targeting doctors. In the late 1990s, drug advertising rules were loosened, and we began to see an explosion of what are called direct-to-consumer (DTC) ads, mostly on television and in popular magazines and on the Internet. A direct-to-consumer ad is basically a commercial for a prescription drug, targeting everyday people instead of doctors or other medical professionals. These ads can appear on TV, on the Internet, or in magazines—in any everyday form of mass media.

We've all seen these DTC drug ads. An older man walks along the beach throwing a tennis ball to his golden retriever. A voice says, "Ask your doctor about" insert-drug-name-here. When I first saw these ads on TV, they really got my attention. Ask my husband! When I saw one, I would laugh out loud and proclaim, "But, it doesn't even say what the drug is used for!" I was amazed.

Time after time, I heard the ad line, "Ask your doctor if 'Drug X' is right for you." I wondered aloud, would a patient really go into her doctor's office and ask earnestly, "Doctor, is 'Drug X' right for me?" Without even knowing what condition it treats? And is the patient happy when she learns that she could use some Plavix or saddened when she learns that Propecia is not right for her? It seemed crazy to me, but now I know that it works for the drug companies. DTC ads are profitable.

Again, these marketing practices raised eyebrows to the extent that the government had to get involved. In 2005, the Congressional Research Service published a report to Congress on DTC ads for prescription drugs.[27] The report indicated that the drug industry spent $3.2 billion on DTC ads in 2003, primarily for its top 50 drugs. The drug most advertised in DTC ads was the heartburn drug Nexium, also known as the "little purple pill." Wow. When you think about it, giving the consumer an oh-so-easy, cute name like "little purple pill" implies that the consumer is like a child who needs a very easy name in order to remember it. If it were true, should such people really be responsible for choosing their own drugs, one wonders? Other drugs on the most-DTC-advertised list included sleep aid Lunesta, cholesterol drug Crestor, and allergy drug Nasonex. I bet you recognized most of those names, as I did, which shows the power of those ad dollars at work.

Drug companies say that these ads encourage people to visit their doctors and to take a more active role in their treatment. Critics say the ads can be misleading. For example, according to the report, "In September 2004, Merck & Co. withdrew its anti-inflammatory medication Vioxx from the market because studies had shown an elevated heart-attack and stroke risk with prolonged use. Questions were raised at a November 2004 Senate Finance Committee hearing about whether earlier studies by the company and others had suggested this risk in Vioxx."[28]

Research has found that seeing DTC ads does influence consumer behavior. Consumers are more likely to talk with their doctors about the drugs and to ask for a prescription after seeing DTC ads. A 2002 study[29] found that DTC ads influenced not only the doctor's prescribing the drug in question but also the diagnosis of the condition implicated. The authors found a trend that the more the drug company spent on the DTC ad, the greater the payoff in prescriptions. They noted that this was more likely to work for some drugs—seasonal allergy meds, for instance—than for others. One concern is that increases in requests for prescription drugs causes tax increases and increased healthcare costs to employers. In other words, ads targeting consumers create demand for a specific drug.

STRAIGHT TO THE HEART OF THE MATTER

Well, we know that advertisers will go a long way to get to the heart of the consumer, but this story, reported in the *Chicago Tribune*,[30] takes that sentiment to a whole new level. Ever resourceful, advertisers, it appears, are now marketing medical equipment like home heart defibrillators, making an estimated $50 million in profits from direct-to-consumer ads, up from $0 a decade before. The company Medtronic is marketing a device that shocks the heart, selling it directly to consumers for a heart-shocking $20,000 to $30,000. According to the *Chicago Tribune*:[31]

> In the campaign, dubbed "What's inside," a soft voice tells viewers they will find inside the device "10,000 more kisses ... 200 more football wins," saying it will "always be there for you—close to your heart with the power to restart it in case of sudden cardiac arrest." Dr. Sidney Wolfe, head of consumer group Public Citizens' Health Research Group, said he considers the ad highly misleading. "This is trying to frighten people and you are going to have people who are scared and uniformed saying, 'Let's not take a chance.'"

Whether it is marketing junk food to children or marketing problematic diet pills or prescription meds to adults, the one thing these advertisers have in common is businesses profiting to the detriment of the consumer. If allowed, marketing like this can have an adverse effect on the physical and mental well-being of the country in general. Persuasive messages seek to define normative behavior and ideals such as the habit of asking your doctor for a drug you've seen advertised on TV. According to what we see in the media, losing weight is easy, and eating high-fat foods isn't fattening. We're unconscious and uncritical of the power of media to move us to watch more than we want, to induce us to buy more than we want, and to take over our free time in ways that do not enrich us or make us happy. When it comes to your health, it pays to be smart about advertising.

Media and Social Identity

Our relationship with media and the ideas and things we see presented there is very personal. William James, the great American psychologist, noted that we extend our sense of self even to material goods. Advertisers can take advantage of this psychological tendency by encouraging us to think of our favorite brands as part of ourselves.

A team of researchers[1] wanted to better understand the consequences of making a favorite brand part of our self-concept. They discovered that people who identified with Starbucks, for example, responded to threats to Starbucks almost as if they had been personally threatened. Those who identified more with Starbucks showed a tendency to actually *increase* their positive attitude toward Starbucks after reading an article that was critical of Starbucks, compared with those who identified less with the brand. Furthermore, those who already had poor self-esteem were more likely than those with high self-esteem to show this pattern of defensiveness.

If you've ever wondered why people sometimes get angry and defensive when you say something negative about their favorite band, film, or show, this phenomenon is probably partly responsible. Teenagers, for instance, tend to prefer music to other media types and may feel personally offended when you question their favorite band or genre. They take it personally—because, psychologically, it is personal to them. If you insult my favorite movie hero, you've insulted me. Anyone who insults me is against me, and therefore I may not like you any more.

Of course, not everybody's the same. For some, their car is part of their identity, while for others, a car is just a practical necessity. For some people, a sports team is part of their identity, while others in the same town don't think about the team at all. (I remember in college, people would sometimes ask me if I was going to "the game" that night. I would think to myself, "Game? Huh?!")

To me, advertising is an interesting area psychologically. I believe that one can be an ethical advertiser, selling products and services that really improve one's quality of life. I also know that there are some who would sell cigarettes to a child if they could turn a profit (and some who have done just that). Also, "brand" is a broad term and could apply to a political party, a religious or charitable group, or even, roughly, to a lifestyle. Maybe there are brands that are worthy of having as part of one's identity. On the other end of the spectrum, some build the foundation of their business on the concept of creating need where there was none. Some purposefully want to make us feel bad about ourselves as long as we then buy their product as a remedy for what's "wrong" with us.

Brene Brown studies shame and vulnerability. She is well known for doing some viral TED Talks. In one of her TED talks, she says that vulnerability comes from the fear that we may not be worthy of social connection. This fear of unworthiness can come from many places, but a common one is the fear that something about our appearance makes us unworthy. It's perhaps no surprise, then, that advertisers like to press the "not worthy" button to get us to go buy that product that we hope will make us more worthy of social connection.

> Advertisers program an uneasy self-consciousness into our minds so that we are on the lookout for products that will make us look, feel, and smell better.
>
> —W. James Potter[2]

How do you feel about yourself? Women, are you thin enough, sexy enough, pretty enough? Men, are you concerned about your abs, your baldness, your, um, size? These are common concerns in great part because making us self-consciousness is profitable for media executives.

Social psychologists study how self-image and self-esteem are shaped by the mass media messages that pervade our social worlds. Because far from being just entertainment and far from not mattering at all, those screens relentlessly feed you messages about your place in the world and how you *should* feel about yourself. As Potter puts it, media "constantly program the way we think about ourselves."[3] How right he is!

On the one side, we have the producers of mass media. Their overarching goal is to get our attention so that we will be moved to buy their advertisers' products. They want to matter to us deeply. They want our money; therefore they need us to care—to be magnetically attracted so that we point our faces at their screens. On the other side, there we sit. We are drawn in by their psychology, but we're largely unaware—or in denial—about how much their messages have come to matter to us. They call us "consumers," and this is a term so commonplace that we have come to accept that perspective unquestioningly.

Is that who we are? Consumers? Is a main function in our lives really to use products that advertisers sell us?

Earlier I told you a story about a business expert who advised that the best way to get what you want out of a person is to find out what's most important to that person and exploit it for your own gain. One of the things we care most deeply about is our place in the social world. Are we good enough? Are we competitive for the most important resources in life—for example, winning a mate and an esteemed position in society? Clearly, mass media executives have tapped the self-worth gold mine over and over. It's because self-worth is such a basic human need that businesses so eagerly and successfully use it against us. If you shake our foundations you motivate us to do whatever it takes to set them right, and that, of course, includes spending money.

DOES SIZE MATTER? OR, HOW TO MAKE MEN NEUROTIC

Speaking of self-esteem, what better way to hit men below the belt than to target them, well, below the belt? In a society where men are the dominant group, men's issues tend to get less attention, but let's do something a little different and start with an example in which mass media have harmed men by targeting their sense of self-worth. And as long as I'm talking about men, I might as well go right ahead and jump into a conversation about penises.

One of the most common types of SPAM e-mail messages are those promising to enhance penis size. If one were to take the frequency of such ads as social information, then one would assume they are generated due to a major problem many men have. Of course, if you've ever been bored enough, curious enough, or tired of working enough to actually read one of these ads, you know that the ads themselves are decidedly unsubtle in telling men they have a problem. Personally, I find it particularly amusing when an ad features a quote, supposedly from a real woman, enthusiastically claiming that whatever product the company is selling has rocked her world. (I visualize these quotes as actually being written by middle-aged men in cubicles.) Of course, this is a very straightforward example of applying basic learning theory to marketing. The message is that if a man buys the product, his sex life and his masculinity will rise to all new highs. Women will find him irresistible.

As we have seen, it is often the ads themselves that create a state of want or inadequacy. Researchers from Cal State and UCLA wanted to find some reality in this media-fueled culture where masculinity and power have been equated with having a large penis. The researchers write:[4] "The flourishing penis enlargement industry indicates that at least some men worry enough about penis size to spend money on costly products and on potentially risky surgery to boost their self-confidence."

Here comes the great part. This research team—God love 'em—reports findings sure to provoke sighs of relief from many quarters. They tell the absolute truth about how big real men's penises are, and what real women actually think about penis size. I would add that an underlying assumption of this work must be that Mother Nature created the average man to be, so to speak, up for any task for which he was designed.

Let me be a part of what I consider a public service announcement and share their news. For your information, everyone, the average erect penis is 5.3 inches long, with most men ranging from 4.6 to 6 inches. Other than porn stars (done with mirrors?) or Aerosmith's *Big Ten Inch Record*, less than 3 percent of men have erect penises that are 6.9 inches or longer. There you have it. As I say to my students, don't say I never taught you anything.

As for women's attitudes, the great majority of women were satisfied with their partner's penis size. Graciously, only 6 percent of women said their partner's penis was smaller than average. In fact, the women were significantly more satisfied (85 percent) with their partner's penis than the men themselves were (55 percent). What we can take away from this, I think, is that a cultural belief—generated in great part by mass media—has caused men to lose confidence and have a distorted view of their own bodies as well as their value as men. These negative and misleading portrayals have unnecessarily harmed men's views of themselves. This case in particular is interesting because the industry was able to take advantage of a general ignorance created when people treat basic sex education as a taboo topic. It's easier to create a mythology when the facts have become obscured.

Talking about adult sexuality is one thing, but now we move to a discussion of how marketers have targeted children's basic social motives to be valued and wanted by using sex to sell them things. In the last chapter, we discussed how governmental deregulation has allowed marketers to target children directly, to the detriment of their health. We've seen how fiercely they have taken to this task, how they sell high-calorie fast food meals with toys, create whole TV shows to sell toys, and pay athletes to market junk food. Now we move into another territory that big business is using to make a profit from unsuspecting children: marketing sex and sexiness to them.

READY OR NOT, HERE THEY COME

Hey kids, are you ready to be sexy? That sounds dumb, doesn't it? But it represents the direction in which mass media are taking our children. Everywhere you look, marketers are selling sex and sexiness to younger and younger children. Now, I'm not a prude, and I don't have a problem with media content for adults that talks about sex and relationships. I'm guessing I probably don't even need to say that, after just having an extended conversation about penises, but just in case. But seriously, *not* discussing those topics with adults would be unhealthy, in fact. No, it's not even sex that is the issue, but rather the *marketing* of sexiness to children that is unhealthy. Our kids—little girls in particular—are being sold the notion that they are supposed to be sexy.

The very ubiquity of this marketing strategy may have desensitized us to its inappropriateness, at least partially. So, let's take a look at this situation for what it is by starting with a premise I think we can all agree on: it is not healthy for children to be having sex. Sexuality, ideally, develops as a child grows to maturity. In a healthy environment, children are curious about relationships and about sex and have caring adults to support their development. What they see around them supports a natural unfolding of their understanding of sexuality. But that is what takes place ideally—in a *healthy* environment. How would you describe the cultural environment in which we are raising our children when it comes to sex?

Sharon Lamb and Lyn Mikel Brown, the authors of *Packaging Girlhood: Rescuing Our Daughters from Marketers' Schemes*, are experts on the subject. They very astutely explain how girls are sold very limited notions of what it means to be a girl. A little girl is told that she is supposed to want to be a pretty pink princess. I'm sure you are familiar with this, but if not, go to the toy department of your local big box store and find the aisle that is completely pink. This is supposedly the aisle that represents what little girls all want: Barbies, Bratz, and pink princesses all the time.

Media and marketers now sell even the littlest girls on the idea that a girl's identity is wrapped up in being "sexy." There are many ways that American girls get told that this is who they are or who they should be. If you read the slogans on T-shirts sold to girls, you get the idea of the very limited identity marketers are prescribing for them. Lamb and Brown[5] give examples of these prescribed "choices," including becoming a "professional drama queen," or a "pretty princess beauty queen," or "delicious." Girls are supposed to be "hot," "sexy," "divas," and "beauties." T-shirt slogans[6] quip: "Official cheer bunny: we're hip, we hop, we're always on top," or "Come to cutie summer camp—feel the nature," or "Recess flirt—meet by the swings when the bell rings," the latter with a picture of lips in the background.

Have you looked at kids' Halloween costumes lately? Lamb and Brown point out that it is common now to see little girls' costumes that are designed to be "sexy," or to present them as little "divas." Boys' identities, as suggested by their clothes and costumes, are also very restricted. Boys are sold as tough and aggressive or even violent. I walked into my son's preschool one Halloween when he was about three and I was struck with the false division between the sexes that I was seeing. There seemed to be two choices: princess or tough guy. Boys had superhero costumes with fake "six packs" and bulging biceps. They had gritting, angry *Hulk* teeth. Girls wore gossamer pink fabric with glittery tiaras and delicate slippers. The Halloween costumes I remember from childhood were much more diverse and also much more likely to be homemade. Therefore, they really were about choosing who you wanted to be and exercising your own creativity. This was, however, not nearly as profitable to businesses that sell Halloween costumes.

I am struck by the same heavy-handed prescription for gender roles, whether it is in the toy aisles at the local big box store or in the drive-through at the fast-food restaurant. The girls' toy aisle is pink and Bratzified (yes, I made that word up). The boys' toy aisle is dark and full of ripped, muscular bodies, weaponry, and characters that fight and show off their muscles.

I've had conversations about this with my son since he was old enough to talk. I have asked him, "Jason, are there really two kinds of people in the world? Are girls really all princesses? Are boys really all aggressive?" I've told him over and over that his mom fits neither category. I wouldn't be attracted to a princess doll or a doll that shoots people. And I've noticed that Jason gets interested and involved when we have these kinds of conversations. For example, at about age five, he came home from a friend's house claiming that he was just playing a video game, "but it wasn't a 'violent video game,' mom." He made the quotation mark signs with his fingers when he said "violent video game." There's a kid who has his mother's number. But my point is that from my experience, kids appreciate it when their parents start a conversation about the kinds of things that really matter. Even if it doesn't all come out just right, it shows them that you care.

IS IT OK TO SELL LITTLE GIRLS' PANTIES THAT SAY "EYE CANDY"?

Diane Levin and Jean Kilbourne discuss selling little girls on sexuality in their book *So Sexy So Soon: The New Sexualized Childhood and What Parents Can Do to Protect Their Kids*.[7] These experts very clearly state that the problem is not that kids are learning about sex. The problem is that the media and marketers target children with sexualized images that are confusing and that undermine their healthy sexual development. Their book is filled with the real-life stories of parents and teachers who are struggling to deal with unprecedented situations, like the seven-year-old who asks what a "blow job" is, or the five-year-old who is suspended from school for saying he wanted to "have sex" with one of his classmates. In a world where there is now a series of Barbie dolls who model lingerie, where there are T-shirts for toddler boys that say "pimp squad," and where "mainstream national chains ... are selling padded bras and thong panties for young girls that feature cherries and slogans such as 'Wink-Wink' and 'Eye Candy,' the problem is not sex, but the widespread practice of undermining children's healthy sexual development for money."[8]

This raises the issue of where boys fall in this discussion. The experts say that in this environment boys learn early, even before they really know what sex is, that girls are sex objects. Girls are supposed to focus on their looks and try to please boys by looking sexy or "hot." When marketers send these messages to boys, they have already undercut boys' ability to have healthy, respectful relationships with girls. When a girl is an object rather than a person, one is pretty much as good as another.

WHY DO SEXUALITY AND AGGRESSION DRAW KIDS' ATTENTION?

Some answer criticism about selling girls a vision of themselves as sex objects with the reply that sex is natural and therefore any sexual content in the media is, by extension, only natural, too. Again, it is not sex or sexuality that is unnatural, but it is targeting children with ideas they are not ready for and packaging sexuality as sexual objectification that are the issues. A big question that is necessary to understand in this debate is why children are attracted to these sexual messages. Why does selling kids with sex draw them in? According to the authors of *So Sexy So Soon*, developmental psychology has answers for these questions, and they have to do with the way children think, feel, and react to the world around them. Any information that is unfamiliar and dramatic will grab a child's attention. Children are also drawn to concrete visual stimulation. Even if dramatic, sexy imagery or stories are somewhat scary to a small child, still she will be drawn in. She will focus on the concrete image that has been prepackaged for her, rather than questioning it or putting it in context. For instance, when a child sees another child dressed sexually in an advertisement, the child probably doesn't understand that the girl in the ad is an actress who has been paid to pretend to be a certain way. The child certainly does not know that the entire ad was the idea of some executives who most likely were wealthy White men, or that it was created to make someone money. Also, if the actress in the ad is smiling or having fun, the child looking at the ad will tend to take it at face value—that this is what the child in the ad wants and enjoys. And since children do not understand media messages as well as adults can, they will not naturally analyze and resist them in the way that would best protect them from other people's agendas.

Another reason I think that selling with sex works is that sex and belonging are basic needs. They get our attention because we are organisms designed first and foremost to survive and reproduce. These responses are adaptive and tend to sustain the species. What is not adaptive is when businesses exploit and twist our natural tendencies for their own financial gain.

SHOULD KINDERGARTEN GIRLS WEAR THE SAME CLOTHES AS TEENS?

It used to be that clothes for kindergarten girls were different from clothes for teens, but this has changed. Marketers are now often selling the same styles to the five-year-olds as to the 15-year-olds. As authors Lamb and Brown rightly emphasize, big business is now selling our little girls on an idea called "girl power," which is patently not about real power. Is a nine-year-old in a camisole or a shirt that shows her belly powerful in any substantive sense? Today's girls are being sold "very limited choices about who they can be alongside continuous pleas for them to shop, primp, chat, and do the things girls are 'supposed to do.'"[9] While girls should be supported and encouraged to be real individuals, they are sold this fake image of who it's OK to be.

As with sugary breakfast foods, bubbly beverages, and candy, marketers sell a brand of sexuality to children knowing that it is not healthy for them, knowing it will make them anxious. They *hope* their targets become so anxious that they will be motivated to buy the products that will supposedly "fix" them.

"While products aimed at tween girls promise perfect faces and bodies, friends and boyfriends, the marketers and manufacturers don't have to confront the negative impact on girls: the confusion about sexuality and romantic relationships, the anxiety about weight and appearance, the struggle with popularity and fitting in. No, they leave that to you [the parent]. . . At a time when daughters could be developing skills, talents, and interests that will serve them well their whole life, they are being enticed into a dream of specialness through pop stardom and sexual objectivity that will derail other opportunities."[10]

HOW NOT TO DRESS YOUR DAUGHTER

In her book *Stop Dressing Your Six-Year-Old like a Skank*, comedian and mother Celia Rivenbark recalls an experience that's been shared by mothers of daughters across the country. Leaving behind softer, sweeter clothing designed for the littlest girls, Celia found herself staring down the racks of clothes designed for her now size 7 daughter and was seriously dismayed. It did not make sense to her that her six-year-old was now supposed to dress in the same clothes as an 18-year-old heading for college. She astutely noted that if, as these "choices" imply, you are supposed to dress your little daughter like a young woman going clubbing, then your daughter will miss the fun of being a child, among other things. When she told the store clerk that all these clothes looked like prostitute wear, she was told that all the moms say that. Like moms everywhere, Celia is uncomfortable with little girls wearing shorts with the words JUICY or DELICIOUS across the rear end. She does not want to shop in a department she thinks should be called "L'il Skanks" or to buy the "little ladies of the night" look for a daughter who should be dressing for the monkeybars, not for the runway or the street corner. Here's how Celia put it: "I get it. Now that my kid is practically of child-bearing age (is six the new seventeen?) I must choose … from t-shirts that scream things like BABY DOLL and JAIL BAIT not to mention a rather angry GIRLS RULE AND BOYS DROOL where an embroidered flower and buzzing bee should be. When did this happen? Who decided that my six year old should dress like a Vegas showgirl? And one with an abundance of anger issues at that?"[11]

My colleague sociologist Beth Wright and I have team-taught a course on gender in society. In this course, we have had our students form teams and go to different types of stores, looking for clothes for boys and girls of different ages. Our student reporters come back and tell the class about what they've seen. They show pictures of the clothes on the market today for children of various ages. I am struck by how these college students are really interested and concerned about what they are seeing. They, too, think the clothes designed even for the littlest girls look like they are made for prostitutes, and they don't like it that their little sisters have mostly bad options to choose from. My female college students have also been very honest and frank about how they navigated these issues themselves. The young women talk about feeling the pressure to wear what everyone is wearing, while at the same time feeling uncomfortable with it. Some talk about coming to a point at which they decided they needed to present themselves in such a way that people would respect them, rather than going for the oversexed pop star look. And the male college students are outspoken as well, talking about how they see that girls who dress with the oversexed look are attracting guys who want to use them, not guys who would care about them. And that's an excellent point, because this is not just about sex. It is about how males and females understand and relate to each other in all kinds of ways.

I've talked with moms of little girls, and they, too, are distressed about the lack of good choices and the abundance of inappropriate items made available to them by marketers. Several of my friends and colleagues who are moms and grandmas of little girls have a problem with the clothes being offered to their girls. Moms have told me over and over about the conversations they have with their daughters in clothing store dressing rooms while overhearing other moms and daughters in nearby dressing rooms having the same conversations. Moms and dads have told me that they have taken to buying shorts from the boys' section for their little daughters because the ones in the girls' section are too short. Friends have said they order shirts and shorts for their little girls from classic catalogues like Land's End, which they consider one of the last bastions of "non-skank" wear for their little girls. When I hear this, I feel bad because I know not everyone can afford to order from a higher end catalogue. Along the same lines, less-educated people may be more likely to accept what they are being offered as normal and healthy. Or they may know that they don't like what they see in the stores, but they may not have the skills and knowledge to understand what the effects of dressing their daughters in the typical oversexed-kitten girl wardrobe might be. And if they do, they may well feel powerless to change the system. And do you know what? Dressing your little girl should not be this hard! Marketers should not be allowed to undermine our parenting, let alone our children's health.

THE AMERICAN PSYCHOLOGICAL
ASSOCIATION MAKES A STATEMENT

The American Psychological Association (APA) is the largest association of psychologists in the world. Central to the APA's mission[12] is to use psychology in the public interest in order to advance public health and welfare. This means using psychological knowledge to benefit society and to improve people's lives.[13] In that spirit and with public concern over the issue increasing, in 2005 the APA established the Task Force on the Sexualization of Girls. Their charge was to report on the current psychological understanding of the influence of the sexualization of girls by mass media and popular culture. In their report, they were to make recommendations for everything from public awareness to new research and public policy.

What did the task force find? From TV and movies, to video games, the Internet, and magazines, they found a deep and pervasive sexualization of girls and women across virtually every popular form of media. Females were much more likely than males to be sexualized. The task force published a definition of sexualization, which included presenting a person's value as coming from his or her sexuality. According to the task force, a sexualized girl is an object of other people's agendas, rather than an agent actively asserting her own will. When a girl is sexualized, others have imposed sexuality on her, and have narrowly defined a specific physical appearance she must attain and have equated it with sexiness.

What is the cost to girls and young women when the mass media and the broad culture represent them consistently as being valued for their appearance and their worth as sex objects? The APA Task Force reports clear and demonstrable damages that undercut both the physical and psychological well-being of girls and women. The sexualization of girls and women promotes eating disorders. Girls change the way they eat because of how media portray who they are supposed to be. Psychologically, exposure is associated with depression and low self-esteem. Girls and women feel badly about themselves because they compare themselves to this media image of who they are supposed to be, and they feel that they do not measure up. As a consequence of this narrow view of what it means for a girl or a woman to be a valued member of our culture, females experience greater self-image problems. They deal with emotional issues such as shame and anxiety. They deal with body shame. Finally, they develop an unhealthy sexual self-image. Being a psychologist, I could tell it to you in more detail from a scientific perspective, but it comes to this: we are making our girls and women sick by tolerating the pervasive misrepresentation of femininity in the mass media.

HOW DID IT GET THIS WAY?

Ultimately, this is *not even about sex*. It is about money. Advertisers don't care about our sex lives; they care about getting their hands inside our wallets and purses. Simply put, in the current social order, it is advantageous for mass media to make us feel bad about ourselves so that we are motivated to spend money to fix what's "wrong" with us. Mass media are tapping into a bottomless pit of motivation because if we are always losing, we are always highly motivated to get on a winning path. For example, as noted media scholar Jean Kilbourne[14] so rightly points out, there are beauty standards set for women that are so high we are virtually all doomed to "fail." But that doesn't stop us from spending money trying not to fail. And nobody cares if this unending failure robs us of our self-worth, not to mention time, energy, and money.

As a college professor, I have worked with many young women over the years. I have talked with them and I have read their journals. I can tell you that there is a lot of pain out there and a lot of distorted self-images. If I were to make a list of what motivates me most strongly in my career, among the top motives would be the desire to help take away this deep pain that so many are suffering. I think about how these young women's lives could be happier and healthier and how their attention could be more focused on the positive and I want to help them get there. I think about my own daughter, and I want to make it better for her, too.

BIG MONEY CHANGED THE RULES FOR THE LITTLE GUY

We can look back at US history and see pretty easily how this happened. Historically, the US government—through groups like the FCC and FTC (Federal Communications Commission and Federal Trade Commission)—has been in the practice of protecting children from harmful products and advertising. However, lobbyists for big media and marketing companies successfully moved the US Congress to deregulate how they sell to children. Deregulation basically means fewer rules that restrict big companies. For our kids, that essentially means that the government bowed to the lobbyists and decided it was open season on selling to children. This "no rules" kind of environment put the fox in charge of the henhouse, with predictable results. Advertisers started meeting openly to discuss how best to target children. For example, they started the practice of making entire TV shows for kids that were just commercials to sell toys featured in the show, something that hadn't been possible under the previous rules. They began the cross-marketing strategies that are so prevalent now that we may have forgotten the days when they didn't exist. Cross-marketing, as discussed in the section of Chapter 6 on food marketing and children, involves selling a theme across products. For example, it's cross-marketing in action when your child's fast-food meal, breakfast cereal, fruit snacks, and school folder all sport the same TV star or characters from the latest movie.

"TELLING STORIES" ABOUT OTHER PEOPLE

I grew up in the Midwest, but I've lived in the American South now for over a decade, so I claim dual citizenship. Southerners have a delightful way of phrasing things, and since I love language, my ears perk up when I hear an interesting one. Southerners love indirection. If you are a liar, it wouldn't be neighborly to call you one, so we'll say something more charming. We'll say, for example, that you are "telling a story." So "telling a story" means lying. And if you are cheating, you are not "having an affair," you are "stepping out" on your spouse. I love that one! It sounds so quaint! But back to the quaint habit of "telling stories"—this is a great characterization for media scholars because it captures so beautifully how the media can misrepresent people by the stories they tell about them.

Bad Rap

We've talked about how we form our personal identities as a consequence of who the media tell us we should be. Now let's look at a couple of examples that show how we form impressions of other people or groups through the mass media. Recently Melinda Burgess, Beth Wright, and I[15] investigated the "stories" that rap music tells about women—especially African American women—and about African American men. One reason it is particularly important to study media representations of numerical minorities is that White people often live in rather segregated neighborhoods and don't always have much racially diverse contact. If you don't have many face-to-face interactions with people who are different from you, you may rely more heavily on the stories the mass media tell you about who members of other groups are.

Focusing on "hardcore" or "gangsta" rap, we asked college students what typical songs in this genre are about, what the typical video shows, what the rappers are like, and what rappers say about women in the songs. It's a common mistake (an urban legend?) to believe that most people who listen to hardcore rap are African American. In fact, as the industry is well aware, their target audience is White—young White males, specifically. Our sample of about 200 college students (75 percent White, which is similar to the general US population) also believed that African American men are most likely to listen to hardcore rap. When I gave expert testimony to Congress in 2007, the big media executives (mostly older, White men) and rappers were there. The big media chief executive officers (CEOs) and rappers were aware of the idea that one thing that sells rap music to White suburban kids is the appeal of the "dangerous minority" Black stereotype. Whites want to vicariously enjoy a subculture that they see as cooler and edgier than theirs. Another thing that came out of the discussion was the argument that rap benefits the community that it comes from. Actually, research out of Vanderbilt University[16] documents that at its start, hip-hop and rap were evocative of the culture from which they emerged, and were also anti-corporate. It's only when the rich, White CEOs saw that rap was marketable (to White suburbanites) that rap content changed into the stereotypical violent and misogynistic brand that is now widely criticized.

Our study showed that our sample of college students believed strongly that the rappers and the industry benefit from rap music, not the community from which the music came. What did these college students think about rappers? In order of frequency, they described the typical rapper as a gangster, Black, a thug, rich, and disrespectful to women. Of the respondents who listed "Black" as a characteristic of rappers, 20 percent used a variation of the "n" word. What did they think rap songs were about? The most common responses were sex, drugs, women, and violence. These themes match up with research that has analyzed the content of top-selling rap songs. When asked how the rappers refer to women, the top answers were ho/whore, bitch, slut, "shawty," and sexy.

In general, this group of 200 college students thought that hardcore rap portrays African American women and men in very negative ways. They believe rap songs and videos characterize the men as dangerous, violent, criminal, disrespectful to women, and focused on money and acquiring things in a pretty stereotypical and tasteless way—flashy cars, prostitutes, and "bling," for instance. They think the genre shows a vision of Black women as sexualized and degraded. Let's take a closer look at the words they believe rappers call women: whore, bitch, slut, shawty, and sexy. First, "shawty," if you haven't heard, is a derivative of shorty, which used to refer to a child but now is used as a term of affection for a friend or girlfriend. In mainstream culture, a bitch is an overbearing, mean woman. When you "bitch" about something, you are complaining. Talking about "bitches" in rap music, the word takes on a different meaning. It means someone you dominate and use. If you are "my bitch," you are my servant, sexual and otherwise. A group of "bitches" are the sex objects in the brood of a player or hustler. Whore/ho and slut are words that degrade female sexuality, making the argument that women's sexuality is dirty, promiscuous, and predatory.

Actually, you know what word perfectly describes the characterization of women in rap music? Rapacious. No, really. I love plays on words, but you have to admit, this one is pretty perfect. According to the Encarta World English dictionary, "rapacious" means "greedy and grasping, especially for money, and sometimes willing to use unscrupulous means to obtain what is desired." Though I take great delight in word play, I'm actually heading toward something deeper here. Characterizing a woman as your bitch and as a whore is sending out the message that women are rapacious. When you call someone a whore, you're putting out this degrading image of women as playing men for money and as using their sexuality to do it. Even your girlfriend, or a member of your promiscuous brood of women, is your "bitch." She does what you want, sexually and otherwise. As the APA Task Force on the Sexualization of Girls and Women rightly points out, when you make someone an object, you are saying that she is really worthless in that she is to be used and then tossed aside. Any one of them will serve the purpose.

DOMESTIC VIOLENCE MEDIA COVERAGE: HOW BOOKS, TV AND MAGAZINES HAVE INFLUENCED HOW WE UNDERSTAND AND ADDRESS INTIMATE PARTNER VIOLENCE

Now, let's move on to another issue that affects the identities of thousands of women in the United States alone: intimate partner violence (IPV). Intimate partner violence (also known as domestic violence) did not begin in the 1970s, but public consciousness of the issue did emerge in a very real way in that decade. In 1974, Englishwoman Erin Pizzey published *Scream Quietly or the Neighbours Will Hear*[17] . On the cover were pictures of physically abused women, beaten and bruised. *Scream Quietly* brought public attention to domestic violence, which at that time was more likely to be called wife beating, wife battering, or wife abuse. Erin Pizzey also opened the first shelter for victims of domestic violence in a London suburb in 1971. Around the same time, Woman House, the first battered women's shelter in the United States, opened its doors and what became known as the shelter movement began.

Intentionally and unintentionally, both helpful and harmful media messages get sent and received. Messages about domestic violence are communicated in a variety of ways, ranging from news reports to more detailed accounts like those that appeared in Pizzey's book, to those from less serious outlets like entertainment magazines. What we choose to talk about and what we choose to ignore all contribute to public opinion about intimate partner violence. Part of the reason that public opinion about intimate partner violence is important is that it shapes public policy, which, in turn shapes how the police respond to victims and influences financial support for shelters and other social services. Another reason that mass media coverage of intimate partner violence is important is the teaching component. It is a way for people to better understand one aspect of relationships, to be aware of potential problems, and to know more effective ways of responding. This is important for current and future victims, for friends and family, and for members of the culture at large. More broadly, it is a way for us all to understand one aspect of the human condition.

Once I attended a yoga class sponsored by my local Women's Resource Center. After doing yoga together, the group of women sat down to a light lunch and we began socializing. A local woman, roughly my own age, had brought her mother to the event. The mother heard that I was a psychologist who had done some research on violence, which sparked a passionate soliloquy on intimate partner violence. She said she'd recently read a magazine article about an abused wife. She was emphatic that *she* would never have allowed her husband to beat her. If he tried, she would have left him immediately. What was wrong with these women who let themselves be abused? Metaphorically, my jaw dropped when I heard these opinions. Didn't this lady know that intimate partner violence situations are much more complicated than she was suggesting? Didn't she understand that there are many reasons women don't leave abusive situations? I told her I was fortunate to have never been a victim of intimate partner violence myself, but I understood that it was a complex picture. To blame the victims is really to do them a disservice—literally adding insult to injury.

Also at the table with us was my friend, who was the director of the women's center. She had seen many women come to her doors to escape a violent, abusive situation. We tried to explain gently that the women who are victims of intimate partner violence are not unintelligent, masochistic, or really fundamentally different from any other woman. Abusive relationships are often characterized by a larger pattern of coercion. Abusive men control their partners' lives using strategies such as limiting their access to transportation and communication, thus keeping them isolated from friends and family and from the benefits of a social support system. An abuser can sabotage his partner's attempts to work or to get an education, thus keeping her financially dependent. A common tactic is for an abuser to criticize his partner, saying she is unattractive, unintelligent, or unworthy, and lucky to have a man at all. If he thinks she might try to escape the situation, he uses other coercive tactics, such as threatening to take the children or to harm or even kill her or the children. The terrible fact is, abusers do often harm or kill their ex-partners after the partner has left. They do continue to stalk or threaten the victim and to involve the children.

So victims of intimate partner violence are often not in a situation in which they can walk out the door so easily. As Evan Stark explains eloquently in his 2007 book *Coercive Control: How Men Entrap Women in Personal Life*[18], intimate abuse goes beyond the physical to psychological manipulation and coercion. In fact, victims report that the mental anguish they experience can be worse than the physical pain. Often the victim entered the relationship as a young woman and the abuse came on gradually. Part of the cycle of coercion is a pattern whereby the abuse starts slowly and is often followed by expressions of sorrow and vows never to repeat the abuse. Women want to believe this of the men they love, and many do and get caught in the trap. It is a psychological bind. All of this makes it harder for police and other interested parties to understand the total situation and makes it more likely for the victim to be blamed.

One-third of American women report being physically or sexually abused by a husband or partner at some time in their lives. Current estimates are that approximately 4 million women are abused each year. Reports have indicated that about 25 percent of females who go to the emergency room for treatment are the victims of domestic abuse. A third of teenagers say that they know someone who has been punched, kicked, slapped, choked, or otherwise physically hurt by her partner. (Visit loveisnotabuse.com for these and more facts about domestic and dating violence.) Given these statistics, I wondered at the time why this mother was so quick to blame the victims of intimate partner violence. Why, in this country where intimate partner violence is so commonplace, was it possible that women can have very little knowledge about these important issues?

How has the public learned about abusive relationships, and what are the implications? To address this question, Kathryn Thill and I[19] investigated how popular American magazines have talked about intimate partner violence over a 30-year period. As it turned out, this investigation became a multimedia story because the magazines covered issues and events that took place or were documented in other media, such as on television. We began with 1974, the year *Scream Quietly or the Neighbours Will Hear* was first published and also the year that the first battered women's shelter in the United States opened its doors, collecting all the American popular magazine articles on intimate partner violence that were published that year. Moving forward, we did the same for the years 1984, 1994, and 2004. We did this initially because we wanted to take a sample of articles that was both deep (every article published in every American magazine in that year) and broad (every 10 years so as to cover potential changes over time).

As it turned out, selecting these years made historical sense as well because there were watershed events relevant to intimate partner violence or highly publicized news stories relevant to intimate partner violence that took place in each of the years 1974, 1984, 1994, and 2004. Relevant events in 1974 included the publication of *Scream Quietly* and the opening of the first American battered women's shelter; 1984 saw the broadcast of *The Burning Bed*, a film that sparked public conversation about intimate partner violence. In 1984, Congress passed the Family Violence Prevention and Services Act. In 1994, the world watched and listened to the trial of O. J. Simpson and heard about his past abusive relationship with murdered ex-wife Nicole Brown Simpson. That same year, President Bill Clinton signed into law the Violence Against Women Act—the most far-reaching legislation in modern history concerning intimate partner violence. Later that same year, the world was drawn into another story of an abusive marriage—this time that of John and Lorena Bobbitt. In 2004, Scott Peterson was convicted of the murder of his wife Laci and their unborn child, and later that year President Bush signed the Unborn Victims of Violent Crime law. Sadly, intimate partner violence scholars have long identified pregnancy as a time when partner violence against women *increases*, rather than decreases as one might have imagined.

In 1984, the made-for-television movie *The Burning Bed* garnered wide attention and critical acclaim. *The Burning Bed*, starring Farrah Fawcett, dramatized the true story of Francine Hughes, telling how she met and married Mickey Hughes and how Mickey repeatedly and brutally abused her. One reason the story was so compelling to the public is that one night, after Mickey beat, raped, threatened, and verbally abused her, Francine snapped. As Mickey lay passed out drunk, Francine poured gasoline over him, took their children out to the car, and came back in and lit Mickey and the bed aflame, killing him—thus the title *The Burning Bed*. Also fascinating to the public was the fact that Francine was acquitted of all charges in Mickey's death due to reasons of temporary insanity.

Here we have a true case of intimate partner violence, dramatized on television and discussed in magazines and other media outlets. This story provides an example in which there are layers of media coverage and discourse about an important social issue. Looking back, what can we learn about intimate partner violence from this public discourse? How did American magazines cover *The Burning Bed*? What we found for this case was broadly true of intimate partner violence coverage in American magazines across the 30-year span we studied. When American magazines discuss intimate partner violence, they tend to do so in a way that is sensational or shallow, or both. We found that many times these magazine articles about abusive husbands and abused wives simply retold the lurid and shocking details of episodes of assault or murder. While *The Burning Bed* involved dramatizing Francine's experiences of being beaten, it went beyond that in a way that was potentially helpful to other victims and in a way the magazine articles about the story did not.

If most articles support the myth that abuse is the woman's problem and it is up to her to fix it, then readers may well come to believe it themselves, as the belief is apparently widely accepted. If journalists believe it, and no one contradicts it, it must be true. Also, consensus dictates that if most victims can solve their own problems, I should be able to solve mine as well. Furthermore, the availability heuristic—the idea that the more easily we can think of certain examples, the more typical the examples are—comes into play. If the "typical" intimate partner violence story is for a woman to escape successfully and solve her own problem, then that must be what most women do.

Remember that two of the three primary motives for reading magazines are largely social—to gather information about what people are talking about and to see how your life fits into the picture. Since intimate partner violence affects so many Americans, misinformation in magazine coverage does not satisfy the reader's intended motives in reading the magazine. In one article, for example, readers are misinformed that victims of intimate partner violence are secretly masochistic—a well-known myth. A woman reports that her husband dominated her from the day they met and she always *wanted* to be dominated by him. Social psychologists often cite people's desire to believe in a just world—if women are abused, they must deserve it because the world is a fair place. This myth certainly supports that belief, and by extension it hurts victims again. If it is their fault, why should we help?

FANTASY AND REALITY—MORE GRAY THAN BLACK AND WHITE

After *The Burning Bed* aired nationally, related news stories followed. Shelters received record numbers of calls, from both men and women, wanting counseling about their domestic situations. There were reports of men beating their wives in response to the film. In Chicago, a battered wife watched *The Burning Bed* and then shot her husband.

Again, we go back to a central message of this book on the social psychology of the media. Stories in the media mean something real to the people who watch them. The social messages are complex and interact with the life experiences of the person watching. We have to stop thinking there are two separate notions, one called fantasy and one called reality, and that our processing of fictional stories does not affect this real thing we call life.

The Burning Bed was based on a true story, which has been shown in the social psychologists' laboratory to be more likely to incite aggression in the viewer. To make the point that this applies to fiction as well as nonfiction, let's consider a related, but purely fictional, film. Farrah Fawcett, who portrayed Francine Hughes in *The Burning Bed* to critical acclaim, also starred in the movie *Extremities*, the story of a woman who turns the tables on a rapist who humiliated and tortured her by humiliating and torturing him. One tagline for *Extremities* was the subtle "Alone and vulnerable. The perfect victim ... or so he thought." A less subtle tagline said, "What she did to survive is nothing compared to what she'll do to get even." (For more on *The Burning Bed* or *Extremities*, visit the Internet Movie Database at imdb.com).

BBC reporter Barry Norman interviewed Fawcett[20] at the time of the film's British release, questioning the potential danger of the film's plot, saying: "Any film story which treats women as objects to be brutalized should be handled with extreme care because the world, alas, has more than its share of lunatics and cretins who believe that's precisely how women should be treated." When Norman comments that Farrah's character's torture of the potential rapist makes her just about as bad as he is, Farrah replies, "I tried my best to get down there where you men hover sometimes ... [T]he only way I could see to vindicate myself was to do that ... the only way to make him feel as scared and degraded and inadequate as I had felt." She continued by describing personal experience with physical abuse and humiliation as her inspiration for playing the film role the way she did. When pressed on the point of whether the film might encourage bad men to copycat the crime in the film, she replied that she did not find the portrayal in any way encouraging of violence.

This interview raises a number of important issues. First, we see again an actress being asked to give expert opinion about rape. Being an actress does not bar you from being an expert on rape, but it certainly does not guarantee it either. The interview of the actress about the serious issues explored in the film raises intriguing issues. How does the public separate acting from reality? Is it totally separate? We've already seen that Farrah Fawcett has both personal experience and interest in women's issues and intimate partner violence. She reported herself that she used her own experience to play these roles. Again, are there really two things here—one clearly fantasy and one reality?

I think this line of reasoning invites one to look closer at portrayals and how viewers construe them. In a classic social psychological investigation of attribution—how we explain people's behaviors—psychologists Jones and Harris[21] asked participants to read aloud a speech either defending or criticizing the politics of Cuban dictator Fidel Castro. Other students were asked to judge whether each speaker's attitude was consistent with his or her speech. Remember, the students had no choice as to whether they were defending or criticizing Castro; they were simply asked to do it. Results indicated that the audience generally believed that the speakers endorsed the beliefs espoused by their speeches. This finding is an example of a very common social bias known as the fundamental attribution error—we assume that people's internal attitudes are consistent with their behaviors. The fundamental attribution error is basically synonymous with the term "correspondence bias," which means that we have a bias to think people's behavior matches (corresponds to) their attitudes.

I think we can apply this idea to acting, which of course is one of the main things we watch in all our free time spent staring into screens. We often assume that an actor's behavior matches his internal beliefs and attitudes. So, if an actor often plays villains, we assume he is an evil sort of man in real life. When Farrah plays a victim who fights back, we assume she personally endorses her character's beliefs. This is meaningful for a number of reasons, some of which have been discussed in other contexts. For one thing, when people identify with aggressors, they are more likely to emulate them. When people think what they see on the screen is more realistic, they are also more likely to act like the actor in question. I make these points not to say that people should or should not emulate the character Francine Hughes but to underline the social psychology in action here. We most emphatically do not say to ourselves, "This is acting. It is not related to reality and it has no lessons I can apply in my life." We pretty much believe the exact opposite. In other words, the concept of media as pure fantasy is—well, pure fantasy.

REAL REALITY MEDIA

We know that one-third of women will face domestic abuse in a lifetime. That's a staggering statistic. Given how many of us this issue affects, are there helpful media resources available? There are indeed. In fact, I've mentioned some already. We saw how *The Burning Bed* presented some realistic, important, and pretty novel information about intimate partner violence. Also, the Web site loveisnotabuse.com has some practical information, and there is a special emphasis on teens and dating violence, which is important for the prevention of intimate partner violence. How about magazines? Our study revealed just two articles, one from *Oprah's O Magazine*[22] called "She's Come Undone," and one from *Ladies' Home Journal*[23] called "Wife Beating," that were great resources. Those were too few, given the dozens of articles published in those four years that broached the issue, yet failed to do it service.

Having said that, I want to describe the best magazine resource I have found on intimate partner violence. This magazine did not appear in the years we studied, and if it had, we would not have found it in our search because it is not available everywhere. Even so, happily it reaches many women who can benefit from it. The magazine is called *Diane* and it is published and distributed by the *Curves for Women* fitness centers. In the fall of 2006, *Diane* published an issue on the faces of intimate partner violence. The cover page showed images of 63 women who have survived intimate partner violence. As I read Abigail Esman's story, "If I Could Close My Eyes,"[24] in the issue, I got chills—the good kind. Here was reality. There was no Cinderella story, no blaming the victim, no shallow coverage. Here was a story that explained clearly and directly things that are difficult to understand. What is the abuse really like? How could the beatings not be the worst part of the abuse?

> Four million American women a year are abused by their partners—one every 10 seconds. We've all seen ... the photographs of women made up to look bruised. But they don't tell the real story. The real story is not the blood or the bruises or the shattered bones. The real story is the part you cannot see. It is the part we feel long after we've ceased noticing that it hurts when he hits us. It's the fear, fear that follows us everywhere, rising and falling with the events of the day, looming over us, a black shadow

… that keeps our shoulders hunched as we try to become invisible, recoil from the blows, verbal or physical we know will come.

As to the question of how people end up in abusive relationships, I'll let Abigail tell it in her own words:

The ascent of abuse is gradual. It begins very slightly and gets progressively hotter, so that by the time the bones are shattered in your jaw and you are telling people stories of falling down stairs, it doesn't even seem all that bad.

And there is the question that we seem to always come back to: Why do women stay with abusers? Again, Abigail has a way of speaking directly and with eloquence:

In 1978, the prevailing view was still that battered women were masochists. But I wasn't a masochist. It was just that leaving seemed—and usually is—at least as dangerous as staying. There was the social stigma, the very real fear of retribution. Better, I thought, to endure the beatings—which, I was always certain, wouldn't happen. . . . I loved him even though he didn't exist outside my own imagination. I didn't understand that the man I loved was my own mirage … from one moment to the next he became a different person, a gentleman, a lover, holding me as if the beating had never happened. He even told me sometimes that it hadn't … now … I see that the man who once wept as he held his dying cat in his arms was the same man who had caused its death in the first place—and that this moment was the entirety and the whole of our life together.

Curves is a fitness center for women. As a member at a local *Curves*, I have noticed that *Diane* magazine has often been given away or sold for a dollar, so the magazine is accessible to many women. This special issue on intimate partner violence gave great practical advice and contacts. It listed companies that make special provisions to aid victims of intimate partner violence, tips for helping a daughter or a friend, and practical tips to help a woman cope in an abusive situation (see Box 7.1).

Thus far, I have talked about entertainment magazines that tend to perpetuate myths about intimate partner violence, and those that challenge these myths. My colleagues and I[25] asked the question "What difference can the best and worst women's magazine articles about IPV make to their readers?" In an article titled, "What a Difference a Frame Makes," we report the results of a study about the differences in attitudes and beliefs of people who

Box 7.1.

PRACTICAL ADVICE ABOUT DOMESTIC VIOLENCE

Helping a daughter: Make sure you and your daughter have conversations about what makes a healthy relationship. Advise her to be wary and to talk to you if a boyfriend tells her what she should wear, gives her a cell phone and calls any time, or threatens violence during arguments.

Practical information for domestic abuse victims: pack a bag with important items and consider keeping it at a family member's house; create a code word that means you need the police and tell it to those you trust; in conflicts, try to get to a room you can lock or can leave from. If you have left: give a photograph of the abuser to your coworkers and children's principal and teachers, contact a domestic violence agency for advice on staying safe. Call 1-800-799-7233 for the *National Domestic Violence Hotline.*

To donate a cell phone to a survivor, go to www.ncadv.org/donate.

Adapted from *Diane: The Curves Magazine*, Fall 2006, special report on domestic violence.

read entertainment magazine articles that either perpetuated or challenged these myths about intimate partner violence. As predicted, those who read myth-perpetuating articles were more likely to believe myths about intimate partner violence than those exposed to myth-challenging articles, including the one quoted above from *Diane* magazine. One conclusion of this research is that magazine publishers better serve their readers if they avoid giving misinformation about such serious issues as intimate partner violence. If a magazine would not misinform its readers about breast cancer or depression, it should not misinform them about another serious issue, especially one with such widely documented and devastating costs to women, including its readership.

Before we leave the topic of media and identity, let me share one more study with you, this one on a very different topic. I share this study as another example of the positive side of mediated communications.

We've been talking a lot about how we understand who we are and how this relates to messages delivered via media. One issue that has been well documented in the psychological literature as contributing to the suffering of many is that of body image dissatisfaction. The thing about the body image dissatisfaction literature that struck me was that it communicated a widespread problem that seemed to defy solution. Even well-educated women and feminist women, even thin women, fell victim to body image dissatisfaction. It occurred to me that one approach that had not been tried was meditation. Meditation has been documented as a health practice with a myriad of benefits, both physical and psychological. It also costs little and has no side effects.

With this in mind, Ellen Albertson, Kristen Neff, and I[26] conducted a study in which women of a variety of ages took part in a three-week program addressing the benefits of self-compassion meditation for reducing body image dissatisfaction and increasing self-compassion. Briefly, self-compassion relates to three factors: being kind to yourself, cultivating mindfulness, and understanding that we all share a common humanity. (For more information on self-compassion, go to self-comassion.org.) The meditation treatment was delivered via digital media in the form of podcasts and was delivered to the treatment group first, and then to a wait-listed control group. Results indicated that, compared to controls, the women who meditated increased their self-compassion, decreased their negative body image, and increased their positive body image. One of the specific outcomes we measured was contingency of self-worth for appearance. This factor measures the degree to which women believe our self-worth is related to our physical appearance.

This study demonstrates, among other things, that one's view of oneself and one's healthy relationship to the self can be improved by simply listening to a meditation podcast. This is an example of how media can be used for social good, improving the well-being of women of all ages at little cost to them. With simple podcasts, we were able to show health benefits in an area that had stubbornly resisted treatment in the past.

I hope that one of the messages that you take away from this chapter is that what we expose ourselves to in the media, even in entertainment media, can make a real difference in our lives. Media messages can uplift us and help us live healthier lives, or they can perpetuate ignorance and a debilitating status quo. If someone tells you that the ideas we read about in a magazine or listen to on a podcast don't make any difference in our lives, I hope you will now be able to explain to that person some of the ways it makes quite a difference.

The Social Psychology of Political Coverage

In 2013, the US Congress held hearings to discuss whether or not to send missiles into Syria to intervene in the ongoing war there. While attending a congressional hearing on this issue, Senator John McCain was caught by the *Washington Post* playing poker on his iPhone. The *Washington Post* shared a photo of the senator's iPhone screen on their live blog of the event. Senator McCain responded by tweeting: "Scandal! Caught playing iPhone game at 3+ hour Senate hearing—worst of all I lost!"[1] Later, in an interview with CNN's Wolf Blitzer, McCain smiled, cringed, and repeated that the worst thing was that he lost money in the game. The Daily Show created an animated GIF of the McCain smile-and-cringe "you caught me!" moment. David Letterman quipped, "Senator John McCain, during a Senate session on whether we're going to teach Syria a lesson, was caught playing online poker. I was stunned. John McCain knows how to use a computer? Really?"[2] Citizens posted the image of McCain playing poker, adding captions like "Syria: so boring," or "I'm 'all in' on bombing those bastards." A group of supporters started a Facebook page called the "McCain poker club." Others tweeted photos of McCain playing poker with dogs; sometimes the dogs were other members of Congress.

This is an example of one discreet event in the news cycle and how it was discussed by a spectrum of sources, from the *Washington Post* and CNN to the political comedy shows, to citizens. Notable is how the story quickly crossed a variety of media and how the images and issues of the story were presented, transformed, and re-created. This is the era of new political media that we live in. For years, many read the paper and listened to the evening news. Some still do. But now coverage is continuous, interactive, and perhaps more partisan than ever. There are definitely minefields to navigate in the land of media literacy, but also new opportunities to join the conversation.

It's difficult to write a book chapter on a topic like news media in a climate where technology and preferences change so rapidly. So, although I'll pepper this chapter with recent examples, I generally prefer the McLuhan approach to media analysis—talk about the underlying concepts, theories, and ideas, and the particular incarnation will matter less. True enough, tweets and vines have their own particular characteristics that are interesting. But those characteristics, such as sharing short messages and video, will likely last for some time, though the most popular outlets are likely to change more rapidly. Another consideration is that we now live in an era of media convergence, where the same content is accessed via multiple devices. In a way, this media convergence also draws our attention away from the differences in platform and toward the content itself. Now, let's move on to a discussion of one of the enduring characteristics of media psychology—that of parasocial relationships.

POLITICAL CONNECTIONS

On Friday June 13, 2008, I walked into a restaurant to eat dinner with my family. Glancing up at the plasma TV on the wall, I couldn't quite take in what I was seeing. Tim Russert, *NBC News'* Washington bureau chief and long-time moderator of *Meet the Press*, had collapsed at work and, at the age of 58 and in the prime of his career, had died from a heart attack. What I felt was a visceral sense of loss, sadness, and the kind of wish to make it not true that one feels upon learning of the sudden death of a friend or a cherished uncle.

What I felt might seem absurd, I know. Tim Russert and I had never met. Why should his death send me reeling? I think this is an example of what is good and human about mass media. As an excellent journalist, Tim made a difference in our lives because he provided us with a service that we couldn't do for ourselves. On *Meet the Press*, he was known for pressing politicians on the tough questions—on questions that mattered to us as everyday citizens. He forced the politicians to do their homework so they would have the answers Americans needed to hear. Through watching him do what he loved, the viewers felt they had come to know something of Tim Russert as a person, too. And that's why the relationship between Tim and his audience was not absurd, and why his death mattered to viewers like me.

Many felt similarly upon hearing the news of entertainer Robin Williams's death in the summer of 2014. Because images are so powerful and evoke such strong emotions, they are sometimes very helpful when people have a need to share feelings over the passing of a public figure. For example, one editorial cartoon showed drawings of the comedy and tragedy masks, each recognizable as bearing the face of Robin William. As a comedian who had struggled

with substance abuse and depression and who ultimately committed suicide, Williams's life seemed aptly summed up by the opposing emotions of
those masks.

POLITICS ON THE SCREEN—DECIDING
WHAT'S FAIR AND BALANCED

What is political journalism? At its best, political coverage helps keep the
general public informed of the most important issues and events happening
in the country. And lest we forget, the press also shapes American politics.
One example is that after the presidential election of 2008, the state of North
Carolina was deemed too close to call for the Republicans or the Democrats.
Eventually it was the Associated Press that analyzed the situation and publicly
pronounced Obama the victor. Of course, on Election Day, the presidential
candidates themselves watch the returns on television to find out who won and
they act on that information. The Electoral College does not vote until later,
but we use the press as a source of election information. The American press is
allowed access to government proceedings so that they can pass along relevant
information to citizens. In countries without a free press, government, religious institutions, corporations, or other groups can control the information
the press reports on, either by omission or by misrepresentation. Of course,
even with a free press, there is a manipulation that can and does occur. I'm
a social psychologist, not a journalist, so I'm going to give you my vision of
political coverage as a citizen and overlay that with what I think is important
about it from a social psychological perspective. In analyzing the psychology
behind political coverage, what we'll end up doing will be a valuable exercise
in media literacy.

> A new form of "politics" is emerging, and in ways we haven't yet noticed.
> The living room has become a voting booth. Participation via television
> in Freedom Marches, in war, revolution, pollution, and other events is
> changing everything.[3]
>
> —MARSHALL McLUHAN

It's not always easy to know what a so-called fair and balanced representation of a political story is. A "straight reporter" strives to present a story that
covers "just the facts," without bias. She gives equal time to the relevant stakeholders. For example, a straight political reporter or program might attempt
to interview both the Republican and Democratic candidate for office and ask
them both the same questions. Beyond straight reporting, there is also news

analysis and commentary. Analysis and commentary, by definition, present judgments about events, ideas, and people in the news. If done well, news analysis offers something more than straight reporting. It offers an educated perspective on what's happening. Imagine, for instance, that you hear that Russia has invaded Georgia (the republic, not the state). What are you to make of this fact on your own? Unless you happen to be a historian or political scientist, you are probably at a loss to understand what this event means to you personally or to the world at large. Good political reporting goes beyond the role of a telegraph that transmits only the barest information by helping us make sense of the news.

Let's look at a key example focused on the notion of fair reporting in a domain where politics and science collide: global climate change. In the scientific community, the consensus is that global climate change is real. However, political reporting in the last half decade might not always make it look that way. One reason that science reporting doesn't always give an accurate account of scientific consensus is the misapplication of a fairness rule. This rule is that there are two sides to every story and that good journalists report the two sides to make a report balanced. Anderson and Bushman wrote about this in the *American Psychologist* in a report titled "Media Violence and the American Public: Scientific Facts Versus Media Misinformation."

This rule of journalistic fairness rings true at first. One can almost see a scale with the two sides balancing, implying truth and justice. The problem is that the two sides in any given scientific debate just might not be equal. In fact, this will happen any time there is general scientific consensus on an issue, which is—well, often.

In 2014, the BBC not only acknowledged this flaw in their reporting, but took effective steps to change how their staff deals with this problem in scientific news coverage. The BBC Trust enlisted the help of Steve Jones, a genetics professor at University College-London, who conducted an independent analysis of the BBCs scientific coverage and found this misapplied fairness rule. This would mean, for example, pitting the views of a well-respected and well-published scientist against those of a fringe science denialist and presenting them as equal in credibility and presumably equal in the degree to which those "in the know" agree with one or the other of them. Another example would be to present the views of a scientist who has published piles of research data in peer-reviewed journals against the opinion of a person writing a blog on the subject with no similar credentials. The BBC concluded that rather than presenting two opposing opinions as equally valid, they would, in the future, set their sights on presenting balance in terms of "due weight," based on factors such as credibility and consensus in the field.

While, at first blush, presenting "two sides of the story" might seem like justice, it turns out that presenting a variety of viewpoints while considering their proper weight and context trumps the "every story has two equal sides" approach. Here's hoping that other news sources follow the BBC's lead on this.

PERSUASION: WHICH BRANCH OF THE ELM TREE WILL YOU TAKE?

Before we go any further, any conversation about the persuasive ability of the mass media would be incomplete without a review of one of the most important models of persuasion in social psychology: Petty and Caccioppo's Elaboration Likelihood Model of persuasion, or ELM. I mentioned the ELM earlier, but want to go into more detail in this chapter. Basically, the ELM says that we can be persuaded either substantively or peripherally. If we really care about an issue, and we have the skill and the time to think about the relevant information, then we will take the ELM's Central Route to persuasion. Simply put, we'll process the arguments and make a reasoned decision based on the arguments. But, if we don't really care or don't have the resources (time, skill) to process the argument, we'll go the Peripheral Route. Since peripheral means "side," as in peripheral vision, this means we'll use less important aspects of the argument to make our decision. For example, if a speaker is attractive, well dressed, and charming, we'll more likely believe him regardless of the quality of his arguments. If we feel good—like at a political rally where we hear uplifting music, eat free food, and receive free gifts—we will be more likely to support the candidate.

With political content in the mass media, these sorts of shallow "look good" and "feel good" elements can be present, too. For example, let me make fun of myself by sharing with you a time when I took a walk down the peripheral path to persuasion. In 1992, I was 22 years old—a graduate student in my first semester of a social psychology Ph.D. program. I almost never watched TV during college or graduate school (no time). I also remember that I didn't have cable (no time, no money). But right before the presidential election, feeling an obligation to pay *some* attention to the election, I took a break from work by firing up the TV to watch political coverage. I happened to see what I could only term an "infomercial" for one of the presidential candidates. It featured "feel-good" shots of the candidate and his political promises—kind of a video version of kissing babies—feel-good music and warm fuzzy interviews. In short, it was very astutely and professionally produced to take advantage of the psychology of persuasion. I voted for that candidate and I have since believed that I was motivated quite a bit by that political "infomercial." I tell this story to underline that political media messages such as political ads are very powerful and can "get to us" even when we maybe should know better. They play on emotions by using many psychological techniques—camera angles, lighting, music, color schemes, jump cuts, and attractive spokespeople—to persuade the viewer.

The more media literate you are, the better the chances that your vote will represent what you really value, as opposed to representing the hype often generated by mass media of all sorts. Does this matter? According to recent reports, more than a quarter of voters vote for a candidate who does not share their basic substantive beliefs. In a democracy you can vote for whomever you want, whether that person agrees with you on substance or not. When it comes to mass media and politics, though, media hype can take precedence over substance. And it seems to me that, as important an adult decision as voting is, we should be raising a generation of future voters who at least know something about all of this.

Reality leaves a lot to the imagination.

—John Lennon

You know, politics may be just the perfect topic to study if you want an understanding of the social psychology of the media. For starters, politics is serious business in that what politicians do matters to the people they govern. But political information is complex, and ordinary citizens mostly cannot learn about politics and government through firsthand experience. Enter the mass media, where legitimate journalists try to do the service of supplying important information to their audiences. But in analyzing the events of the day, social psychology necessarily enters the picture. We see smart, successful people offering analysis and interpretation—opinions—and we are swayed by those opinions. The media literacy knowledge needed to make the best decisions about all this political coverage really is quite high.

THINKING ABOUT WHAT GOES ON BEHIND THE SCENES

Behind the scenes, pundits could be quite literally bought off by those who have financial interest in the politician or issue being covered. If not bought off, they may be influenced by other factors. For instance, networks may instruct teams of journalists to select the questions or issues that might generate the most emotional interest from viewers since their job is to keep an audience. Even reporters with good integrity can be influenced by the agenda of the commercial success of the network, magazine, or conglomerate they work for. On the other hand, there are factors that influence coverage for the good, such as independent awards and honors for journalistic integrity, and the ability of a report to be fact checked and analyzed by other news sources.

POLITICAL COVERAGE AND SOCIAL INFLUENCE

Political coverage can shape how you think about issues and candidates. For instance, if you read the headlines, you would infer that at a friend's party you should not yell out, "Recycling bin! Why bother!" When we hear so often about "going green," global warming, Al Gore's Nobel Prize, and so on, it tells us what behaviors are socially acceptable, especially for "people like us," however we construe that. There are other social cues we respond to in the media. Polls are a good example. If a candidate is ahead in the polls, that carries momentum because it puts consensus behind the candidate who is out front, inviting voters to jump on the winning bandwagon. Another example involves the social cues we receive from watching pundits discuss and debate in the media. News commentators often talk among themselves, and the reaction each commentator and each position provokes from the panel gives us social information. It suggests whether we'll be likely to be rewarded or punished socially for holding similar views. Furthermore, since one motivation for watching political coverage is keeping up with current information and common beliefs, we may adopt the perspective of a pundit we heard on television, hoping it will play well around the proverbial water cooler the next day.

THE LANGUAGE OF PERSUASION

What factors might persuade us to adopt the perspective of a particular pundit we see on TV or on the Internet? One answer is how the pundit "frames" the issue. To frame something means to place it in perspective. For example, is a particular drop in the stock market a "blip," a "crash," or a "meltdown?" Are Democrats liberals or progressives? Are Republicans conservatives or right-wingers? Is gay marriage a political, religious, or financial issue, or none of the above? When you frame an issue, you are telling people what to think about it. From a social psychological perspective, reporting carries with it certain social inferences. For instance, if the press consistently reports on gay marriage, it sends the social message that gay marriage is an issue that many people care about. That may or may not be true, but either way it causes you to think that if others care so much about it, maybe you should care about it, too. This is a form of agenda setting, as discussed in Chapter 6. The media set the agenda by defining what issues are important enough to talk about and, by inference, what most people are concerned about. This type of political agenda setting has been shown to be persuasive to viewers, influencing what they report caring the most about—not to mention that it encourages you in general to conform to the opinions you see broadcast consistently. If four perspectives on gay marriage are typically discussed, you might choose one of those based on factors like your similarity to the people who hold the particular view in question. Of course, there are more than four ways to think about gay marriage, but particularly if you are only shallowly processing the messages broadcast (taking the peripheral route), it might pretty much seem like there are only four.

Let's take a deeper look at persuasive language. If I call the stock market drop a "crisis," I am implying any number of things. For instance, I'm implying that there is cause for concern, that you may be hurt either now or in the future, and even that people who understand finance have judged that what occurred was a crisis. If it is the responsibility of journalists to inform the public on matters that are in their interest to know, then it can be very appropriate and responsible to call a particular event a financial crisis. Politicians are often the primary purveyors of persuasion, and the press must navigate that minefield. On the other hand, if you as a news source call an event a crisis in order to increase your ratings or sales, then it's a very different situation. Then your coverage becomes like those sensational promos for local news that ask questions like, "Is our water supply toxic? We'll answer that at 11." Just as lobbyists for businesses manipulate politicians, businesses and politicians sometimes manipulate the press directly and intentionally. I make these points not for their own sake but in the context of a discussion of media literacy. If you don't know these things are possible, you're not able to read what you see nearly as well.

From our perspective as an audience, there is no magic filter that helps us see through the persuasive language. For example, think about the difference in framing when you use the terms "pro-choice" and "anti-choice" versus the terms "pro-abortion" and "anti-abortion" or "pro-life" and "anti-life." If you support *Roe v. Wade*, are you for reproductive rights, a woman's right to choose, or a pro-abortion position? Which is most accurate? There is no litmus test for accurate political language. Beyond that, there is no single political reality out there. The inherent ambiguity of the topic allows ample room to manipulate perceptions. And probably we just accept whatever language we are used to hearing. There are also those who clearly use language in order to be provocative. For example, when conservative Alaska radio host Eddie Burke referred to organizers of the "Alaska Women Reject Palin" rally as "a bunch of socialist baby-killing maggots," he presumably knew that was inflammatory language. Some pundits offer extreme views and make inflammatory statements in order to get attention and thus boost ratings.

If your job were to write a headline about the news that a senator was sleeping with a woman other than his wife, what would you write? What would be fair? The same event can be labeled a scandal, a private matter, or irrelevant information by different news sources. The very fact that we believe it is our business to write or say *anything* about it is a judgment. There is a whole lot of gray area in determining what constitutes the public's need to know about a given story. What is for sure—at least to me as a social psychologist—is that the decisions that are made influence how the public understands the story and how they potentially act on the news.

Political Ads

During an election year, the public is exposed to many political advertisements, and there has been debate about whether negative or positive ads are more effective. Greer and Greer[4] emphasize that people do not necessarily remember the content of an ad, but they remember their own mental construction of the content of the ad. For example, the researchers studied memory for both positive and negative radio ads about both Republicans and Democrats. They found that people remembered information in the positive ads relatively well. However, for the negative ads, people tended to fill in their own opinions without necessarily realizing that they were doing so. Emotional content is used in the media in order to get people's attention; however, as this study shows, it sometimes may backfire. This actually reminds me of a study by Brad Bushman and Colleen Phillips. They studied memory for products advertised during violent TV programming and found that, as the article's title puts it, "If the Television Program Bleeds, Memory for the Advertisement Recedes."[5] Watching violent programming decreases memory for the products advertised during these programs. The authors suggest that part of the reason for this is that violence can induce anger and anger management, both of which interfere with memory. I would say that the same is true for political ads. I know that some attack ads make me angry!

Interestingly, these days one can avoid watching ads by using a DVR. However, I have noticed that TV and Internet news sources actually cover and analyze the day's top political ads, making them harder to avoid. Sometimes, thankfully, political comedy shows lampoon the ads, helping us laugh off the anger they may produce. For example, during the Democratic primary race of 2008, Senator Hillary Clinton ran an ad suggesting that when the phone rings in the White House at 3 A.M., we need a president with the experience and judgment to respond to such a call. *Saturday Night Live* spoofed the Clinton ad, showing Senator Clinton answering the phone wearing curlers in her hair, night cream on her face, and a grandmotherly robe. In one such parody, President Obama phones Senator Clinton at 3 A.M. to ask her what he should do about the emergency.

The Colorful Language of Getting Elected

I remember discussions during the presidential primary of 2008 in which the press referred to Obama voters as the "latte-sipping" crowd and Clinton voters as the "beer-drinking" crowd. Later, Republican vice-presidential nominee Governor Sarah Palin referred to herself as a "hockey mom," and John King of CNN used the term when mapping out voter demographics. Terms like "hockey mom," "latte-sipping crowd," and the "boutique" voters versus the "Joe Six Pack" demographic are characterizations that alter perceptions. People like familiarity and consistency. Voters ask themselves, "Am I like the beer drinkers or the latte sippers? Which group is more socially powerful, acceptable, or impressive? Do people like me vote for this candidate?" and it potentially influences their views.

Front-Page News?

Another factor that influences perception revolves around which stories are covered and how much attention each story is given. "Front page news" literally means a story is important because it was placed on the front page of a newspaper, while a story that is "buried" is put toward the end of the newspaper section and might also be covered with less detail. Whether a story gets buried or gets presented as front page news is up to the journalists—the reporters, the editors, and other staffers at the newspaper. The same basic premise holds for television news shows that highlight the importance of certain news by making issues "top stories," or labeling them with a red banner that reads "breaking news." A red "breaking news" banner implies that this news is something you need to know about. This is another form of agenda setting.

It's reasonable to ask yourself whether news outlets are focusing too much or too little on a particular story. Furthermore, it's also smart to question whether the news source is framing a story in a way that is fair. For example, one study of intimate partner violence reporting in Australia found that when the perpetrator was male, the word "murder" was not used in the headline, but when a female perpetrator was involved, that was the only instance of using the term "murder."[6] This is a good example of how media psychologists, whether coming from a psychological, sociological, or communications perspective, can help citizens by drawing their attention to the way news media frames an issue or a bias in reporting an issue. Media literate citizens can then apply this mindset when they read other stories.

As in other chapters, we see that because we are a media-saturated culture, it is in our best interest to be media literate. Viewers should understand the many ways that political coverage frames the public debate. After all, what we're talking about here is the relationship between government leaders and citizens. Leaders will be elected, laws will be passed, and your tax money will be spent, so political coverage is relevant to everyone. Those who are ignorant of these issues make themselves vulnerable to manipulation.

Pointing out that journalists and how they cover stories have a lot of power to shape the way ordinary citizens think is not an indictment of journalism. To be sure, there seem to be a lot of persuasive pitches being offered in the world of political coverage. But recall that I started the chapter by celebrating Tim Russert's contribution to his audience and his country. The best journalists have to be both terribly smart and terribly articulate. Simultaneously, they must be informed and nuanced thinkers and must be able to translate what they understand back into simple but strong language.

THE PARTISAN PART OF THE PICTURE

There is some meaningful social psychology to explore behind the idea of partisan news coverage. When you tune in or log on, there is a choice in the perspective of the source where you find your political information. And modern news outlets seem aware of this, often commenting on each other's coverage. Some outlets are considered highly partisan. Whatever your political bent, all of this opens up a really exciting debate with some fascinating questions. What is the effect on viewers when programs or whole networks are seen as partisan? If networks or shows are partisan, have they taken their stance in order to increase their ratings? I don't claim to have all the answers, but just having the debate is an excellent exercise in media literacy.

For starters, social psychologists have long documented a basic tendency that people have to divide the world into "us" versus "them"—called the ingroup and outgroup, respectively—and the consequences of those divisions. Studies show that even when we randomly assign people to two groups, you will like the members of your own random group more and you will give them more resources when you have the opportunity. It's kind of like extending your "me" bubble out so that you treat the people who are "yours" better. You favor them, you like what they say. There's a classic study in social psychology that showed the same quotation will be liked more if attributed to a favored political figure like Abraham Lincoln than if the same quotation is attributed to a less favored person. So even if a journalist from a show or network you think is on "the other side" said something sound, you might well reject it because you see it as negative or dumb just because it came from them. Research has also demonstrated a hostile media bias—the perception that media reports are biased against "your side."

Social psychology can help us dig deeper into what happens when news sources are seen as taking sides—either Republican or Democrat. The "us" versus "them" divide we find in news coverage is supported by sound social psychological theory. For one thing, we like people more who share our attitudes, including beliefs and values. If you take a group of people and measure their attitudes, you can reliably predict that they will like other people who share those attitudes. It doesn't matter if you do the measurement before they meet these other people or after, the phenomenon is robust. The total proportion of similarity you share with a person predicts your degree of liking for that person. It follows then, for news coverage, that if we like certain journalists, if we share a high degree of similarity with them, then we will want to watch their shows. We want to "spend time with them," so to speak, because it will make us feel good and will bolster our confidence in our own attitudes. One reason for this is that finding a journalist, show, or Web site that agrees with our perspective validates us. It shows that smart, successful people agree with us and that we therefore must have good judgment and a solid grip on reality, or at least that our conclusions are "normal."

It's also true that we find dissimilar attitudes repulsive; in other words, liking decreases to the degree that two people don't think the same way. So, not only might we seek out journalists who think like we do, but we are repelled by those who hold dissimilar attitudes, beliefs, and values. Some theorists think that the strong negative emotions produced by dissimilarity are evolutionary throwbacks to the time when humans were hunter-gatherers. Basically, it paid to focus on potential enemies in that attacking them, preemptively even, eliminated the possible harm they might unleash on you.

In *Seducing America: How Television Charms the Modern Voter*,[7] Roderick Hart argues that watching political coverage serves our emotional desires—among them, the desire to feel clever and important. Television helps us feel informed and it also wards off our fear of being obsolete—making us feel a part of the process in an intimate way. Hart also thinks that cynicism is the natural language of political coverage on television and so encourages political cynicism in viewers. He worries that watching political coverage deepens cynicism and substitutes for real involvement.

The bottom line for mass media outlets may well be their actual bottom line. In a media climate where networks look for "niche audiences"—special interest groups—what bigger "news niche audiences" could there be than Republicans and Democrats? So, it may be smart from a money-making perspective to supply sources of partisan reporting.

TAPPING THE PSYCHOLOGY OF PARTY AFFILIATION

I have to say that I have often found it a distasteful premise that there are only two kinds of people in the world—Republicans and Democrats (OK, maybe three if you count Independents). Surely the world is more complex than that! Well, research tends to go against my sensibilities on this one. There is a strong body of evidence accumulating that there are reliable differences in a number of domains based on political party affiliation. Personality research indicates that liberals tend to prefer "flexibility over stability and progress over tradition."[8] There is also a growing body of research that supports the utility of the Republican-Democratic distinction, even at the physical level. See what you think.

Your Body Is Taking Sides

A group of political scientists[9] believe that a person's physical makeup can predict his or her party affiliation. These researchers showed scary pictures like spiders and maggots to self-described Republicans and Democrats. They measured skin sweat, which is a sign of the fight or flight response, and found that the Republicans had more pronounced startle responses than Democrats. Then they startled participants with loud noises and measured blinking—another startle response. They found that Republicans blinked more than Democrats in response to the noise. Those who startled more easily tended to have more conservative views on political hot-button issues such as the Iraq war and immigration.

The scientists concluded that people who are more sensitive to physical threats are also more sensitive to psychological threats and therefore take a more defensive, risk-averse stance on political issues. In an interview[10] about their research, the authors said that they were not trying to characterize conservative threat responses as better or worse than those of liberals. One could argue that it is risky to ignore threat as easily as arguing that it is weak to be too frightened by threat. The broader characterization is that some people are more risk-focused and more risk-averse than others. If you have the perspective that something is risky, you may well react differently to it than someone who is not focused as much on the risk factor, but on other factors. For example, those who think about immigration in terms of risk will make different decisions from those who think about it in terms of social justice. Politicians can capitalize on this knowledge by evoking fear and suggesting that they are the only ones who can save you from disaster.

Manipulating Fear of Death Changes Political Positions

One study demonstrates that whatever your party affiliation, reminders of your own mortality can change how you view a candidate. Social psychologists Solomon, Greenberg, and Pyszczynski and their colleagues have studied the influence of thinking about death on political outcomes. In one investigation, they had 100 participants think about television and another 100 think about the September 11, 2001, terrorist attacks; then the researchers asked them about their opinions of then President George W. Bush. When thinking of a neutral topic, the participants did not approve of Bush or his policies in Iraq, but in a dramatic reversal, thinking about 9/11 created very strong approval of Bush and his policies in Iraq. This group of researchers has also demonstrated that thinking about death caused increases in wanting to vote for Bush versus John Kerry in the 2004 presidential election. These scientists noted that as a matter of public record, it was a Bush campaign strategy to remind the public of the terror attacks of September 11 and the concept of domestic insecurity.

In their book *In the Wake of 9/11: The Psychology of Terror*[11] Pyszczynski, Solomon, and Greenberg use terror management theory to explain the pattern of reactions that results from thinking about your own death—that is, "mortality salience." Since we are the only animals who anticipate and are terrorized by the specter of our own deaths, we develop coping strategies to deal with this fear. Fear of death makes us more likely to cling to charismatic leaders who reinforce a worldview in which our great and right country wages an epic battle against "evildoers." These characterizations assuage our fears and bolster our self-esteem by making us feel part of something meaningful that is bigger and more enduring than we are. Furthermore, people with high self-esteem do not need to stomp down others in order to make themselves feel better. Aside from whether the candidate's positions make sense from a perspective of governing, they make sense from a psychological standpoint because such positions can win elections.

Another crucial aspect of the psychology of terror management theory is that by its nature it is not conscious. Here, we return to our theme of media manipulation without awareness. When a political strategy causes citizens to focus on death, they are not aware that their current feelings or arousal level have changed. In fact, the effect is stronger when tested after a time delay. I must underline, the theory is not that we look to the candidate who is rationally more capable of being a strong leader; rather, we look to the candidate who offers rhetoric that soothes our fears. As a case in point, President Bush's policies in Iraq were widely criticized by Republicans as well as Democrats and were mirrored in very low approval ratings by citizens. Arguably, poor leadership by President Bush made the world more vulnerable to terror, so it was not what he really offered the country that was appealing, but rather the very astute use of rhetoric based on the psychology of fear. What is clearest to me as someone interested in advancing media literacy is that there is no doubt that politicians and journalists take advantage of this psychological information when wondering what will make their target audience respond most passionately.

PUSHING THE HOT BUTTON: EMOTION VERSUS REASON

Psychologists have long studied emotions and have found that they are highly motivating. In fact, psychologists assume an inextricable link between emotion and motivation. Fear, as we have seen, is one of the most basic emotions and one that has been manipulated by the media and by politicians. Social psychologist Jack Brehm[12] has studied the utility of emotions, citing, for example, the idea that anger motivates a response to the provocation while sadness may tend to motivate disengagement or withdrawal.

Research in political psychology has compared the relative influence of emotions versus knowledge in forming political opinion. Drew Westen of Emory University and his colleagues were curious as to whether emotions or ideas would win out in voters' assessments of the Clinton-Lewinsky scandal. This scandal revolved around a sexual relationship between then-President Clinton and a young White House intern, Monica Lewinsky, and whether Clinton lied about it. The researchers measured people's emotional reactions to President Clinton, to the Democratic and Republican parties, and to affairs in general. Months later, the researchers asked the same people to make a factual assessment as to whether Clinton had met the criteria for impeachment set by the US Constitution. Eighty-five percent of the time, they were able to predict how voters responded to the factual question from knowing how they felt about the issue. The scientists concluded that what voters *feel*, and not the facts, predict their political beliefs and actions.

You Can't Fight Feeling with Fact

Sometimes our attitudes are based primarily on facts—for example, if we choose which car to buy based solely on gas mileage. What the participants in the Clinton-Lewinsky study described earlier demonstrated was that they had emotion-based attitudes. Those who believed Clinton met the criteria for impeachment based their assessments not on knowledge of the criteria but on a dislike for Clinton. Social psychologists who study persuasion have long found in their research that you can't change an emotion-based attitude with facts. In fact, research actually shows that when you present facts that run contrary to people's feelings about a candidate, it actually motivates people to justify their endorsement of the candidate. That cognitive dissonance and justification, in turn, cause their original feelings to be even stronger.

In his book *The Political Brain: The Role of Emotion in Deciding the Fate of the Nation*,[13] Westen describes research in which he and his colleagues performed brain scans on Democrat and Republican partisans as they read contradictory statements attributed to John Kerry and George W. Bush just prior to the 2004 presidential election. The partisans were able to identify the contradictions in the opposing party's statements. However, when they read inconsistent statements from their own party's leader, they did not see the contradictions. Their brain scans showed that they went through a process of being threatened by the contradictory information, then attempting to regulate that emotion, then resolving the conflict. One of the main theses of *The Political Brain* is the notion that we think of people as rational decision-makers, but emotions are what is central to our decision-making processes. In other words, rather than being *rational*, it's perhaps more fitting to say that we are *rationalizers*. When we hear something threatening, we rationalize and we are not aware that we are doing it. By now, I hope this sounds familiar to you.

Emotions Have a Place in Decisions

All of this is not to say that emotions have no legitimate role in decision-making. Psychologists who study emotional intelligence find that, contrary to the accepted position that the best decisions are purely rational, the decisions that are objectively stronger tend to balance emotion and rationality. For example, if you chose to buy a car by making a list of all the "facts"—the crash test reports, gas mileage, and so on—this would not at all guarantee that you would be choosing the car that is best for you. However, persuasive media coverage seeks to manipulate the power of emotions to influence decision-making. For example, associating a candidate with someone undesirable—even in the most shallow way—can change citizens' views of the candidate in part because they are processing in a peripheral way. Smear ads are an attempt to associate the candidate in a very basic way with whatever evokes a negative emotional response, while positive ads tend to evoke greater feelings of engagement with constituents. Videos of candidates hanging out with voters, bowling and drinking beer, are intended to capitalize on the finding that voters prefer what is familiar to them and to trust candidates who are familiar or "like me." Though it is a tenuous notion that a candidate for president is ever very much like the average voter (or whether, indeed, they should be), staffers know that this is a profitable illusion because it presses all the right emotional buttons.

HEY GOOD-LOOKIN', LET'S TALK POLITICS!

Speaking of the psychology of form over substance, perhaps nowhere is that more evident than when one analyzes the power of physical attractiveness to win the hearts and minds of people. Attraction theory says that we like people who make us feel good. Of course, there are lots of ways people can make you feel good, including the aforementioned shared attitudes, but physical attractiveness is a particularly potent motivator. This argument actually works both for candidates and for the journalists who cover them. For example, CNN's Anderson Cooper made *People Magazine*'s 2005 list of "sexiest men alive." The female reporters and anchors on *Fox News* have also raised commentary due to their conspicuous brand of physical attractiveness. Some have called them the "news babes," "anchorettes," and "foxy ladies" while wondering aloud at their collective degree of blondeness. Believe it or not, researchers have studied blondeness on TV and found that it is much more common than in the real world, probably due to its association with youth and attractiveness. Though the physical attractiveness of the *Fox* "news babes" surely helps garner an audience, it has called into question their credibility. There is a difference between someone who seems to represent the stereotype "babe" and someone—for example, like MSNBC's Nora O'Donnell—who is attractive but whose appearance is professional. Research has shown that when it comes to physical attractiveness, people differentiate between "attitude prototypes" like "the babe"—empty-headed and shallow—and competent, attractive professional women like Nora O'Donnell or MSNBC's Alex Wagner. While

attractiveness in general is an asset, it can become a liability when it is presented in such a way that it undermines the respectability and credibility of
the source.

To continue our discussion of the power of physical attractiveness in politics,
let us turn to a historic example, the 1960 Nixon-Kennedy presidential debates.
These contests marked the first televised presidential debates in US history.
Perhaps because of the newness of televising debates, Nixon did not take his
physical appearance as seriously as would a modern candidate. He was recover-
ing from an illness and had lost 20 pounds, and he refused the offer of makeup.
Some said he was pasty, sweaty, and surly looking, and that he had a five o'clock
shadow. Kennedy, on the other hand, looked tanned, healthy, and confident.
Kennedy, of course, had Nixon beaten by a long shot in both the handsome and
the charming categories. Because of all this, those who listened to the first debate
on the radio judged Nixon the winner, whereas those who watched the debate
on television (which, remember, was a new thing) judged Kennedy to have won.

All of this may be hard to imagine in an era when there is so much visibility
for politicians. Pictures and videos of modern candidates are ubiquitous. If
you want to hear or see a particular comment from a particular day, there are
many sources readily available. For example, if I want to see the State of the
Union address, I know I can go to YouTube and any number of other sites and
find that video. I can save the coverage on my DVR and burn it to a disk. I can
search on endless blogs and Web sites, or through magazines, or even on TiVo
or my iPod and watch videos of the event itself and of discussions and com-
mentaries on the event—even those from ordinary citizens. In terms of media
coverage of politics, it is a completely different world from the that of pre-1960.

IN POLITICS AS IN ROMANCE, LOOKS MATTER

Although we like to say that looks do not matter, years of social psychological
research documents just the opposite. For example, research has shown that
college students matched up on dates want to see their date again only if the
date is physically attractive; other features such as shared interests are irrelevant. Also well documented by research, people generally believe that "what
is beautiful is good." In other words, if a person is good-looking, we attribute a
whole host of other positive characteristics to him, ranging from the belief that
he has great social skills and is fun to be around to having great intelligence
and even great character! Simply put, when we see good-looking outsides, we
infer that the person is also better inside.

What are the consequences of mass media's role in politics vis-à-vis
attractiveness and other physical characteristics of candidates? In October

1992, *Time Magazine*'s cover featured the top three presidential candidates of that year: George H. W. Bush, Bill Clinton, and Ross Perot. The image contrasted the relatively handsome, strong appearances of Clinton and Bush with a silly, big-eared image of Perot. Not only did the cover mock his big ears but also his height, since Clinton and Bush were nose to nose, while Perot's head poked up between the two, dwarfed by comparison. The cover became an iconic representation of Perot as physically inferior to Clinton and Bush. In fact, this joke at the expense of Perot's height represents a political reality: there has been a relationship between height of (male) presidential candidates and their electability, with the taller candidate winning about two-thirds of the time.

Today, media-savvy political staffers make efforts to present their candidates' physical appearance to its best advantage. In the televised presidential debates of 2004, care was taken to remove John Kerry's height advantage over George W. Bush. (Kerry is 6'4", while Bush is 5'11"). John McCain, a skin cancer survivor, reportedly spent $5,000 a year on makeup during the 2008 presidential campaign. Of course, sometimes fussing over your looks gets attention as well, as was the case when the media reported that Senator John Edwards spent $400 on a haircut and mockingly dubbed the senator "the Breck girl" for primping over his hair. And Republican vice-presidential nominee Sarah Palin was widely criticized for spending over $150,000 on clothes for herself and her family at high-end stores in the midst of one of the worst financial crises in American history—a story that may well have lost votes for the ticket. President Obama was variously teased for wearing jeans that were too hip for his age, for wearing "mom jeans," and for wearing a tan suit three days before Labor Day. And Hillary Clinton was teased about her campaigning pants suits. Of course, many rightly argue about whether this shallow view of our leaders is worth our time. Like it or not, the fact is that our candidates are scrutinized on their appearances, and it's a factor in who gets elected.

THE ROLE OF POLITICAL COMEDY IN PUBLIC DISCOURSE

But comedy is just entertainment, right? Comedians have no real role in politics or public policy. Actually, major figures like Letterman and Jay Leno, Jon Stewart, and Stephen Colbert have strong followings, and when they slash a political figure with rapier wit, they can draw blood. There is a growing body of scholarly research that demonstrates very real political effects of political comedy. For example, when a political comedian mocks a candidate, the candidate's ratings show declines.

Politicians have made news by announcing their candidacies on political comedy shows. For example, Senator John Edwards announced his presidential candidacy on *The Daily Show* and McCain announced on *The Late Show with David Letterman*. Hillary Clinton did a surprise appearance on the Colbert Report in 2014 when she released her book *Hard Choices*, considered by most a sign of her upcoming candidacy for the 2016 presidential race. An appearance on the top comedy shows is now a must for presidential candidates, and when well timed can create a bump in their poll numbers. A study conducted in California found evidence for the "Colbert bump"—a month after an appearance on *The Colbert Report*, candidates got significantly higher campaign contributions than those who had not appeared on the show. Such appearances also give Americans a chance to see the candidate in a different light, interacting with a host that the viewers have come to like and trust.

In the world of political comedy, one show stands out as a unique and endlessly intriguing case study in the social psychology of political coverage. I'm talking about *The Daily Show with Jon Stewart*. *The Daily Show*, billed as "fake news" and claiming no journalistic responsibility, has a regular audience of around a million and a half viewers. The audience of political comedy shows like *The Daily* Show and its spin-off *The Colbert Report* tend to be relatively young and well educated. These programs assume a working knowledge of current popular culture, including people, events, and language. Since pop culture is, to a great extent, youth culture, it makes sense that younger viewers would learn more political information from political comedy shows than viewers who are older. If young people are more familiar with popular culture references and language, they should be able to understand, process, and remember the information presented better than older viewers.

Research has shown a relationship between watching *The Daily Show* and *Politically Incorrect with Bill Maher* and increased political knowledge, especially for younger viewers.[14] In 2007, the *New York Times*[15] reported that a survey by the Pew Center for the People and the Press revealed that those who were most knowledgeable about current events were likely to be viewers of *The Daily Show* and *The Colbert Report*, whereas those who knew the least were likely to watch *Fox News* or local TV news. Scholarly research has also shown that more highly educated people learn more from political comedy shows than do less educated people. This is partly because more highly educated people have a greater knowledge base to build on, and they also have stronger skills for processing that information.

FAKING IT, OR FAKING FAKING IT? OR IS THAT EVEN THE RIGHT QUESTION?

In interviews, Jon Stewart has claimed that *The Daily Show* is only in the business of telling jokes, that they don't have journalistic responsibilities, and that they have no agenda of political influence. On the other hand, Lizz Winstead, co-creator of *The Daily Show*, told NPR that it is the satirist's job to be skeptical of politicians who have amassed power and to keep them in check with humor. *Newsweek* named Jon Stewart one of the 25 most influential voices in the 2004 presidential election. An Emmy and Peabody Award winner, *The Daily Show* has also won journalistic awards such as the Television Critics Award for outstanding achievement in news and information.

Now this is where I, as a social psychologist studying media influence, rub my hands together in glee. It's not because I want to reveal the sinister agenda of *The Daily Show, The Colbert Report*, or *Saturday Night Live*. Not at all! In fact, I'm a big fan of all of them. No, I get excited because this is one of the most brilliantly complex media literacy debates that we could have. We can start by asking what the intentions are of the host and writers. We can also talk about the idea that, regardless of intention, shows like these exert a real influence on political thought and action in our country. But I agree with political rhetoric scholar Aaron McKain,[16] who says that it's not a simple black and white issue of whether *The Daily Show* is real or fake news. Instead, the intellectual exercise involves talking about how these new political comedies differ from other forms of news and what the implications of those differences are. For example, we tend to categorize network news as serious business, but a recent content analysis showed that traditional network news is relatively short on substance, emphasizing instead political "hoopla and hype."[17] Could there, in fact, be a reversal, so that "real" news is more "fake" than the supposedly fake news? I can just imagine Jon Stewart delighting in the question, cupping his chin in his hands, grinning and asking, "Is fair foul and foul fair?"

PBS's Bill Moyers interviewed Jon Stewart in 2003 and 2007[18] to explore Stewart's views on political journalism and the place of *The Daily Show* in the journalistic landscape. Stewart explained that in the days of the Nixon-Kennedy debates, the media had the upper hand over politicians, but now the politicians have the upper hand. According to Stewart, the 24-hour cable news networks "don't have time for journalism,"[19] and so end up just reading what the government feeds them. Others have noted that big media simply point their cameras at government and the big newsmakers and report what they are being given, rather than thoughtfully seeking out news on their own. Stewart goes on to describe what is essentially a kind of journalistic freedom that *The Daily Show* has, saying that they do not have to pretend to be objective.

AUTHENTICITY MATTERS

Now some may find a lack of pretense about objectivity to be an indictment of *The Daily Show*, but I think it speaks to one of the show's greatest attractions: the feeling of authenticity Stewart and his team capture. Interestingly, *Comedy Central* used the tagline, "Something approximating election news with something approximating honesty" on their *Daily Show/Colbert Report* Web site. When you think about it, it's a very weird thing—from a social perspective—to listen to straight reporters and wonder how they think or feel about what they're talking about. Reporters can seem robotic, cold, and distant when they are robbed of the power to interpret, analyze, and react to what they are reporting. Contrast this with Jon Stewart watching a news video with his audience and then looking horrified and yelling expletives at the video. He's modeling for the audience an opinion and a feeling about the rhetoric we all face on a daily basis.

Whether you agree with the specific opinion or not, it feels real, while "real" news often feels fake. I think we want our journalists to react with human authenticity. After all, great reporters know the people they cover, they understand economics and government and politics better than we do as ordinary citizens. For one thing, it's their job to understand those things. For another, they had to be pretty smart—and by that I mean both book smart and people smart—to get a gig on TV. So we look at our screens at these smart, capable people and we wonder what they really think and that sucks the authenticity out of the transaction between journalist and audience. No wonder people find Jon Stewart so attractive.

As a case in point, I cite Stewart's reaction to the shooting in Ferguson, Missouri, of Michael Brown in the summer of 2014. Brown was an unarmed Black teenager who was shot by a White Ferguson police officer. In analyzing the media coverage of the Ferguson tragedy, *The Daily Show* presented a video montage where talking heads lamented making everything "about race." The message was that the anchors were tired of hearing about the role of race in the story. Jon Stewart gave an impassioned speech in which he underlined the very real racism faced by African Americans still today. He said, "Do you not understand that life in this country, is inherently different for white people and black people?" He went on to say, "I guarantee you that every person of color in this country has faced an indignity, from the ridiculous to the grotesque to the sometimes fatal ... because of their skin color."

Stewart went on to cite, as an example, a story about one of his correspondents and a producer going to do a shoot in the "liberal bastion" that they live in—New York City. He said that the producer (a White man) was dressed in "homeless elf attire" and the anchor (a Black man) was dressed "resplendently in a tailored suit." Who was stopped and questioned? Stewart went on: "Who do you think was stopped? Let me give you a hint: the Black guy. And that sh*t happens all the time. Race is there and it is constant. You're tired of hearing about it? Imagine how f****ing exhausting it is living it." You can watch the full segment (titled RACE/OFF) here: http://thedailyshow.cc.com/videos/ufqeuz/race-off.

The authenticity factor is part of what makes the top pundits attractive to their audiences. To be fair, it's probably what draws some people to more extreme perspectives like those of Rush Limbaugh as well. Even if we don't like what he's saying, we must admit that he appears to mean it. Although people have criticized the growing number of people—especially young, educated people—who get their news from political comedy shows, in "a landscape in which 'real' news is becoming increasingly harder to identify or define,"[20] I think it is actually an astute social judgment to choose a source that offers authenticity. Given the level of media literacy needed to even begin to sort through the complexities of political coverage, one element of the authenticity we seek is the honest voice of someone who can help us figure it all out. This excerpt from the Bill Moyers's interview of Jon Stewart addresses that issue:

> *Moyers*: I do not know whether you are practicing an old form of parody and satire ... or a new form of journalism.
> *Stewart*: Well then, that either speaks to the sad state of comedy or the sad state of news. I can't figure out which one. I think, honestly, we're practicing a new form of desperation where we just are so inundated with mixed messages from the media and from politicians that we're [the writers and cast of the show] just trying to sort it out for ourselves.[21]

THAT'S FUNNY: ANALYZING POLITICAL HUMOR

Now for some psychological analysis of political comedy. Some psychologists believe that when we laugh, we are releasing tension. While "real" news may increase our stress over serious topics like war, terrorism, and economic crises, "fake" news gives us a chance to release tension through laughter. Even if we're laughing at the absurdly bad way politicians sometimes take on serious issues, at least we're laughing. Furthermore, since humor is emotional, it has a special power to change attitudes beyond the power of the facts. When you mock someone, you get away with an attack by covering it with humor, hence the term "rapier wit"—a humorous attack that cuts like a blade. Such rapier wit is also powerful because—as we've seen—attitudes that are based on emotions are resistant to change through factual argumentation but are open to change through emotion-based persuasion. In addition, since humor accesses our emotional system and emotional information is easier to remember, that means we're more likely to remember what we see on a political comedy show than on a traditional news report. This may be one reason that those studies show greater political knowledge among viewers of political comedy. Another reason is that it's far easier to remember something presented in an interesting way than something presented in a boring way.

POLITICAL COMEDY AND ELECTION COVERAGE

When I wrote the first edition of this book, it was in the days surrounding the 2008 presidential election, and it couldn't have been a more perfect time to talk about the social psychology of political comedy. For one thing, this is a new world of political coverage that we live in. YouTube, offering 24-hour accessibility to politics, media coverage, and public commentary, is pretty much brand new. It didn't exist as we know it today in previous presidential elections. Blogging as we know it today is also brand new, too, in the grand scheme of things. The rise of cable over local and network news is another new phenomenon. And when you add all the issues I have already raised about how to interpret all this information that is available to us, it makes one's head spin. One way many people get some perspective on politics, in addition to some well-needed laughs, is by turning to political comedy.

Looking back on the 2008 presidential election, I think one of the main things people will remember about what we saw in the media will be Tina Fey's spot-on parody of Republican vice-presidential nominee Governor Sarah Palin on *Saturday Night Live*. *SNL* is famous for its impressions of journalists and politicians, including Darrell Hammond's amazing imitations of figures like President Bill Clinton and *Hardball's* Chris Matthews. In the fall of 2008, as fate would have it, the very talented Fey—longtime "co-anchor" of *SNL's* news spoof "Weekend Update"—also happened to resemble the Republican vice-presidential candidate. Fey parodied Palin's speeches, debate performances, and some interviews by Katie Couric that had been widely criticized in the media. When CNN's Wolf Blitzer and John King discussed the Fey impersonation,[22] Blitzer commented that he couldn't remember another time when *SNL* relied so heavily on direct quotes from the candidate to get laughs. King reported that behind the scenes, even Palin's own campaign staffers believed the Katie Couric interviews were disastrous. Of course, on the other side of the debate, one reason the Palin impressions were popular was because the candidate herself had developed a passionate following.

Videos of the Couric interviews and the Fey impersonation circulated on sites like YouTube and attracted millions of viewers. This example also highlights cross-coverage, when one news source discusses another—even a comedy source. Other examples of cross-coverage include *Hardball*'s "Sideshow" segment where *SNL* skits are often chuckled over by Chris Matthews and his guests. The fact that "real" news sources regularly cover political comedy sketches speaks to their broad influence and appeal. So popular were the *SNL* political comedy skits during the 2008 election that NBC launched a new show called *SNL: Weekend Update*, which played on Thursday nights during the last month of the 2008 presidential campaign.

Make no mistake, *SNL*'s political skits are very powerful. The staffers who work for the campaigns must watch the skits and try to diffuse negative characterizations. Because of the nature of humor, as we've discussed, portraying a candidate as an idiot in a political comedy skit can be much more damning than to question the candidate's intelligence or qualifications in a straight news story. Whereas one can attack a journalist's straight reporting or commentary, it doesn't play well to be affronted by a skit that is "all in fun." The McCain campaign tried to characterize Palin's disastrous interviews as "gotcha" journalism, but there was little they could say about the Tina Fey impersonation. In fact, the governor actually said she'd only *watched* the Fey impression but did not *listen* to it, probably at least in part so that she would not be asked to comment on the content.

SNL continued their brilliant parody with a spoof on the Biden-Palin vice-presidential debate. During the actual debate, when Palin and Biden shook hands, Palin could be overheard asking Senator Biden if she could call him "Joe." In the *SNL* parody of that debate, Palin asks Biden the same question and, when he answers in the affirmative, responds, "OK, because I practiced a couple zingers where I call you Joe." In the debate, Senator Biden (see Figure 8.1) said he considered rival John McCain a personal friend, but he waged repeated attacks against the Republican presidential nominee. Jason Sudeikis, spoofing Biden,[23] said, "I love John McCain. He's one of my dearest friends. But, at the same time, he's also dangerously unbalanced. ... As my mother would say, 'God love him,' but he's a raging maniac."

Figure 8.1 Jason Sudeikis of *SNL* mocked the inherent contradiction of Senator Biden's stance in the vice-presidential debate that he both considered John McCain a personal friend and found him unfit for office. Sudeikis spoofed Biden's position, saying, "OK, let's be frank. John McCain—and again, this is a man I'd take a bullet for—is bad at his job, and mentally unstable."

The Power of Parody and Satire

Our modern mass media versions of political comedy stand on the strong shoulders of literary satirists. In 1729, Jonathan Swift published *A Modest Proposal: For Preventing the Children of Poor People in Ireland from Being a Burden to Their Parents or Country, and for Making Them Beneficial to the Public*, long considered one of the greatest examples of political satire in history. The crux of Swift's *Modest Proposal* is to attack the poverty problem in Ireland by encouraging poor Irish to sell their babies to the rich for food. In so doing, it mocks political decision-making and the attitudes of the day. Swift's *Modest Proposal* is a masterpiece because it brilliantly employs rhetoric to provoke an emotional response in the reader and thereby fuel political attitude change. For example, it provokes ire against Irish landlords and pity for the poor, leaving readers in a trap that the author so expertly set. How can they disagree with his perspective when put in such a way?

Today's political comedy, such as the parody interviews on *The Daily Show* and *The Colbert Report*, are in that same rhetorical tradition. When Colbert interviews a gay man with dark, provocative questions and offers him reasons to "go straight," he is doing a parody of news interviews while trying to make a point that there is folly in extreme social positions. Of course, *The Colbert*

Report is one giant parody because Colbert's approach is to say the opposite of what he means while mimicking "his mentor" Bill O'Reilly. When a caricature artist draws a person's likeness, she amplifies individual characteristics. In the same way, the satire and parody done by political comedy shows identify legitimate points of concern through exaggeration.

In the midst of the parody and satire, Jon Stewart throws in a new brand of political interviews. Recently, he interviewed former prime minister of England, Tony Blair. The *London Guardian* covered the interview, noting that the "format of his [Stewart's] influential show allows him to sting with mockery and false chumminess."[24] The *Guardian* noticed that Stewart alternated between penetrating questions and diffusing the tension with humor. The *Guardian* also commented on the role of what they term our "satirical news show" in the landscape of American political coverage: "Perhaps it says something good about *The Daily Show*—or bad about the rest of the American television news media—that anyone might ever have expected a comedy talk show to penetrate deeply into a topic such as Blair's motivations for going to war in Iraq."[25]

Imagery

Another important way we deliver news and political content is via the editorial cartoon and other forms of imagery. The editorial cartoon has a rich history as a powerful way of communicating messages, using humor and drama and the art of encapsulating an idea in a single panel. Today we are used to sharing images on the Internet via social media and other sites. We could think of these images, often with captions, as the evolution of editorial cartoons, where the editors are sometimes the public and the skill is in using the combination of a particular image and caption to convey a thought and an emotion. Let's take a look at some recent editorial images and think about the impact of these various forms of visual communication.

Users share images via social media such as Facebook, Instagram, or Pinterest. Similarly, short videos can be shared via Vine, YouTube, or other video-sharing sites or apps. In this way, the image or video "goes viral" as those that capture the imagination are shared from friend to friend to friend.

Figure 8.2 shows two traditional editorial cartoons, both related to Hillary Clinton's presidential candidacy. The first depicts Bill Clinton's problem as philandering and Hillary Clinton's as lying (represented by Hillary Clinton embracing Pinocchio). Art has a way of getting under our skin and sticking with us. Images evoke powerful emotions. Cartoons or memetic images simplify an issue in a way that is provocative and persuasive.

Figure 8.2 A political cartoon aimed at Bill and Hillary Clinton.

NEW MEDIA AND INCIVILITY

Let's move now from the light side to the dark side of civic participation. We all know that where there are blogs, there are comments, and these comments can become uncivil. We saw this in Chapter 5 with the harsh commentary directed toward feminist vblogger Anita Sarkeesian and a game developer who agreed with her about representations of women in video games.

In a recent study related to online trolling in the video game community, researchers Michael Kasumovic and Jeffrey Kuznekoff conducted some research[26] that shines some needed light into what I think is the somewhat mysterious world of Anita Sarkeesian trolls. Sarkeesian has received many death threats and rape threats for calling out the gaming industry for its portrayals of female characters. The mystery, to me, is why the response that is all out of proportion to the "crime" and who of all the mild mannered gamers I know would actually be making these outlandish comments. Well, Kasumovic and Kuznekoff may have one answer. Of course, it's not all gamers who would make rape and death threats (we did know that much). But, who is it then? In studying Halo 3 players, these researchers discovered that it is, in fact, the guys who are the least skillful players are the most positive towards other men and the most negative towards women. Wired magazine published an article about this research, which they titled, "Gamers who troll women are literally losers."[27]

On the subject of incivility in news or entertainment, about 40 percent of users reported deciding to stay away from an interactive site, such as a news outlet or fan site, due to incivility of the comments there. Hlavach and Freivogel[28] recount an event where a triple murder was reported briefly in an online news forum affiliated with the *Chicago Tribune*. Many rude comments were posted on the story, such as commenters criticizing the car of the victims and telling the victims' parents to "stop breeding." Finally, a family friend begged posters to stop making "disgusting" comments. Hlavach and Freivogel assert that these sorts of harsh online comments would never pass muster with print journalists. They ask about the reason for the double standard. This is a good question in light of the fact that emerging research suggests that the negativity of comments (also known as trolling) can influence the perceived credibility of the source, whether or not the aspersions cast are justified.

Political campaigns are also taking advantage of (especially younger) constituents' habit of text messaging. Obama was the first presidential candidate to inform his supporters about key campaign developments using text messaging or e-mail, whichever the voter chose. Obama's Web site included links to new media sources such as Facebook, Twitter, and LinkedIn. In Chapter 3 I mentioned that young people prefer text messaging over e-mail because they can reach their friends wherever they are. The Obama campaign took advantage of new media use and profited by sending text messages to individual supporters. This astute use of the new media probably helped Obama with record registration of new voters and with voter turnout, which helped him win the election.

New forms of media are evolving rapidly. No doubt in future elections, candidates who understand how to use new media most astutely will continue to be at an advantage. Voters with higher media literacy levels will be at an advantage as well.

From the Passenger's Seat
to the Driver's Seat

We deal in illusions, man. None of it is true. But you people sit there day after day, night after night, all ages, colors, creeds. We're all you know. You're beginning to believe the illusions we're spinning here. You're beginning to think that the tube is reality and that your own lives are unreal. You do whatever the tube tells you. You dress like the tube. You eat like the tube. You raise your children like the tube. You even think like the tube. This is mass madness—you maniacs! In God's name you people are the real thing, WE are the illusion.

—*Fictional anchorman Howard Beale in the film Network*[1]

In the United States, we spend two-thirds of our waking lives plugged into mass media. Our children spend more time staring at screens than they spend in school. Throughout this book, we have seen many examples of how we are influenced by mass media and how we are often unaware of this influence. For example, college students transported into the world of a story believed false assertions embedded in that story, such as the idea that exercise weakens the heart and lungs. And while their confidence in these new beliefs lagged at first, over time they forgot where they learned the false information and their confidence rose to normal levels.

Of course, the social influence of the mass media goes beyond learning factual information, either rightly or wrongly. We are bombarded by images and attitudes, constantly learning and constantly being persuaded. Our view of race and gender roles is informed by the stories and images we see before us on screens and pages every day. Kids watch ads showing that top athletes eat junk food and young girls are sex objects. Magazines spin illusions about domestic violence that do not serve their many readers who need help with a truly overwhelming problem. Violence is glamorized and sanitized. When we are transported by the world of fiction, our attitudes and beliefs change, becoming more consistent with the ideas and claims that take place within the story. We suspend our disbelief, and in so doing we open ourselves up to absorbing involuntarily the belief system dramatized in the fictional world[2,3] and to acting on those beliefs and ideas. Many times what we see on the screen provokes a change or a response outside our awareness. This is how the fantasy world of media shapes our realities.

We may believe that, though others risk being negatively affected by mass media, we do not. Furthermore, fans of a particular medium are the least likely to believe that its negative content has harmful consequences. For example, males who play more violent video games are the least likely to believe that these games have harmful effects,[4] despite decades of scientific research suggesting that exposure to media violence increases aggression, hostility, and aggressive thoughts in those exposed.[5] Reading romance novels has been shown to increase negative attitudes toward condom use.

But there are also studies showing the benefits of exposure to positive health information incorporated into dramatic storylines. A team of breast cancer experts served as consultants on a Spanish language *telenovela* designed to educate viewers about this disease.[6] A study conducted after the program was aired showed that viewers had developed greater knowledge about breast cancer and were more likely to take positive steps, such as calling 1-800-4-Cancer for information. Furthermore, viewers who identified with the characters in the *telenovela* were more greatly affected than those who identified less with the characters. We are moved by what we experience in mass media. Sometimes we are moved in positive directions and sometimes in negative ones, but media engage us deeply and have great power to change us. As Marshall McLuhan said, "All media work us over completely."[7]

I opened this chapter with a quote from Paddy Chayefsky's multiple Oscar-winning drama *Network*. The American Film Institute ranked *Network* among the 100 greatest American films, and the Library of Congress selected it for preservation in the *National Registry of Films* of cultural, historical, or aesthetic importance.

Even if you haven't seen *Network*, you probably know about one of its most famous scenes. Anchorman Howard Beale has had an epiphany: he sees the folly of a television industry unconcerned with quality and substance but focused on banalities designed to boost ratings. He sees the audience as sheep, eating up whatever the industry serves them. Beale tells his audience: "I don't know what to do about the depression and the inflation and the Russians and the crime in the street. All I know is that first you've got to get mad. You've got to say, 'I'm a HUMAN BEING, Goddamnit! My life has VALUE!' So I want you to get up now. I want all of you to get up out of your chairs. I want you to get up right now and go to the window. Open it, and stick your head out, and yell: 'I'M AS MAD AS HELL, AND I'M NOT GOING TO TAKE THIS ANYMORE!' "[8]

Network was released in the 1970s, and like Marshall McLuhan's *The Medium Is the Message*, published in the 1960s, it has an uncanny resonance today. One of the marks of a fine work of art is its universality. The classics in literature and film have this universality. It is rather astonishing that Chayefsky and McLuhan both managed to write about mass media in a way that would continue to endure, despite the rapid changes in media and technology. One reason that I think they both accomplished this was that they spoke about the underlying psychology and the basic relationship between people and mass media. Not only are these elements that have endured, but they also represent what is fundamentally important to understand when approaching any form of media.

Now, I want to underline what might appear to be an unintended irony here but is actually an intentional one. In this chapter, I am asking you to rethink your relationship with mass media. In doing that, I am invoking a film and a book—two forms of mass media. This is no mistake. Chayefsky's and McLuhan's thinking has influenced, excited, and energized me. In exposing myself to their thinking, I am changed, and I think it's for the better. This book is not about defining media messages as bad; it's about defining them as influential—including both positive and negative influence. It's also about taking a look at how much of your time on this planet you spend hooked into other people's messages and how much time you devote to doing your own thing. To paraphrase Howard Beale, it's your life that is real. I'm not going to ask you to go scream out your windows (though, go ahead if you want). I'm going to gently suggest that if your life ever flashes before your eyes, I don't think you will want to see endless images of yourself staring into screens. We're happier when we're playing basketball, talking with our friends, or doing something creative. We're happier when we're getting into something we love like playing the guitar, volunteering for a cause we believe in, throwing a Frisbee at the park, or walking the dog.

There are absolutely delights to be had through the mass media. There are films, shows, and songs that have moved me and taught me things. There are apps and devices that have made my life happier and more productive. Today's technological advances also increase the ease of media access. And media can sometimes offer unique experiences. My family plays games on the Nintendo Wii together. I love watching my daughter Regan swing her virtual tennis racquet. My son Jason and I have bonded while playing *Guitar Hero* together. I was proud of him when, at age six, he used the practice mode to painstakingly get better and better at the game. I've played *Guitar Hero* in Italy in the living room of my friends Carlo and Ximena, and I imagine I'll remember that experience for a long time. In my classroom, I play an NPR podcast of an interview with scientist Robert Sapolsky called "Does Age Quash Our Spirit of Adventure?" that excites me every time I hear it. And every time I play it, I can't wait to hear what my students will say about it. I play another delightful podcast called "Darwin and the Floating Asparagus," which always makes my students laugh but also teaches them some things about history and psychology that are harder to teach in other ways.

Media messages are not uniformly bad or troubling. Again, my message is that media are powerful, persuasive, and influential, and that we are passively staring into screens more often than actively living our own lives. Given that this is the case, I have some recommendations. These ideas are designed to move you, as a consumer of mass media, from the passenger's seat to the driver's seat. I focus on making you more in control and less vulnerable to influence. Use these as a starting point, and customize them to fit your situation.

RECOMMENDATIONS

Always Assume That When You Are Plugged In, the Media May Be Influencing You

Throughout this book, we have seen how media influence us outside our awareness. Media can evoke reactions that are automatic and unconscious. This may be one reason that we seem to think that media do not affect us, but that they do affect others. Other times, we may be conscious of media's influence over us, but deny it because we need to reduce the discomfort of cognitive dissonance.

Think about your media diet like you do your food diet, in the sense that everything you take in becomes a part of you and influences how you feel, think, and behave. This shift in perspective may seem inconsequential, but I believe this seemingly small change has the potential to make a significant difference in your life. The ancient Greek philosopher Heraclitus said that the nature of a thing is to hide its nature. Television shows, movies, video games, and songs may seem trivial, but they are not. The percentage of our lives that mass media now take up should tell us all we need to know about media's influence. Be smart about it.

Limit Your Exposure

Given the psychology of media influence, it follows logically that one major way to reduce it is to limit our exposure. There are many ways to approach this goal. I will offer a few tips. I will follow the model of the Ad Council's "Small

Step" approach, based on the research that suggests that recommendations are more effective when people have suggestions for little ways they can change, rather than goals that seem too large to be doable.[9,10] For example, you might start by keeping a log of what you watch and when. Add up your exposure in, say, a week's time and see where you are. Then make a plan. You can start with little changes. You might decide, for instance, that you will watch a half hour or an hour less of TV per night. As a side note, Americans are sleep deprived, and sleep deprivation is correlated with reduced immune functioning, reduced concentration, and even obesity. You might simply decide to turn the TV off an hour earlier and go to bed earlier. I bet if you do, you will feel better almost immediately. Or you might decide to do some regular chores or read a book in the hour before you go to bed.

For children, the American Academy of Pediatrics recommends no more than one or two hours of screen time per day. Experts believe that simply limiting screen time in society will have positive effects, such as reducing aggression.[11] As we have seen, increased screen time is also associated with other health factors, such as increased obesity and reduced attention span in children. Clearly, one of the best things you can do for your children's health is to reduce their overall screen time. Also, when parents talk with their children about what they are seeing on the screen, and they criticize violent content, children have less interest in media violence and less aggressive attitudes.

An organization formerly known as TV Turnoff Network, now called the Center for Screen Time Awareness (at screentime.org) sponsors a media turnoff week every year in an effort to promote health and awareness of media effects. I have participated in TV Turnoff Week in the past, working with local schools on the initiative. I remember two things most strongly from these experiences: (1) that youth initially had very little idea what to do with themselves without electronic screens, and (2) that after an initial period of complaining, the participants were amazed at how good they felt and wanted to turn off the screens more often. Isn't it telling that our youth are so plugged in to the matrix of mass media that they honestly don't know what to do without it? The organizers even published lists of TV-free activities (wash the dog, fly a kite, climb a tree, etc.) to give kids an idea of where to start without media.

The Italians have a pleasurable habit of taking after-dinner walks. Italians are known for their arts and letters, for their cuisine—for high culture and high society in general. Whether it is cooking, fashion, or even conversation, Italians embrace *la dolce vita*—the sweet life. Whereas Americans have high alcoholism rates, Italians drink wine and aperitifs with dinner as a way of enjoying life. In America, we are concerned with becoming a society of couch potatoes. In Italy, there is the lovely tradition of the *passeggiata*, or evening stroll. Every evening, between about 5 P.M. and 7 P.M., Italians take a little stroll and see their neighbors. Part of the point is to see and be seen and to *fare la bella figura*—or, as the English say, to cut a dashing figure. It is a charming social event—to be outside on the sidewalks and in the public squares, to meet up with friends, to walk and talk. I have lovely memories of walking with my friends Carlo and Ximena in Rome, gazing out over the Spanish steps at dusk (of almost falling in the fountain at the foot of the Spanish steps—OK, that wasn't very "lovely" of me, but it *was* funny), and of walking in the neighborhood most closely associated with *la dolce vita*.

I mention the Italian habit of the *passeggiata*, or "little stroll," to point out that some cultural habits are much healthier and more enriching—both societally and individually—than others. We have come to a point in the United States where media consumption *is* life for many of us. While I think media use can be *part* of a healthy lifestyle, I question the intelligence of the imbalance that we have allowed to creep into our lives. We also seem largely unaware that we have let media take us over. I suggest that we start to question this and add some balance to our lifestyles as a society. Of course, not all Americans are couch potatoes. Some lead interesting, active, engaged lives. But too many of us have slipped into an unhealthy imbalance. Not only does the imbalance make us less active, less interesting, and less likely to contribute anything of lasting value to society; it also opens us up to being manipulated by what we see when we stare into those screens. Habits like after-dinner walks make life richer, and they are healthier and more memorable than time spent staring into a screen. Whatever you enjoy, do that. It might be taking a run with your dog, playing cards with your neighbor, or doing crafts or gardening with your preschooler.

Another approach would be to make a plan to do a screen-free activity you really like once a week. For example, on Thursdays you will play basketball with some friends, rather than watching TV or playing video games. You can make a list of the things you most enjoy doing and add one of those activities to your week. Or you can make a list of new things you want to try or learn. Take a class in yoga or photography or whatever it is you've always wanted to learn. Do that once a week instead of watching TV. I bet that if you do, five years from now you will remember playing basketball with your friends or learning photography much more than you'd remember watching some extra TV. I bet you'll get more pleasure out of it, too.

In *Finding Flow*, Csikszentmihalyi says that according to his research, it is not watching TV or even retiring that makes us happy, contrary to popular opinion. What makes us happy is engagement—doing something that consumes us and makes us feel alive. It's worth stopping for a moment to address why we choose screen time above those things that make us happier. As Csikszentmihalyi explains, his research finds that hobbies are about two and a half times more likely to produce a state of heightened enjoyment than TV does, and active games and sports about three times more. Yet these same teenagers [in his studies] spend at least four times more of their free hours watching TV than doing hobbies or sports. Similar ratios are also true for adults. Why would we spend four times more time doing something that has less than half the chance of making us feel good?[12]

The answer, according to his data, is that the most enjoyable activities require some investment in time and energy to get started. It is easier to passively watch TV, even though we find it less enjoyable. And the more we watch, the less we enjoy it. Another motive for passive entertainment is to distract us from things that are causing us anxiety. The problem with that motive, he says, is that in the end we are still left with a sense of "listless dissatisfaction."[13] The fact that young people participating in TV Turnoff Week didn't expect how good they'd feel without media, I think, underlines what Csikszentmihalyi's research tells us: counterintuitively, spending more time with media does not make us happier; in fact, it makes us less happy and more discontent. I would suggest finding that sweet spot of media consumption that uplifts you rather than drags you down.

Make Smart Choices About Which Media You Use

With mass media, there are a veritable plethora of choices. The research documented in this book suggests content to avoid. Use ratings and content descriptors to help you make choices. You can also look for sources that are critically acclaimed. For example, I mentioned the American Film Institute's list of the 100 greatest films (available at AFI.com). The AFI also has lists for other film genres, like the 100 greatest comedy films. Like the classics in literature, great films can be influential in a positive way. If you are interested, you can read more about the arguments behind the film or about cinematic techniques used to produce it. That way, you are more actively engaged with what you are watching.

Of course, not everything need be critically acclaimed for you to enjoy it. Sometimes I'm in the mood for silly humor rather than an Academy Award nominee. And, of course, some critically acclaimed films don't do anything for you. (I have repeatedly fallen asleep while trying to watch *The Big Sleep*. Sorry, Bogie!). Your own personality and experiences play a role in these choices. If you aren't already in the habit, pay attention to how your different mediated activities make you feel. If you watch a police procedural before bed, do you sleep more poorly? If you play a casual video game for five minutes between tasks, does it perk you up (while if you play for an hour before bed, it makes you feel scattered and tired)? Listen to what your body is telling you.

Speaking of the classics in literature, I recommend that you read more and watch less. Reading a book before bedtime might be a habit you'd enjoy developing if you haven't already. There are so many engaging and enriching choices out there. Try the classics, the *New York Times* bestseller list, or new works in a favorite genre. There are multiple sources that list great books to read. Modern Library polled readers and developed lists of the 100 Best Novels and the 100 Best Nonfiction books in the English language published since 1900. You can find these lists and more online at http://www.randomhouse. com/modernlibrary/100best.html. Teachersfirst.com lists the best books for children and youth, compiled by the National Education Association. And why not join a book club so that you can not only read a good book but also discuss it with a group of intellectually stimulating people?

Another recommendation I have is that when you are watching TV, choose what you are going to watch in advance, rather than surfing the channels. This can help you keep track of your viewing time, which will make it easier to manage how much you watch. A DVR service like TiVo can help with this. Watching prerecorded shows will allow you to fast-forward through commercials, thus avoiding those direct attempts at influence. Skipping commercials or segments that don't interest you can also help reduce your TV time. When you choose shows to watch in advance, you are also better able to tailor your viewing to your interests. For example, I love to do creative projects around the house. I watch home and garden shows for inspiration and ideas, while recognizing that those shows are sponsored by businesses that sell home improvement products. Maybe you, like me, like to see shows where people are creative, and then try out their ideas yourself, or adapt them for your lifestyle.

Seek Alternative Viewpoints

It's easy to be swayed by a person you connect with in the media, or a perspective that you hear most commonly. Challenge yourself by seeking out alternative viewpoints. For example, after watching a presidential debate on television, compare how various news outlets scored who won the debate. Look at blogs online and newspaper articles. Talk to a variety of people about how they saw it. Resist the urge to see things only one way.

Approach Your Media Diet Like You Would Your Diet of Food

Watching films, playing games, and searching the Internet can enhance your life, but you have to be smart about it. As noted earlier, it is helpful to think about your media diet like you think about your diet of food. What you eat and how much you eat are factors in your long-term health and in how good you feel right now. If you eat lots of junk food, you are taking in too much of what is not healthy and not enough of what is healthy. You will feel worse and put yourself at risk for further problems. If you eat in moderation, and eat things that are good for you, you feel better and are at less risk for problems. The same is true for your media diet, and you have to make similar choices. Consuming the wrong things and consuming too much put you at risk for less healthy outcomes. These would include increased aggression, decreased empathy, impaired social and intellectual skills, and obesity.

When I was pregnant with my first child, a nurse at my obstetrician's office dutifully sat me down and played me a video that I since have referred to as the "propaganda video" for new moms. In this video, a young pregnant mother, surrounded by her well-behaved children, prepared a meal of steamed broccoli and plain, broiled chicken, to everyone's general delight. I call this the "propaganda video" jokingly because it was less helpful to the extent that it didn't seem realistic. Now, I did eat more broccoli and healthily prepared chicken and fish when I was pregnant with Jason, but I didn't eat them plain and I didn't have older children pretending they would eat them that way either. While I understand that the video was trying to make a good point, I think it's more helpful if we can meet parents (and everyone else) where they really are. I know, for example, that you are not going to watch *only* excellent films and TV shows, just like you are not going to eat *only* broccoli and tofu. That doesn't mean that you can't have a healthy, or even just a *healthier* media diet. I confess that sometimes I watch trash TV. A prime example would be that Japanese show where people run obstacle courses while announcers say things that would make 14-year-old boys guffaw. In the overall picture of my media diet, I guess shows like this would be like drinking a soda instead of water or eating cheese puffs instead of carrot sticks. It's OK to have some fat in the system, I think. But overall, to be healthier, you should reduce the overall intake and improve the quality of what you do take in. Again, try to notice how you feel after you consume something, including the amount of time you spent doing it. If you are what you eat, then you also are what you consume on screens.

Increase Your Media Literacy Skills

If you have read this book, then you have already increased your media literacy skills. There are other books, Web sites, and films that can help. There are also lots of activities you can do—by yourself, with friends, or with your kids—to move from the passenger's seat to the driver's seat, increasing your control of your mass media diet and your understanding of how it influences you. While you watch, ask questions. Ask, "What ideas are they trying to sell me on? What assumptions are they making? What beliefs, values, or ideas does this program promote? Where do I agree and where do I disagree?"

You can talk with your kids about the media that target them. What are the characters like? What seems important to these characters? How are the characters the same and how are they different from the real people you know? What characters or brands do you see everywhere, and why do you think this is? I talk to people a lot about mass media, and I often hear the idea that if you raise your kids right, they will be fine. I think that what we need to come to grips with is that in our current media-saturated culture, raising our kids right includes raising them to know something about media's power to influence us.

Your "Daily" Dose of Media Literacy

A fine example of media literacy education comes from James Trier, media scholar at the University of North Carolina at Chapel Hill.[14] Trier recommends using *The Daily Show* to teach critical media viewing. I'll summarize some of his recommendations for you. Trier's activities focus on the satire news update section of *The Daily Show*, following the beginning monologue habitually given by Jon Stewart as the host at the time of his writing. An important media literacy lesson from the satiric news update is how *Daily Show* conventions differ from mainstream media conventions. Specifically, the mainstream media try to appear dispassionate, using sound bites about 10 seconds long that conform to specific criteria, such as being grammatically correct and without long pauses. *The Daily Show* breaks with these conventions. Furthermore, Stewart talks back to the speaker in the sound bites, using a technique called *detournement* or "reversal of perspective" to challenge or shift meaning. For example, Trier cites a *Daily Show* segment called "Progress Defined," which presents a series of quotes from President Bush about the Iraq war. The quotes begin in 2007 with Bush complaining that Congress is trying to block him just as the country is beginning to make progress in the war. Stewart talks back to Bush, noting that he thinks progress has just begun, then undercuts this by playing several past clips in which Bush says that we are making progress in the war, ending with Bush's infamous "mission accomplished" statement about the war in 2003.

There are many activities you could do from this starting point, either by yourself, with your children, or in a classroom with students of a range of ages. Trier recommends starting by asking why the video is funny. He also suggests beginning a class by defining *detournement* and then asking students to find other segments that use this technique. Later, he recommends comparing coverage of the same person or event on a show like the *Nightly News with Brian Williams* to its coverage on *The Daily Show*.

Can you think of other media literacy exercises that compare political comedy or satire to mainstream political coverage? The possibilities for this topic and others are endless. For example, you could analyze the reports from mainstream news media, looking for language that is persuasive in one way or the other. Some claimed that mainstream media reported in a way that favored Obama over McCain in the 2008 presidential election. It would be profitable to discuss the notion of whether coverage that favors one candidate does so because of bias or because the facts are on the side of a particular candidate. Might coverage be biased toward the candidate who is ahead in the polls in order to please viewers? What other reasons can you think of that reporting is or seems biased? Ask other questions, such as who produces the show and what is the target audience. Search out trustworthy sources and find their perspective. For example, NPR does a show called *On the Media* that critiques media coverage.

Growing a Country of Media-Literate Citizens

One of the most important steps we can take to make broad change is to begin teaching media literacy skills in our schools. Some say there is no time to cover media literacy in schools. The end result is that American children spend most of their time with media, yet we have not addressed this by teaching them to be smart consumers of media. When we do that, we leave them vulnerable to influence at the hands of profiteers. We have seen examples of the weakness of this position. For example, the deregulation of advertising to children has had such negative effects that governments are feeling the urgent need to respond and make change. This is not a book about educational reform, but I assert that we do, in fact, have time to teach our children the things that will equip them best to be successful in life. It would be a mistake to miss the opportunity to teach them how to navigate the waters of the culture in which they are immersed.

If you are a teacher, there are also great resources available from places like the Center for Media Literacy, Children Now, and the Media Education Foundation. For example, the Center for Media Literacy has a video and curriculum (made to fit the common core) called *Beyond Blame: Challenging Violence in the Media*. (See their Web site, medialit.org, for details.)

WE ARE ALL STAKEHOLDERS

After giving expert testimony before Congress two times as a media psychologist, I was invited by the Organisation for Economic Co-operation and Development (OECD) and the Korea Education and Research Information Service (KERIS) to come to South Korea and take part in an expert meeting. My role was to talk about how scientists and policymakers communicate. I was thrilled at the invitation. I was thrilled because the invitation meant going on an adventure halfway around the world and visiting South Korea for the first time. This was a promise that did not disappoint—the trip was both exciting and a sublime pleasure. But I was also thrilled because I had been asked to talk about something that I really care about that I don't think I'd ever been formally asked to talk about before. I had the opportunity to talk about communicating about science to different stakeholders. This was fun for me because what the topic addresses is basically the social psychology of social psychology!

I took the liberty of broadening my topic, not just to how scientists and policymakers communicate but also to how four groups who have interest in understanding mass media research communicate. Those four groups are scientists, the public, policymakers, and business (see Figure 9.1).

Communication is a real issue because these four groups speak different languages and have different motives. The four stakeholders also often have a poor understanding of each other, and when you don't understand someone, how can you communicate? In the *Eleven Myths of Media Violence*, James Potter[15] said that after over 50 years of public hearings about media violence, we have done little but spin our wheels over the issue. There continues to be concern and discussion, but to no real effect. I think a big part of why we find ourselves stuck, unable to make forward progress, is a lack of effective communication between the interested parties. Therefore I want to make some recommendations. To extend the driving metaphor, I want to recommend how we can get some traction and drive out of the rut we find ourselves in. In order to get there, I am going to get some help from an artist who knows something about science.

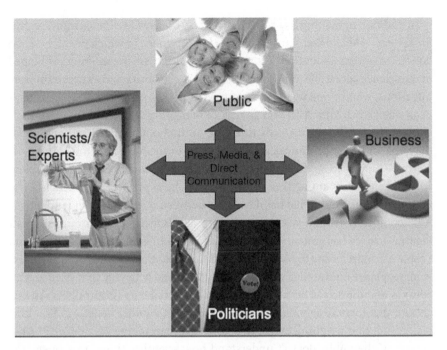

Figure 9.1 The public, scientists and experts, policymakers, and businesspeople are all stakeholders who have an interest in mass media and its influence. Scientists and other experts must learn how to communicate more effectively with all interested parties in order for their work to be most helpful.
(With permission from Family Huddle (*8421366*): © Katrina Brown—Fotolia. com, VOTE (*7502670*): © Michael Flippo—Fotolia.com, Scientist (*1468559*): © Yuri Arcurs—Fotolia.com, Business (*1538103*): © Iryna Petrenko—Fotolia.com)

Earlier I recommended exposing yourself to different viewpoints in high-quality media. You really never know what you will discover when you take this advice. I find fascinating connections to my work everywhere. On a long airplane trip, I fired up my iPod and listened to *Things I Overheard While Talking to Myself*[16] by Alan Alda. In this book, the actor talks about the content of commencement addresses and other speeches he's given throughout his life. I thought I had been listening primarily for pleasure, but I stumbled upon something so intellectually imperative that I want to end my book discussing it.

Alan Alda is famous for playing Hawkeye Pierce in the TV show *M*A*S*H*, and I can hardly think of a character who was brought to life more brilliantly by an actor. In fact, as a side note, when I read some reviews of *Things I Overheard While Talking to Myself* on Amazon.com, one commentator opined that anyone over 30 *unconsciously* [emphasis added] believes Alan Alda *is* Hawkeye Pierce! Well said.

In addition to making our collective fantasy of Hawkeye Pierce into a reality, for 11 years Alda hosted *Scientific American Frontiers*, in which he interviewed famous scientists about their discoveries. *Scientific American Frontiers* helped make science accessible to nonscientists. Alda's curiosity and enthusiasm were infectious, whether he was finding out what makes peppers hot or what happens when we dream. And his experience of helping scientists talk about their work with clarity informed his thinking both about science itself and about the need for better communication of science to the public.

This is the topic he discussed in a commencement address to young scientists and engineers at Cal Tech. In this speech, he explained why there is a real need to heal the breach that has developed between scientists and nonscientists. Alda compared art and science to the two hemispheres of the brain, suggesting that science has gotten a reputation as cold, while art is warm and human. People are more prone to rely on magical thinking than on scientific evidence. And people are confused if scientists disagree, often believing that science is an opinion and the scientific community just can't make up its mind. "We're in a culture that increasingly holds that science is just another belief. . . . We don't really get it that weighing evidence is different than taking on a belief."[17] And, he says, if the public doesn't understand how scientists think, that opens the door to call solid research junk science and to dismiss it. If the public thinks science is just another opinion, then this labeling by politicians takes on a weight that is equal to the science.

As discussed earlier, Bushman and Anderson[18] presented a case that as scientific evidence for a link between media violence and aggression became stronger, the press began to report that the link was weaker. One reason for the flawed coverage was the misapplication of a journalistic principle of fairness. The press commonly presents a scientist and an industry representative as holding two equal sides of an argument, ignoring both the nature of science and the vested interest of the businessperson. As Alda so aptly put it, this reflects a deep lack of understanding that science is based on evidence rather than opinion. Another reason for the flawed coverage, according to Bushman and Anderson, is that big companies that own newspapers and news magazines may also be in the business of selling violent media, such as video games and DVDs. As I mentioned earlier, as of this writing, the BBC has recognized publicly that they do this, and has explicitly made it a policy to stop doing it. If others follow suit, that would represent a meaningful shift in the quality of science coverage we consume.

And what of the public's view of scientists? The American Academy for the Advancement of Science (AAAS) offered grants to filmmakers in order to encourage them to portray scientists as real people rather than stereotypes.[19] Why? Because the public forms their view of scientists from the mass media rather from real experience with scientists! And scientists in the mass media tend to fall into stereotypes such as the nerd, the cold fish, or the mad scientist. (And yes, I resemble some of those, but that's just a coincidence.) The AAAS simply wanted films to show scientists as real people, people who go fishing, have families, and are sometimes attractive—and that scientists can be women. This underlines what Alda said about science having the reputation of being cold and rather inhuman. The public mistrusts distant, robotic scientists who speak from an ivory tower. That brand of science becomes a smug and incomprehensible opinion.

So how can we get the public to understand and value science? How can we get the public to see that scientists are human, often warm even? In his address to Cal Tech, Alda said that to open the channels of communication between scientists and the public, scientists must communicate their work in a way that causes people to fall in love with science. More specifically, in talking about research, scientists should lead people through the three stages of love, defined as (1) lust, (2) infatuation, and (3) commitment.

"Lust for science?" I can hear you thinking. "What would that involve, exactly?" Lust for science is that stirring of excitement that comes when we hear about a scientific advance that amazes us. It makes us feel like we live in a world where science might just make us live longer or better. Our pulse quickens and the world feels fresh and exciting. To seduce an audience with a lust for science, Alda says, the attraction must happen right away. The scientist should begin by focusing on tone and body language. Be conversational and interesting in a way that a lay audience can understand. Avoid slipping into lecture mode; watch your vocabulary. Show human warmth and feeling; use facial expression. If you speak with your authentic, human voice, the audience will get the sense that you are genuine human and not a god from Mount Olympus. Did you know that most professors never study teaching, and most scientists never study how to communicate with the public? Isn't that amazing? I guess the accepted idea was that smart people would figure out by themselves how to communicate. But, of course, there are different ways of being smart. Some people are natural communicators, but great communication can and should be taught to scientists.

The next stage of falling in love with science is infatuation. Making a story emotional helps us remember it. Alda suggests that scientists frame their work as a detective story. Mysteries are dramatic. They involve blind alleys, ups and downs, and the desire for a breakthrough. It's important not to leave out the mistakes because they make the story more human.

I think that's so true. Scientists often don't publish the studies that don't work. We actually have a term for this: the "file drawer problem"; this means that studies that didn't show significant results end up in the file drawer rather than being published. But when we never talk about what didn't work, it seems that we are elite, flawless—again, inhuman. The audience doesn't know that this study they are hearing about is exciting to the scientist in part because it worked! They may not know that lots of studies don't work. I can tell you that when you run your data and you see significant results—and remember, this is after much thought and work have gone into the process—when you see those numbers come up as you predicted, there is a palpable sense of awe and wonder, not to mention joy, that you feel. Those are some of the human things that get lost when we just skip to the end. It makes something that was so hard seem so easy.

Finally, the last stage of falling in love with science happens when the scientist gets the audience to commit. Committing to a person means you have found real value in that individual. Committing to science, then, means you truly understand its value. Here Alda calls for simplicity and clarity of communication. He quotes Leonardo Da Vinci, who said that simplicity is the ultimate form of sophistication, and Albert Einstein, who said that science should be explained so that a child could understand it. Perhaps my favorite line comes from physicist Richard Feinman, who said that if the scientist can't explain his work, he probably doesn't understand it himself. In my experience, that's often true.

Experts note that one reason public policy has not been better informed by the psychological literature on media is that interested parties, like the press, the courts, and the general public, do not understand basic scientific concepts, such as how scientists understand cause and effect.[20] This problem was put into sharp relief for me when, the night before I testified before Congress in 2007, I was advised that politicians do not understand the scientific meaning of cause and effect. I was told that members of Congress treat research findings like poll data. Again, this frames scientific findings as a matter of opinion, rather than an understanding that scientific findings are based on evidence and not conjecture.

HUMANIZING SCIENCE

When scientists publish their data in journals, the communication follows prescribed standards that are impersonal. As Alda puts it, this is because the scientific community believes that the cult of personality should not rule. A fundamental principle of science is objectivity; therefore, subjective content such as personality and feelings are unwelcome in scientific communications. This is understandable because objectivity is an important and appropriate goal. But it is not the appropriate model for how scientists should communicate with those outside the scientific community.

The public usually hears about scientific findings through the media. If the scientist gives an interview or testimony that is broadcast on television or the radio, for example, then the public gets to hear the scientist speak in her own words. Any time scientists communicate a message through the media, they should not speak in the same way as they would in a scientific journal. Here the scientist has the opportunity to do what Alda suggests: to speak with feeling, to put the personal back into the equation, and to speak with clarity so that a child, or at least a layperson, can understand it. This is what I try to do when I speak about science. I give the facts, but I give them with feeling and in context. This is why I told you something about my life story, about where I come from and why I do what I do. It's why I let you see my goofy side along the way. I want you to know that scientists are also real people. We're parents, taking our kids to one more birthday party at Chuck E. Cheese, dreaming of the day they will go to college. Often we are really hard workers, in part because we believe that what we do matters. To the scientists out there who study mass media, I say that we have to work even harder. We have to concentrate on communicating our findings to the public in a way that is clearer and more engaging.

To the public, digesting scientific information, I assert that science is not just another opinion. Science is also not a cold, inhuman enterprise. Science means gathering evidence about what's true, as well as we can decipher the truth. It is not practiced by robots or heartless snobs. It is practiced by smart people who have a hunger for the truth. These are people who want to make the world a better place by finding answers that are worth knowing. And, unlike the situation with business, scientists are not trying to get your money.

I want to thank you for taking this journey with me and for learning more about the social psychology of mass media. I hope you are primed to take greater control of your relationship with mass media. I also hope you understand better the science behind mass media's influence. You will get more pleasure out of life and you will be happier with the choices you made if you unplug more and actively do whatever engages you. You will also be happier and less vulnerable to other people's agendas if you are more educated about the media that take up so much of our time. According to *Finding Flow,* "it is how we choose what we do, and how we approach it, that will determine whether the sum of our days adds up to a formless blur, or to something resembling a work of art."[21] Life is short and it is precious. To put it metaphorically, up to now we have often consented to ride shotgun while media drive us where they choose. It's time we hopped into the driver's seat and mapped out our own journey. I hope your journey is full of fun and adventure!

CHAPTER 1 FANTASY AND REALITY

1. Kilbourne, Jean. *Killing Us Softly 3*. Northampton, MA: Media Education Foundation, 2000.
2. House Committee on Energy and Commerce, Subcommittee on Commerce, Trade and Consumer Protection. *From Imus to Industry: The Business of Stereotyopes and Degrading Images*, September 25, 2007.
3. Brenick, A., A. Henning, M. Killen, A. O'Connor, and M. Collins. "Social Evaluations of Stereotypic Images in Videogames: Unfair, Legitimate, or 'Just Entertainment'?" *Youth and Society* 38, no. 4 (2007): 395–19.
4. "Poll Says Games Are Safe." 1999. Retrieved February 1, 2000, from http://pc.ign.com/articles/068/068231p1.html.
5. Glasser, Ira. "Television and the Construction of Reality." *Applied Social Psychology Annual* 8 (1988): 44–51.
6. Haney, Craig, and John Manzolatti. "Television Criminology: Network Illusions of Criminal Justice Realities." In *Readings on the Social Animal*, edited by E. Aronson. San Francisco: Freeman, 1980.
7. Appel, M., and T. Richter. "Persuasive Effects of Fictional Narratives Increase over Time." *Media Psychology* 10, no. 1 (2007): 113–34.
8. Dill-Shackleford, Karen E., Green, Melanie C., Scharrer, Erica, Wetterer, Craig, and Shackleford, Lee E. "Setting the stage for social change: Using live theater to dispel myths about intimate partner violence." *Journal of Health Communication*, (in press) doi:10.1080/10810730.2015.1018622
9. Green, Melanie C. "Linking Self and Others Through Narrative." *Psychological Inquiry* 18, no. 2 (2007): 100–102.
10. Prentice, Deborah A., Richard J. Gerrig, Shelly Chaiken, and Trope, Yaacov. "Exploring the Boundary Between Fiction and Reality." In *Dual-Process Theories in Social Psychology*, 529–46. New York: Guilford Press, 1999.
11. Smith, Elaine, and Jessica Whiteside. "TV Sitcom So Transforms Use of English." *University of Toronto Magazine*, Spring, 2004, available at http://www.magazine.utoronto.ca/04spring/leadingedge.asp.

12. Deaux, K., and R. Hanna. "Courtship in the Personal Column: The Influence of Gender and Sexual Orientation." *Sex Roles* 11 (1984): 363–75.

13. Gutierres, S. E., D. T. Kenrick, and J. J. Partch. "Beauty, Dominance and the Mating Game: Contrast Effects in Self Assessment Reflect Gender Differences in Mate Selection." *Personality & Social Psychology Bulletin* 25, no. 9 (1999): 1126–34.

14. Gutierres et al., "Beauty, Dominance and the Mating Game," p. 1133.

15. Festinger, Leon, and J. Merrill Carlsmith. "Cognitive Consequences of Forced Compliance." *Journal of Abnormal and Social Psychology* 58 (1959): 203–10.

16. Gosling, P., M. Denizeau, and D. Oberle. "Denial of Responsibility: A New Mode of Dissonance Reduction." *Journal of Personality and Social Psychology* 90, no. 5 (2006): 722–33.

17. Kubey, Robert, and Mihaly Csikszentmihalyi. "Television Addiction Is No Mere Metaphor." *Scientific American, Special Edition* 14, no. 1 (2004): 48–55.

18. Kubey et al., "Television Addiction," 48–55.

19. Bushman, Brad J., and Craig A. Anderson. "Media Violence and the American Public." *American Psychologist* 56, no. 6–7 (2001): 477.

20. Great thanks to an anonymous peer reviewer for suggesting this historical perspective on manipulation.

21. Bargh, John A., and Tanya L. Chartrand. "The Unbearable Automaticity of Being." *American Psychologist* 54, no. 7 (1999): 462.

22. Chartrand, Tanya L., and John A. Bargh. "The Chameleon Effect: The Perception-Behavior Link and Social Interaction." *Journal of Personality and Social Psychology* 76, no. 6 (1999): 893–910.

23. Prentice et al., "Exploring the Boundary."

24. Appel and Richter, "Persuasive Effects of Fictional Narratives."

25. Nisbett, R. E., and T. D. Wilson. "Telling More Than We Can Know: Verbal Reports on Mental Processes." *Psychological Review* 84, no. 3 (1977): 231–59.

26. Nisbett and Wilson, "Telling More Than We Can Know."

27. The course was taught by Craig Anderson.

28. Zimbardo quote from the Discovering Psychology film series Constructing Social Realities, Annenberg Center for Public Broadcasting.

CHAPTER 2 FANDOM, FANTASY, AND REALITY

1. Bielby DD, Harrington CL, Bielby WT. Whose stories are they? Fans' engagement with soap opera narratives in three sites of fan activity. J Broadcast Electron Media. 1999;43(1):35–51. doi:10.1080/08838159909364473.

2. Pearson R. Fandom in the Digital Era. Pop Commun. 2010;8(1):84–95. doi:10.1080/15405700903502346.

3. Booth P. Rereading Fandom: MySpace Character Personas and Narrative Identification. Crit Stud Media Commun. 2008;25(5):514–536. doi:10.1080/15295030802468073.

4. Jenkins H. Superpowered Fans. Boom A J Calif. 2011;2(2):22–37. doi:10.1525/boom.2012.2.2.22.22.

5. Vorderer P, Steen FF, Chan E. Motivation. In: Bryant J, Vorderer P, eds. Psychology of Entertainment. Mahwah, NJ: Lawrence Erlbaum; 2006:3–17.

6. Moyer-Gusé E. Toward a Theory of Entertainment Persuasion: Explaining the Persuasive Effects of Entertainment-Education Messages. Commun Theory. 2008;18(3):407–425. doi:10.1111/j.1468-2885.2008.00328.x.

7. Igartua J-J, Barrios I. Changing Real-World Beliefs With Controversial Movies: Processes and Mechanisms of Narrative Persuasion. J Commun. 2012;62(3):514–531. doi:10.1111/j.1460-2466.2012.01640.x.

8. Greenwood DN. Are Female Action Heroes Risky Role Models? Character Identification, Idealization, and Viewer Aggression. Sex Roles. 2007;57(9-10):725–732. doi:10.1007/s11199-007-9290-5.

9. Igartua J-J. Identification with characters and narrative. Communications. 2010;35(2010):347–374. doi:10.1515/COMM.2010.019.

10. Green MC, Brock TC. The role of transportation in the persuasiveness of public narratives. J Pers Soc Psychol. 2000;79(5):701–721. doi:10.1037//0022-3514.79.5.701.

11. Green MC, Dill KE. Engaging with Stories and Characters: Learning, Persuasion, and Transportation into Narrative Worlds. In: Oxford Handbook of Media Psychology. New York: Oxford University Press; 2013. doi:10.1093/oxfor dhb/9780195398809.013.0025.

12. Green MC, Garst J, Brock TC, Chung S. Fact Versus Fiction Labeling: Persuasion Parity Despite Heightened Scrutiny of Fact Fact Versus Fiction Labeling: Persuasion Parity Despite Heightened Scrutiny of Fact. 2009;(792621630). doi:10.1207/ s1532785xmep0803.

13. Mazzocco PJ, Green MC, Sasota J a., Jones NW. This Story Is Not for Everyone: Transportability and Narrative Persuasion. Soc Psychol Personal Sci. 2010;1(4):361–368. doi:10.1177/1948550610376600.

14. Busselle R, Bilandzic H. Measuring Narrative Engagement. Media Psychol. 2009;12(4):321–347. doi:10.1080/15213260903287259.

15. Brockmyer JH, Fox CM, Curtiss K a., McBroom E, Burkhart KM, Pidruzny JN. The development of the Game Engagement Questionnaire: A measure of engagement in video game-playing. J Exp Soc Psychol. 2009;45(4):624–634. doi:10.1016/j. jesp.2009.02.016.

16. >Nabi RL, Moyer-Gusé E. The Psychology Underlying Media-Based Persuasion. In: Oxford Handbook of Media Psychology. Oxford University Press; 2013. doi:10.1093/oxfordhb/9780195398809.013.0016.

17. Nabi RL, Moyer-Gusé E, Byrne S. All Joking Aside: A Serious Investigation into the Persuasive Effect of Funny Social Issue Messages. Commun Monogr. 2007;74(1):29–54. doi:10.1080/03637750701196896.

18. Csikszenthihalyi M. Finding Flow. (Basic Books, ed.). New York; 1998.

19. Moyer-Gusé E, Nabi RL. Explaining the Effects of Narrative in an Entertainment Television Program: Overcoming Resistance to Persuasion. Hum Commun Res. 2010;36(1):26–52. doi:10.1111/j.1468-2958.2009.01367.x.

20. Holland NN. The Willing Suspension of Disbelief: A Neuro-Psychoanalytic View The Willing Suspension of Disbelief: A Neuro-Psychoanalytic View. PsyArt An Online J Psychol Study Arts. 2003:1–5.

21. Bourdage M. Not just "another humourless bitch": feminist fans' reception of Mad Men. Continuum (N Y). 2014;28(2):164–175. doi:10.1080/10304312.2014.888 038.

22. Scannell P. Television and the Meaning of Live. Polity; 2014.
23. Kaufman GF, Libby LK. Changing beliefs and behavior through experience-taking. J Pers Soc Psychol. 2012;103(1):1–19. doi:10.1037/a0027525.
24. Boucher G. James Cameron: I want to compete with "Star Wars" and Tolkien. L.A. Times. http://herocomplex.latimes.com/movies/james-cameron-i-want-to-compete-with-star-wars-and-tolkien/. Published August 25, 2010.
25. Piazza J. Audiences experience Avatar blues. CNN.com. http://www.cnn.com/2010/SHOWBIZ/Movies/01/11/avatar.movie.blues/. Published January 11, 2010.
26. Langton S. Pride and Prejudice. UK: BBC; 1995.
27. Blascovich J, McCall C. Social Influence in Virtual Environments. 2013;(April). doi:10.1093/oxfordhb/9780195398809.013.0017.
28. Yee N, Bailenson JN. The Difference Between Being and Seeing: The Relative Contribution of Self-Perception and Priming to Behavioral Changes via Digital Self-Representation. Media Psychol. 2009;12(2):195–209. doi:10.1080/15213260902849943.
29. Blascovich J, Bailenson JN. Infinite reality. New York: William Morrow; 2012.
30. Bole C. Hollow Pursuits. 1990.
31. Hayakawa SI. Language in thought and action. New York: Harcourt Brace; 1990.
32. Oliver MB, Bartsch A. Appreciation of Entertainment. J Media Psychol Theor Methods, Appl. 2011;23(1):29–33. doi:10.1027/1864-1105/a000029.
33. Dill-Shackleford KE, Hopper-Losenicky K, Vinney C, Swain LF, Hogg JL. Mad Men Fans Speak Via Social Media: What Fan Voices Reveal About the Social Construction of Reality Via Dramatic Fiction. J Fandom Stud. 2015;3(2):151–170. doi:10.1386/jfs.3.2.151_1.
34. Oatley K. Why fiction may be twice as true as fact: Fiction as cognitive and emotional simulation. Rev Gen Psychol. 1999;3(2):101–117. doi:10.1037/1089-2680.3.2.101.
35. Adalian J, Bernardin M, Buchanan K, et al. The 25 most devoted fan bases. 2012. Available at: http://www.vulture.com/2012/10/25-most-devoted-fans.html#.
36. Pedicini S. Mystery surrounds opening date of Universal's Harry Potter attraction. Orlando Sentinel. http://articles.orlandosentinel.com/2014-06-12/business/os-harry-potter-opening-date-20140612_1_universal-studios-japan-universal-orlando-wizarding-world. Published June 12, 2014.
37. Adams RG, Harrington CL, Bielby DD. Soap Fans: Pursuing Pleasure and Making Meaning in Everyday Life. Soc Forces. 1996;75(1):394. doi:10.2307/2580814.
38. Campbell J. New book series from Intellect - Fan Phenomena. 2012. Available at: http://www.intellectbooks.co.uk/weblog/view-Post,id=51227/.
39. Zaidi N. Top 15 Richest YouTubers Who Make Money by Sharing Videos. smart-earningmethods.com. 2013. Available at: http://www.smartearningmethods.com/richest-youtubers-who-make-money-by-sharing-videos/.
40. Stanfill M. "They're Losers, but I Know Better": Intra-Fandom Stereotyping and the Normalization of the Fan Subject. Crit Stud Media Commun. 2013;30(2):117–134. doi:10.1080/15295036.2012.755053.
41. Larsen K, Zubernis LS. Fangasm: Supernatural Fangirls. Des Moines, IA: University of Iowa Press; 2013.

42. Hills M. Negative Fan Stereotypes (" Get a Life!") and Positive Fan Injunctions (" Everyone ' s Got To Be a Fan of Something!"): Returning To Hegemony Theory in Fan Studies. Spectator. 2005;1(Spring):35–47.

43. Jenkins H. Convergence culture. New York: NYU Press; 2008.

44. Sandvoss C, Gray J, Harrington CL. The Scale and Scope of Popular Communication Research. Pop Commun. 2009;7(2):61–62. doi:10.1080/15405700902776388.

Chapter 3 Old and New Media in Everyday Life

1. Brenner J. The First Cell Phone Call: Excerpt from "Networked: The New Social Operating System." *Pew Internet Am Life Proj.* 2013. Available at: http://www. pewinternet.org/2013/04/03/the-first-cell-phone-call-excerpt-from-networked-the-new-social-operating-system/.

2. Aronson, Elliot. *The Social Animal (9th Ed.)*, The Social Animal (9th Ed.). New York, NY US: Worth Publishers, 2004.

3. Potter, W. James. *Media Literacy.* Los Angeles: Sage, 2008.

4. Roberts, D., and U. Foehr. *Kids and Media in America.* Cambridge, UK: Cambridge University Press, 2004. See also the report of this data released by the Kaiser Family Foundation called *Generation M: Media in the Lives of 8-18 year olds* available from http://www.kff.org/entmedia/entmedia030905pkg.cfm

5. Kubey, Robert, Mihaly Csikszentmihalyi, K. R, and C. M. "Television Addiction Is No Mere Metaphor." *Scientific American Special Edition* 14, no. 1 (2004): 48-55.

6. Csikszentmihalyi, Mihaly. *Finding Flow: The Psychology of Engagement with Everyday Life.* New York: Basic Books, 1998.

7. Randsford, Marc. "Average Person Spends More Time Using Media Than Anything Else" *Ball State University Newsletter*, no. 9/23/2005 (2005), http://www.bsu.edu/news/article/0,1370,7273-850-36658,00.html.

8. McLuhan, Marshall, with Quentin Fiore, and Jerome Agel. *The Medium Is the Massage: An Inventory of Effects.* Corte Madera, CA: Ginko Press, 1967, p. 126.

9. Yellowlees PM, Marks S. Problematic Internet use or Internet addiction? Comput Human Behav. 2007;23(3):1447–1453. doi:10.1016/j.chb.2005.05.004.

10. Cash H, Rae CD, Steel AH, Winkler A. Internet Addiction: A Brief Summary of Research and Practice. Curr Psychiatry Rev. 2012;8(4):292–298. doi:10.2174/157340012803520513.

11. Wilson RE, Gosling SD, Graham LT. A Review of Facebook Research in the Social Sciences. Perspect Psychol Sci. 2012;7(3):203–220. doi:10.1177/1745691612442904

12. Anonymous. 39% of American Public Tuning Out of Social Networks Due to Incivility, According to New Weber Shandwick Survey. New York; 2013. Available at: http://www.prnewswire.com/news-releases/39-of-american-public-tuning-out-of-social-networks-due-to-incivility-according-to-new-weber-shandwick-survey-96971629.html

13. Turan Z, Tinmaz H, Goktas Y. The Reasons for Non-Use of Social Net - working Websites by University Students. Comunicar. 2013;21:137–14510.

14. Cantor, Joanne. "The Media and Children's Fears, Anxieties, and Perceptions of Danger." In *Handbook of Children and the Media*, edited by Dorothy G. Singer and Jerome L. Singer, 207-21. Thousand Oaks, CA: Sage, 2001.

15. Gentile, Douglas A., and David Walsh. "Media-Quotient: National Survey of Family Media Habits, Knowledge, and Attitudes.". Minneapolis, MN: National Institute on Media and the Family, 1999.

16. Singer, Dorothy G., Roberta Michnick Golinkoff, and Kathy Hirsh-Pasek. *Play = Learning: How Play Motivates and Enhances Children's Cognitive and Social-Emotional Growth*, Play = Learning: How Play Motivates and Enhances Children's Cognitive and Social-Emotional Growth. New York, NY US: Oxford University Press, 2006.

17. W. James Potter, Media Literacy, 2008.

18. Walsh D. *Why do they act that way? A survival guide to the adolescent brain for you and your teen*. New York: Atria Books; 2014.

19. Petty RE, Cacioppo JT. *Attitudes and persuasion: Classic and contemporary approaches*. Boulder, CO: Westview Press; 1996.

20. Gerbner G. The stories we tell. *Peace Rev.* 1999;11(1):9–15. doi:10.1080/10402659908426225.

21. Walsh, David. "Mediawise Columns." (2008), http://www.mediafamily.org/mediawisecolumns/index.shtml. Some of Walsh's columns include: All Too Real: ADHD TV and MySpace for the Grade-School Set.

22. Ostrow, Nicole. "Sex on Tv Linked to Teen Pregnancy in Survey of U.S. Teenagers Bloomberg.com: Science, http://www.bloomberg.com/apps/news?pid=20601124&sid=a997bX.pjoWw&refer=science.

23. Walsh, David, and Nat Bennett (Contributor). *Why Do They Act That Way?: A Survival Guide to the Adolescent Brain for You and Your Teen*. New York: Free Press, 2005.

24. Lenhart, Amanda, Mary Madden, Alexandra Rankin Macgill, and Aaron Smith. "Teens and Social Media." Pew Internet and American Life Project (2007), http://www.pewinternet.org/PPF/r/230/report_display.asp.

CHAPTER 4 MEDIA VIOLENCE

1. "Gta 4 Karin Dilettante Hybrid Commercial." 2008.http://www.youtube.com/watch?v=Hnc0obe0NFk Grand Theft Auto 4 by Rockstar Games.

2. Parentingteens.com. "Violence & Video Games." Available at http://www.par-entingteens.com/index/Parent+Forum/Parenting+Poll/Violence+and+Video+Games.

3. Retrieved May 9, 2008, from http://www.whattheyplay.com/features/why-do-young-teens-like-grand-theft-auto/. Quote from teen boy, para. 9.

4. AFP. "Cheers and Fears as Grand Theft Auto IV Revs at the Starting Line." Available at http://news.smh.com.au/technology/cheers-and-fears-as-grand-theft-auto-iv-revs-at-starting-line-20080427-28sv.html, para. 4.

5. Retrieved May 9, 2008, from http://www.whattheyplay.com/features/why-do-young-teens-like-grand-theft-auto/.

6. Thomas, Karen. "Study Ties Aggression to Violence in Games." *USA Today*, May 10, 2000, p. 3D.

7. Funk, Jeanne B., Heidi Bechtoldt Baldacci, Tracie Pasold, and Jennifer Baumgardner. "Violence Exposure in Real-Life, Video Games, Television, Movies, and the Internet: Is There Desensitization?" *Journal of Adolescence* 27, no. 1 (2004): 23.

8. Singer, Dorothy G., Roberta Michnick Golinkoff, and Kathy Hirsh-Pasek. *Play = Learning: How Play Motivates and Enhances Children's Cognitive and Social-Emotional Growth.* New York: Oxford University Press, 2006.

9. Potter WJ. The eleven myths of media violence. Thousand Oaks, CA: SAGE Publications; 2002.

10. Brenick, A., A. Henning, M. Killen, A. O'Connor, and M. Collins. "Social Evaluations of Stereotypic Images in Videogames: Unfair, Legitimate, or 'Just Entertainment'?" *Youth and Society* 38, no. 4 (2007): 395–19.

11. Funk, Jeanne B., and Christine M. Fox. "The Development of the Game Engagement Questionnaire: A Measure of Levels of Engagement in Videogame Playing." In *Meeting of the International Society for Research in Aggression.* Budapest, Hungary, 2008.

12. Gentile, Douglas, and Craig Anderson. "Violent Video Games: The Newest Media Violence Hazard." In *Media Violence and Children,* edited by Douglas Gentile. Westport, CT: Praeger, 2003.

13. Gentile and Anderson, "Violent Video Games," p. 147.

14. Gentile, Douglas, and A. Sesma. "Developmental Approaches to Understanding Media Effects on Individuals." In *Media Violence and Children,* edited by D. Gentile, 19–37. Westport, CT: Praeger, 2003.

15. Huesmann, Rowell, and Eric Dubow. "Leonard D. Eron (1920–2007)." *American Psychologist* 63, no. 2 (2008): 131–32.

16. Huesmann, L. Rowell, Leonard Eron, M. Lefkowitz, and Leopold Walder. "Television Violence and Aggression: The Causal Effect Remains." *American Psychologist* 28 (1973): 617–20.

17. Huesmann, L. Rowell, Jessica Moise-Titus, Cheryl-Lynn Podolski, and Leonard D. Eron. "Longitudinal Relations Between Children's Exposure to TV Violence and Their Aggressive and Violent Behavior in Young Adulthood: 1977–1992." *Developmental Psychology* 39, no. 2 (2003): 201.

18. See also the Web site for the University of Michigan's aggression research program, available at http://www.rcgd.isr.umich.edu/aggr/.

19. Schultz, Duane, and Sydney Schultz. *A History of Modern Psychology.* Belmont, CA: Wadsworth/Thompson Learning, 2004.

20. Huesmann, Rowell, and Eric Dubow. "Leonard D. Eron (1920–2007)." *American Psychologist* 63, no. 2 (2008): 131–32.

21. Huesmann, L. Rowell. "Screen Violence and Real Violence: Understanding the Link." 2003, available at http://www.rcgd.isr.umich.edu/aggr/, p. 20.

22. Potter WJ. The eleven myths of media violence. Thousand Oaks, CA: SAGE Publications; 2002.

23. Anderson, Craig A., Leonard Berkowitz, Edward Donnerstein, L. Rowell Huesmann, James D. Johnson, Daniel Linz, Neil M. Malamuth, and Ellen Wartella. "The Influence of Media Violence on Youth." *Psychological Science in the Public Interest* 4, no. 3 (2003): 81–110, at 81.

24. Bartholow, Bruce D., Marc A. Sestir, and Edward B. Davis. "Correlates and Consequences of Exposure to Video Game Violence: Hostile Personality, Empathy, and Aggressive Behavior." *Personality and Social Psychology Bulletin* 31, no. 11 (2005): 1573–86.

25. Anderson, Craig A., and Karen E. Dill. "Video Games and Aggressive Thoughts, Feelings, and Behavior in the Laboratory and in Life." *Journal of Personality and Social Psychology* 78 (2000): 772–90.

26. Berkowitz, Leonard, and Russell G. Geen. "Stimulus Qualities of the Target of Aggression: A Further Study." *Journal of Personality and Social Psychology* 5, no. 3 (1967): 364–68.

27. Bushman, Anderson. "Comfortably Numb: Desensitizing Effects of Violent Media on Helping Others." *Psychological Science* 21, no. 3 (2009): 273–77.

28. Bartholow, Bruce D., Brad J. Bushman, and Marc A. Sestir. "Chronic Violent Video Game Exposure and Desensitization to Violence: Behavioral and Event-Related Brain Potential Data." *Journal of Experimental Social Psychology* 42, no. 4 (2006): 532–39.

29. Koepp, M. J., R. N. Gunn, A. D. Lawrence, V. J. Cunningham, A. Dagher, T. Jones, D. J. Brooks, C. J. Bench, and P. M. Grasby. "Evidence for Striatal Dopamine Release During a Video Game." *Nature* 393, no. 6682 (1998): 266.

30. Murray, John P., Mario Liotti, Paul T. Ingmundson, Helen S. Mayberg, Pu Yonglin, Frank Zamarripa, Liu Yijun, Marty G. Woldorff, Gao Jia-Hong, and Peter T. Fox. "Children's Brain Activations While Viewing Televised Violence Revealed by fMRI." *Media Psychology* 8, no. 1 (2006): 25–37.

31. Hurley, Susan. "Imitation, Media Violence and Freedom of Speech." *Philosophical Studies* 117 (2004): 165-218 P. 170

32. Chartrand, Tanya L., and John A. Bargh. "The Chameleon Effect: The Perception-Behavior Link and Social Interaction." *Journal of Personality and Social Psychology* 76, no. 6 (1999): 893–910.

33. Giacomo Rizzolatti, and Destro Maddalena Fabbri. "Understanding Actions and the Intentions of Others: The Basic Neural Mechanism." *European Review* 15, no. 2 (2007): 209–22.

34. Nash, J. Madeleine. "The Gift of Mimicry." *Time*, January 29, 2007.

35. Berkowitz, Leonard. "On the Consideration of Automatic as Well as Controlled Psychological Processes in Aggression." *Aggressive Behavior* 34, no. 2 (2008): 117–29.

36. Sacks DP, Bushman BJ, Anderson CA. DO VIOLENT VIDEO GAMES HARM CHILDREN? COMPARING THE SCIENTIFIC AMICUS CURIAE —— EXPERTS || IN BROWN V. ENTERTAINMENT. 2011;106(2010):1–12.

CHAPTER 5 REPRESENTATIONS OF SOCIAL GROUPS IN MEDIA

1. Gerbner, G. "The Stories We Tell." *Peace Review* 11, no. 1 (1999): 9.

2. Saints Row Dev Responds to Feminist Frequency Critique. *Gamespot.com*. 2014. Available at: http://www.gamespot.com/articles/saints-row-dev-responds-to-feminist-frequency-crit/1100-6422014/.

3. Dill KE, Burgess MC. Influence of Black Masculinity Game Exemplars on Social Judgments. *Simul Gaming*. 2012;44(4):562–585. doi:10.1177/1046878112449958.

4. Wilson, C. C., F. Gutierrez, and L. M. Chao. *Racism, Sexism and the Media: The Rise of Class Communication in Multicultural America*, 3rd ed. Thousand Oaks, CA: SAGE, 2003, p. 327.

5. Holtzman, L. *Media Messages: What Film, Television and Popular Music Teach Us about Race, Class, Gender and Sexual Orientation*. New York: M. E. Sharpe, 2000.

6. Burgess MC, Dill KE, Stermer SP, Burgess SR, Brown BP. Playing With Prejudice: The Prevalence and Consequences of Racial Stereotypes in Video Games. *Media Psychol*. 2011;14(3):289–311. doi:10.1080/15213269.2011.596467.

7. Ostman, R. E. "Handbook of Visual Analysis." *Journalism and Mass Communication Quarterly* 79 (2002): 770.

8. Cowan, G. "Content Analysis of Visual Materials." In *Handbook for Conducting Research on Human Sexuality*, edited by M. W. Wiederman and B. E. Whitley. London: Lawrence Erlbaum, 2002, p. 345.

9. Slusher, M. P., and C. A. Anderson. "When Reality Monitoring Fails: The Role of Imagination in Stereotype Maintenance." *Journal of Personality and Social Psychology* 53, no. 4 (1987): 653–62.

10. Slusher and Anderson, "When Reality Monitoring Fails," p. 654.

11. Appel, M., and T. Richter. "Persuasive Effects of Fictional Narratives Increase over Time." *Media Psychology* 10, no. 1 (2007): 113–34.

12. Slusher and Anderson, "When Reality Monitoring Fails."

13. Fiske ST, Xu J, Cuddy A, Glick P. (Dis)respecting versus (dis)liking: Status and interdependence predict ambivalent stereotypes of competence and warmth. *J Soc Issues*. 1999;55:473–489.

14. Amodio, David M., and Patricia G. Devine. "Stereotyping and Evaluation in Implicit Race Bias: Evidence for Independent Constructs and Unique Effects on Behavior." *Journal of Personality and Social Psychology* 91, no. 4 (2006): 652–61.

15. Devine, P. G., et al. "The Regulation of Explicit and Implicit Race Bias: The Role of Motivations to Respond Without Prejudice." *Journal of Personality and Social Psychology* 82, no. 5 (2002): 835–48.

16. Glick, P., and S. T. Fiske. "The Ambivalent Sexism Inventory: Differentiating Hostile and Benevolent Sexism." *Journal of Personality and Social Psychology* 70, no. 3 (1996): 491–12.

17. Glick, P., et al. "Bad but Bold: Ambivalent Attitudes toward Men Predict Gender Inequality in 16 Nations." *Journal of Personality and Social Psychology* 86, no. 5 (2004): 713–28.

18. Fiske, S. T., et al. "A Model of (Often Mixed) Stereotype Content: Competence and Warmth Respectively Follow from Perceived Status and Competition." *Journal of Personality and Social Psychology* 82, no. 6 (2002): 878–902.

19. Fiske et al., "A Model of (Often Mixed) Stereotype Content."

20. Fiske et al., "A Model of (Often Mixed) Stereotype Content."

21. Pohan, C. A., and C. Mathison. "Television: Providing Powerful Multicultural LessonsInsideandOutside ofSchool." MulticulturalPerspectives9, no. 1 (2007): 25.

22. Berdahl, J. L. "The Sexual Harassment of Uppity Women." *Journal of Applied Psychology* 92, no. 2 (2007): 425–37.

23. Das, E., B. J. Bushman, M. D. Bezemer, P. Kerkhof, and I. E. Vermeulen. "How Terrorism News Reports Increase Prejudice Against Outgroups: A Terror Management Account." *Journal of Experimental Social Psychology* 45 (2009): 453–59.

24. Huesmann, L. Rowell, Eric F. Dubow, Paul Boxer, Jeremy Ginges, Violet Souweidane, Maureen O'Brien, Dominic Moceri, and Samantha Hallman. "Relations Between Arab-American and Jewish-American Adolescents' Exposure to Media Depictions of Middle-Eastern Violence and Their Ethnic Stereotypes about the Violent Propensities of Ethnic Groups in America." In *Meeting of the International Society for Research in Aggression*. Budapest, Hungary, 2008.

25. Connell, R. W. *Gender and Power*. Stanford, CA: Stanford University Press, 1987.

26. Connell, *Gender and Power*, p. 185.

27. Glick, P., and S. T. Fiske. "An Ambivalent Alliance: Hostile and Benevolent Sexism as Complementary Justifications for Gender Inequality." *American Psychologist* 56, no. 2 (2001): 109–18.

28. Jost, J. T., M. R. Banaji, and B. A. Nosek. "A Decade of System Justification Theory: Accumulated Evidence of Conscious and Unconscious Bolstering of the Status Quo." *Political Psychology* 25, no. 6 (2004): 881–19.

29. Glick et al., "Bad but Bold.

30. Scharrer, E. "Hypermasculinity, Aggression, and Television Violence: An Experiment." *Media Psychology* 7, no. 4 (2005): 353.

31. Scharrer, E. "Tough Guys: The Portrayal of Hypermasculinity and Aggression in Televised Police Dramas." *Journal of Broadcasting and Electronic Media* 45, no. 4 (2001): 615.

32. Huesmann, L. R., et al. "Longitudinal Relations Between Children's Exposure to TV Violence and Their Aggressive and Violent Behavior in Young Adulthood: 1977–1992." *Developmental Psychology* 39, no. 2 (2003): 201.

33. Huesmann et al. "Longitudinal Relations."

34. Greenwood, D. N. "Are Female Action Heroes Risky Role Models? Character Identification, Idealization and Viewer Aggression." *Sex Roles* 57 (2007): 725–32.

35. Dietz, T. L. "An Examination of Violence and Gender Role Portrayals in Video Games: Implications for Gender Socialization and Aggressive Behavior." *Sex Roles* 38 (1998): 425–42.

36. Dill, K. E., and K. P. Thill. "Video Game Characters and the Socialization of Gender Roles: Young People's Perceptions Mirror Sexist Media Depictions." *Sex Roles* 57 (2007): 851–64.

37. *National Television Violence Study*. Santa Barbara, CA: University of California, Santa Barbara, Center for Communication and Social Policy, 1998.

38. Dill, K. E., et al. "Violence, Sex, Age and Race in Popular Video Games: A Content Analysis." In *Featuring Females: Feminist Analyses of Media*, edited by E. Cole and J. Henderson-Daniel. Washington, DC: American Psychological Association, 2005.

39. Dill, K. E., B. P. Brown, and M. A. Collins. "Effects of Media Stereotypes on Sexual Harassment Judgments and Rape Supportive Attitudes: Popular Video Game Characters, Gender, Violence and Power." *Journal of Experimental Social Psychology* 44 (2008): 1402–408.

40. Brenick, A., et al. "Social Evaluations of Stereotypic Images in Videogames: Unfair, Legitimate, or 'Just Entertainment'?" *Youth and Society* 38, no. 4 (2007): 395–419.

41. Ferguson, T., et al. "Variation in the Application of the 'Promiscuous Female' Stereotype and the Nature of the Application Domain: Influences on Sexual

Harassment Judgments after Exposure to the *Jerry Springer Show.*" *Sex Roles* 52 (2005): 477–87.

42. Milburn, M. A., R. Mather, and S. D. Conrad. "The Effects of Viewing R-rated Movie Scenes That Objectify Women on Perceptions of Date Rape." *Sex Roles* 43 (2000): 645–64.

43. Lanis, K., and K. Covell. "Images of Women in Advertisements: Effects on Attitudes Related to Sexual Aggression." *Sex Roles* 32 (1995): 639–49.

44. Linz, D. G., E. Donnerstein, and S. Penrod. "Effects of Long-Term Exposure to Violent and Sexually Degrading Depictions of Women." *Journal of Personality and Social Psychology* 55, no. 5 (1988): 758.

45. Martino, S. C., et al. "Exposure to Degrading Versus Nondegrading Music Lyrics and Sexual Behavior among Youth." *Pediatrics* 118, no. 2 (2006): 782.

46. *Fetch! with Ruff Ruffman* Web site on pbskids.org. Available at http://pbskids.org/fetch/parentsteachers/program/edu_philosophy.html.

47. Wilson CC, Gutierrez F, Chao LM. *Racism, Sexism and the Media: The rise of Class Communication in Multicultural America.* 3rd ed. Thousand Oaks, CA: SAGE Publications; 2003. Page 134.

CHAPTER 6 ADVERTISING, CONSUMERISM, AND HEALTH

1. Schultz, Duane, and Sydney Schultz. *A History of Modern Psychology.* Belmont, CA: Wadsworth/Thompson Learning, 2004.

2. Schultz, Duane, and Sydney Schultz. *A History of Modern Psychology.*

3. Potter, James. *The Eleven Myths of Media Violence.* Thousand Oaks, CA: Sage, 2002, p. 8.

4. Magazine Publishers of America. "Magazines 24/7, the Magazine Industry's Inaugural Digital Summit Debuts to a Sold-out Audience." Magazine Publishers of America, available at http://www.magazine.org/Press_Room/MPA_Press_Releases/14503.cfm.

5. Lisjak M, Lee AY, Gardner WL. When a threat to the brand is a threat to the self: the importance of brand identification and implicit self-esteem in predicting defensiveness. *Pers Soc Psychol Bull.* 2012;38(9):1120–32. doi:10.1177/0146167212445300.

6. Sutherland, Max, and John Galloway. "Role of Advertising: Persuasion or Agenda Setting?" *Journal of Advertising Research* 21, no. 5 (1981): 27.

7. Wolf, Naomi. *The Beauty Myth: How Images of Beauty Are Used Against Women.* New York: Harper Perennial, 2002.

8. "Marketing Food to Children." *Lancet* 366, no. 9503 (2005): 2064.

9. "Selling to—and Selling Out—Children." *Lancet* 360, no. 9338 (2002): 959.

10. McLellan, Faith. "Marketing and Advertising: Harmful to Children's Health." *Lancet* 360 (2002): 1001.

11. Hyde, Rob. "Europe Battles with Obesity." *Lancet* 371, no. 9631 (2008): 2160.

12. Federal Trade Commission. "Marketing Food to Children and Adolescents: A Report to Congress." Washington, DC: Federal Trade Commission, 2008.

13. Hancox, Robert, Barry Milne, and Richie Poulton. "Association Between Child and Adolescent Television Viewing and Adult Health: A Longitudinal Birth Cohort Study." *Lancet* 364, no. 9430 (2004): 257.

14. Rhodes, Ann. "Legislative Efforts to Combat Childhood Obesity." *Journal for Specialists in Pediatric Nursing* 13 (July 2008): 223.
15. Rhodes, "Legislative Efforts," p. 223.
16. Rhodes, "Legislative Efforts," p. 223.
17. Federal Trade Commission. "Marketing Food to Children and Adolescents."
18. "Liverpool Set to Ban McDonald's Happy Meals in a Bid to Cut Childhood Obesity." *Daily Mail*, 2008, available at http://www.dailymail.co.uk/news/article-517955/Liverpool-set-ban-McDonalds-Happy-Meals-bid-cut-childhood-obesity.html.
19. NEDIC. "Statistics." Available at http://www.nedic.ca/knowthefacts/statistics.shtml.
20. "Are Diet Pills Effective? Fat Chance." *Consumer Reports on Health* 19, no. 3 (2007): 3.
21. "Are Diet Pills Effective?" p. 3.
22. Minjeong, Kim, and Sharron Lennon. "Content Analysis of Diet Advertisements: A Cross-National Comparison of Korean and U.S. Women's Magazines." *Clothing and Textiles Research Journal* 24 (2006): 345–62.
23. Wolf, *The Beauty Myth.*
24. Wolf, *The Beauty Myth.*
25. Taylor, Peter Shawn. "Massaging the Message." *Canadian Business* 79, no. 7 (2006): 12.
26. "Ad Council Announces Collaboration to Combat Childhood Obesity: 'Coalition for Healthy Children.'" *AdCouncil.org* (July 13, 2005), available at http://adcouncil.org/newsDetail.aspx?id=34.
27. Vogt, Donna U. "Direct-to-Consumer Advertising of Prescription Drugs." Congressional Research Service, 2005. Web site: http//www.loc.gov/crsinfo/
28. Rhodes, "Legislative Efforts," p. 223.
29. Zachry, Woodie, Marvin Shepherd, Melvin Hinich, James Wilson, Carolyn Brown, and Kenneth Lawson. "Relationship Between Direct-to-Consumer Advertising and Physician Diagnosing and Prescribing." *American Journal of Health System Pharmacists* 59 (2002): 42.
30. Jaspen, Bruce. "Medical Ads Aim Straight for the Heart." *Chicago Tribune*, January 23, 2007.
31. Jaspen, "Medical Ads Aim Straight for the Heart."

Chapter 7 Media and Social Identity

1. Lisjak M, Lee AY, Gardner WL. When a threat to the brand is a threat to the self: the importance of brand identification and implicit self-esteem in predicting defensiveness. *Pers Soc Psychol Bull.* 2012;38(9):1120–32. doi:10.1177/0146167212445300.
2. Potter, W. James. *Media Literacy.* Los Angeles: SAGE, 2008, 8.
3. Potter, *Media Literacy,* p. 8.
4. Lever, Janet, David A. Frederick, and Letitia Anne Peplau. "Does Size Matter? Men's and Women's Views on Penis Size Across the Lifespan." *Psychology of Men and Masculinity* 7, no. 3 (2006): 129–43, 129.
5. Lamb, Sharon, and Lyn Mikel Brown. *Packaging Girlhood: Rescuing Our Daughters from Marketers' Schemes.* New York: St. Martin's Press, 2006, 16.

6. Lamb and Brown, *Packaging Girlhood*, pp. 26–27.

7. Levin, Diane, and Jean Kilbourne. *So Sexy So Soon: The New Sexualized Childhood and What Parents Can Do to Protect Their Kids*. New York: Ballantine, 2008, 226.

8. Levin and Kilbourne, *So Sexy So Soon*, p. 42.

9. Lamb and Brown, *Packaging Girlhood*, pp. 2–3.

10. Lamb and Brown, *Packaging Girlhood*, p. 6.

11. Rivenbark, Celia. *Stop Dressing Your Six-Year-Old like a Skank*. New York: St. Martin's Press, 2006, p. 28.

12. The full mission statement of the APA is available at www.apa.org.

13. APS, the Association for Psychological Science, is another large organization for psychologists whose mission also includes advancing human welfare. More information is available at www.psychologicalscience.org.

14. Kilbourne, Jean, and M. Pipher. *Can't Buy My Love*. New York: Free Press, 2000.

15. Burgess, M. C. R., Dill, K. E., & Wright, B. A. (2009). You're my bitch: Crude and degrading treatment of women in hardcore rap through the eyes of the predominantly White target audience, *Journal of Current Issues in Media and Telecommunications*, 1, 3/4, available from: https://www.novapublishers.com/catalog/product_info.php?products_id=10552

16. Lena, Jennifer. "Social Context and Musical Content of Rap Music, 1979–1995." *Social Forces* 85, no. 1 (2006): 479–95.

17. Pizzey E. *Scream quietly or the neighbors will hear*. New York: Enslow Publishing; 1974.

18. Stark E. *Coercive Control: How Men Entrap Women in Personal Life (Interpersonal Violence)*. New York: Oxford University Press, USA; 2007. Available at: http://www.amazon.com/Coercive-Control-Personal-Interpersonal-Violence-ebook/dp/B000SMY0CO. Accessed February 17, 2014.

19. Thill KP, Dill KE. Chapter 4 Domestic Violence in American Magazines. In: *Violence Against Women in Families and Relationships: Volume 4, The Media and Cultural Attitudes.*; 2009:81–104.

20. TaggleElgate, "Farah Fawcett BBC Film '86 Extremities Interview." 2007. Retrieved July 30, 2008 from http://youtube.com/watch?v=6LuX2vphPZw

21. Jones, Edward E., and Victor Harris. "The Attribution of Attitudes." *Journal of Experimental Social Psychology* 3 (1967): 1-24.

22. Ball, Aimee Lee. "She's Come Undone." *O, The Oprah Magazine* 5, no. 9 (2004): 300-30.

23. Durbin, Karen. "Wife Beating." *Ladies Home Journal*, June 1974.

24. Esman, A., *If I Could Close My Eyes*, in *Diane: The Curves Magazine*. 2006, Rodale: Emmaus, PA.

25. Dill-Shackleford KE, Vitagliano AA, Burgess MCR, Trivett SR, Hadley SM. What a Difference a Frame Makes: Popular Magazine Coverage of Intimate Partner Violence Influences Attitudes and Beliefs.

26. Albertson ER, Neff KD, Dill-Shackleford KE. Self-Compassion and Body Dissatisfaction in Women: A Randomized Controlled Trial of a Brief Meditation Intervention. *Mindfulness (N Y)*. 2014. doi:10.1007/s12671-014-0277-3.

Chapter 8 The Social Psychology of Political Coverage

1. Kantrowitz A. John McCain unapologetic after Playing iPhone Poker During Syria Hearing. Forbes. 2013. Available at: http://www.forbes.com/sites/alexkantrowitz/2013/09/03/john-mccain-unapologetic-after-playing-iphone-poker-during-syria-hearing/.

2. Newsmax. The best of late night jokes. 2013. Available at: http://www.newsmax.com/Jokes/1013/.

3. McCluhan, Marshall, with Quentin Fiore, and Jerome Agel. *The Medium Is the Message: An Inventory of Effects.* Corte Madera, CA: Ginko Press, 1967, p. 22.

4. Geer, John G., and James H. Geer. "Remembering Attack Ads: An Experimental Investigation of Radio." *Political Behavior* 25, no. 1 (2003): 69–95.

5. Bushman, Brad J., and Colleen M. Phillips. "If the Television Program Bleeds, Memory for the Advertisement Recedes." *Current Directions in Psychological Science* 10, no. 2 (2001): 43–47.

6. Evans, L. (2001). Desperate lovers and Wanton women: Press representations of domestic violence, *Hectate, 27*, 147-173.

7. Hart, Roderick P. *Seducing America: How Television Charms the Modern Voter.* Thousand Oaks, CA: SAGE, 1999.

8. Herbert, Ian. "This Is Your Brain on Politics." *APS Observer* 21, no. 8 (2008).

9. Oxley, Douglas R., Kevin B. Smith, John R. Alford, Matthew V. Hibbing, Jennifer L. Miller, Mario Scalora, Peter K. Hatemi, and John R. Hibbibg. "Political Attitudes Vary with Physiological Traits." *Science* 321, no. 5896 (2008): 1667–70.

10. Vedantam, Shankar. "Startle Response Linked to Politics." Washington Post, September 19, 2008, available at http://www.washingtonpost.com/wp-dyn/content/article/2008/09/18/AR2008091802265.html?hpid=topnews.

11. Pyszczynski TA, Solomon S, Greenberg J. *In the wake of 9/11: The psychology of terror.* Washington, D.C.: American Psychological Assocation; 2003.

12. Brehm JW. The intensity of emotion. *Pers Soc Psychol Rev.* 1999;3(1):2–22. doi:10.1207/s15327957pspr0301_1.

13. Westen D. *The political brain.* New York: Public Affairs; 2008.

14. Cao, Xiaoxia. "Political Comedy Shows and Knowledge about Primary Campaigns: The Moderating Effects of Age and Education." *Mass Communication and Society* 11 (2008): 43–61.

15. Seelye, Katherine Q. "Best Informed Also View Fake News, Study Says." *New York Times,* April 16, 2007.

16. McKain, Aaron. "Not Necessarily Not the News: Gatekeeping, Remediation, and *The Daily Show.*" Journal of American Culture 28, no. 4 (2005): 415–30.

17. Fox, Julia, Glory Koloen, and Volkan. Sahin. "No Joke: A Comparison of Substance in The Daily Show with Jon Stewart and Broadcast Network Television Coverage of the 2004 Presidential Election Campaign." *Journal of Broadcasting and Electronic Media* 51, no. 2 (2007): 15.

18. Trier, James. "*The Daily Show* with Jon Stewart, Part 1." *Journal of Adolescent and Adult Literacy* 51, no. 5 (2008): 424–27.

19. Trier, "*The Daily Show,*" p. 427.

20. Trier, "*The Daily Show,*" p. 427.

21. Trier, "*The Daily Show,*" p. 426.

22. "CNN Laughs It Up over Sarah Palin Interview," 2008, available at http://www. youtube.com/watch?v=zeMypXCUWMw.

23. "Chris Matthews: *SNL* Goes after Biden and Palin," 2008, available at http://www. youtube.com/watch?v=9Ykh93bCQt8.

24. "Iraq, Bush and Cheering: Tony Blair on *The Daily Show* with Jon Stewart." *Guardian politics blog online*, 2008, available at http://www.guardian.co.uk/politics/blog/2008/sep/19/tony.blair.daily.show.jon.stewart.

25. "Iraq, Bush and Cheering."

26. Kasumovic MM, Kuznekoff JH. Insights into Sexism: Male Status and Performance Moderates Female-Directed Hostile and Amicable Behaviour. *PLoS One*. 2015;10(7):e0131613. doi:10.1371/journal.pone.0131613.

27. Greenberg J. Gamers who troll women are literally losers. *Wired.com*. 2015. Available at: http://www.wired.com/2015/07/gamers-troll-women-literally-losers/.

28. Hlavach L, Freivogel WH. Journal of Mass Media Ethics: Exploring Questions of Media Morality Ethical Implications of Anonymous Comments Posted to Online News Stories. (February 2013):37–41.

CHAPTER 9 FROM THE PASSENGER'S SEAT TO THE DRIVER'S SEAT

1. Lumet, Sidney. *Network*. Metro-Goldwyn-Mayer/United Artists, 1976.

2. Appel, Markus, and Tobias Richter. "Persuasive Effects of Fictional Narratives Increase over Time." *Media Psychology* 10, no. 1 (2007): 113–34.

3. Green, Melanie C. "Linking Self and Others Through Narrative." *Psychological Inquiry* 18, no. 2 (2007): 100–02.

4. Brenick, A., A. Henning, M. Killen, A. O'Connor, and M. Collins. "Social Evaluations of Stereotypic Images in Videogames: Unfair, Legitimate, or 'Just Entertainment'?" *Youth and Society* 38, no. 4 (2007): 395–419.

5. Anderson, Craig A., Leonard Berkowitz, Edward Donnerstein, L. Rowell Huesmann, James D. Johnson, Daniel Linz, Neil M. Malamuth, and Ellen Wartella. "The Influence of Media Violence on Youth." *Psychological Science in the Public Interest* 4, no. 3 (2003): 81–110.

6. Wilkin, Holley W., Thomas W. Valente, Sheila Murphy, Michael J. Cody, Grace Huang, and Vicki Beck. "Does Entertainment-Education Work with Latinos in the United States? Identification and the Effects of a Telenovela Breast Cancer Storyline." *Journal of Health Communication* 12, no. 5 (2007): 455–69.

7. McLuhan, Marshall, with Quentin Fiore and Jerome Agel. *The Medium Is the Message: An Inventory of Effects*. Corte Madera, CA: Ginko Press, 1967, p. 26.

8. Lumet, *Network*.

9. Coalition for Healthy Children. "Ad Council Announces Collaboration to Combat Childhood Obesity." *AdCouncil.org*, July 13, 2005, available at http://adcouncil.org/newsDetail.aspx?id=34.

10. Taylor, Peter Shawn. "Massaging the Message." *Canadian Business* 79, no. 7 (2006): 12.

11. Gentile, Saleem M., and Craig A. Anderson. "Public Policy and the Effects of Media Violence on Children." *Social Issues and Policy Review* 1 (2007): 15–61.

12. Csikszentmihalyi, Mihaly. *Finding Flow: The Psychology of Engagement with Everyday Life*. New York: Basic Books, 1998, p. 67.

13. Csikszentmihalyi, *Finding Flow,* p. 65.

14. Trier, James. "*The Daily Show with Jon Stewart,* Part 2." *Journal of Adolescent and Adult Literacy* 51, no. 7 (2008): 600–05.

15. Potter, W. James. *The Eleven Myths of Media Violence.* Thousand Oaks, CA: Sage, 2002.

16. Alda, Alan. *Things I Overheard While Talking to Myself* [Audio Edition]. New York: Random House, 2007, chapter 14.

17. Alda, *Things I Overheard,* chapter 14.

18. Bushman, Brad J., and Craig A. Anderson. "Media Violence and the American Public." *American Psychologist* 56, no. 6–7 (2001): 477.

19. Kaplan, Karen. "Company Town; Scientists Say Movie Image Not a Pretty Picture; Film: Seeking to Counter Stereotypes, Group Offers Grants to Expose Student Filmmakers to Professionals in the Real World." *Los Angeles Times,* November 18, 1998, 5.

20. Gentile and Anderson, "Public Policy and the Effects of Media Violence on Children."

21. Csikszentmihalyi, *Finding Flow,* p. 13.

Page numbers followed by "b", "f", and "t" indicate boxes, figures, and tables.